Transforming Information Literacy Instruction

Transforming Information Literacy Instruction

Threshold Concepts in Theory and Practice

Amy R. Hofer, Silvia Lin Hanick, and Lori Townsend

LIBRARIES
UNLIMITED™
An Imprint of ABC-CLIO, LLC
Santa Barbara, California • Denver, Colorado

Library of Congress Cataloging-in-Publication Data

Names: Hofer, Amy R., author. | Lin Hanick, Silvia, author. | Townsend, Lori, author.
Title: Transforming information literacy instruction : threshold concepts in theory and practice / Amy R. Hofer, Silvia Lin Hanick, and Lori Townsend.
Description: Santa Barbara, California : Libraries Unlimited, [2019] | Includes bibliographical references and index.
Identifiers: LCCN 2018032809 (print) | LCCN 2018036477 (ebook) | ISBN 9781440841675 (ebook) | ISBN 9781440841668 (pbk. : acid-free paper)
Subjects: LCSH: Information literacy—Study and teaching (Higher) | Academic libraries—Relations with faculty and curriculum.
Classification: LCC ZA3075 (ebook) | LCC ZA3075 .H64 2019 (print) | DDC 028.7071/1—dc23
LC record available at https://lccn.loc.gov/2018032809

ISBN: 978–1–4408–4166–8 (paperback)
978–1–4408–4167–5 (ebook)

23 22 21 20 19 1 2 3 4 5

This book is also available on the World Wide Web as an eBook.

Libraries Unlimited
An Imprint of ABC-CLIO, LLC

ABC-CLIO, LLC
130 Cremona Drive, P.O. Box 1911
Santa Barbara, California 93116-1911
www.abc-clio.com

This book is printed on acid-free paper ∞

Manufactured in the United States of America

Contents

Acknowledgments

In the last weeks of completing our manuscript, we took to offering anyone and everyone this unsolicited advice: "No one should write a book." To foreshadow our chapter on the research process, creating novel inquiry—in book form or otherwise—is defined as much by affect (anxiety, uncertainty, discomfort) as it is by scholarly prowess and time at your desk. If, however, you *must* write a book, it is helpful to immerse yourself in a supportive community. With sincere gratitude, we would like to acknowledge the contributions of the following members of our community.

Our editor, Jessica Gribble, and the entire team at Libraries Unlimited and ABC-CLIO. We are grateful for your astute feedback, positive support, and endless patience. We would also like to thank Lise Dyckman for seeing the potential in our work and for guiding us through the book-proposal phase.

Korey Brunetti, our subject matter expert, longtime collaborator, and friend. One sentence from you is worth a hundred sentences from the history of sentences. You made us better, you make us laugh, and we are glad you're on Team TC.

Our colleagues in the Pacific Northwest library community are a thoughtful and supportive bunch. Meredith Farkas and Bob Schroeder, thanks for sharing your work as expert practitioners of our profession (in writing and over drinks). Your contributions have clarified and electrified information literacy for us.

We are also grateful to the open education community for an incredible education on the economics of information as well as the exciting opportunity to think through the overlap between information literacy and open education. Quill West, Candice Watkins, Sarah Cohen, and Michelle Reed, thank you for the challenge.

Our colleagues at LaGuardia Community College (CUNY), who have participated in countless instruction workshops; revised lesson plans galore; and exemplify the value of a community of practice with their curiosity, generosity, and empathy. We would also like to thank the Instruction Curriculum Committee (Ian McDermott, Steven Ovadia, Alexandra Rojas, Chris McHale, Galina Letnikova, and Catherine Stern) for their help with implementing conceptual teaching on a programmatic level; Hong Cheng for being game to try out lots of new activities and assignments when co-teaching LRC 103: Internet Research Strategies; and Dominique Zino, for creating the collaborative space necessary to turn the required library instruction sessions for ENG 101/103 into grounds for pedagogical innovation.

Our colleagues at the University of New Mexico (UNM), who have listened to Lori talk about "the book" for way too long but have always been supportive and kind. We thank the UNM University Libraries Learning Services group, past and present: Robin Potter Nolasco, David Hurley, Jorge Ricardo Lopez-McKnight, Alyssa Russo (information + geography!), and Glenn Koelling (the basket of balls!). Thanks for discussing threshold-y ideas, filling the LSD hallway with silliness and laughter, and generally being smart, caring librarian teachers who inspire. Thanks to the CC Group, a.k.a. Beatrice Fig, Felicity Lemon, and Delilah Papaya, from Agatha Raisin, for bearing with Lori under the weight of genre theory and sometimes infuriating or boring readings—the CC group will solve that conundrum! Thanks to Mark Emmons for noticing us at that first LOEX conference and supporting this research, first as a colleague and then as a supervisor, the whole way through. We would also like to thank Lori's Native colleagues, for keeping her sane and making her laugh: Kevin Brown, for challenging ideas; Paulita Aguilar and Monica Dorame, for encouragement and hope; and Sarah Kostelecky, for being a great friend, mentor, and role model. We also thank the whole Learning and Outreach Services group for the terrific energy and always being willing to give new ideas a try (and also for just letting Lori ramble on sometimes).

NaoMi Bishop Fitzpatrick, Berlin Loa, Karisma Quiballo, and Thomas Cleary for your help with understanding the *Protocols for Native American Archival Materials*.

Amy, Silvia, and Lori are also grateful for the support of their families. Thank you to Marcia, Ricardo, and Jen Hofer; Yuen Su Lin and Joseph Lu; and Virgil and Myrn Townsend. Joe Delwiche, Conor Lin Hanick, and James Markham, for a thousand general reasons and a few specific ones. Joe, for being not just supportive but also genuinely interested in our work, and for listening to Amy read each chapter out loud to him. Conor, for a metaphor about dynamics and musicianship that we ultimately took out of Chapter 7 (sorry, dude), for bringing Silvia slices of Pommes Anna while she worked, and for neatly restacking her piles of paper every morning. James, for being the best co-procrastinator-slash-cheerleader, for puppy wrangling, and for spending hours talking about authority—and thus becoming his own cognitive authority on authority.

Wendell the kitten, Norbert the puppy, and Otis the puppy, who grew alongside this book and provided countless hours of both distraction and delight.

Watson, the most perfect dog who is also a loaf of bread; Rosie, a dog who loves the sound of her own voice; and Fidda, a cat grouchy in all the right ways.

Calvin the cat, Buster the cat, and Sammie the dog: we will think of you always until we meet again on the Rainbow Bridge.

Introduction

This book relies on research and theory, but it was also written by three librarian practitioners who don't talk about themselves as "the authors" and sometimes speak from their own experience. Here is a little bit about who we are.

Amy loves her job as open education librarian for Oregon's colleges and universities. By night she is a fiddler and square dance caller. Amy lives in Portland with her cat Wendell, who has made friends with the cat next door ("Friendell").

Silvia likes concrete examples that clarify conceptual ideas, young adult romances featuring women of color, and filling her Instagram with pictures of her photogenic dogs, Watson and Norbert. She lives in the Bushwick neighborhood of Brooklyn.

Lori is a fan of elaborately constructed sci-fi novels, visually compelling design (she makes our slides), and midday snacks. She bridges the divide in Team TC by being both a dog and a cat person. Lori is a member of the Shoshone-Paiute Tribes of Duck Valley.

About This Book

Librarians have been reinventing themselves for many years. Corinne Stocker Horton (1898) said that modern American librarians represented a departure from the collector or "jealous guardian" of the past. Instead, "there is a growing tendency to regard them as public educator and to demand in them technical knowledge and executive business ability, as well as general literary culture." A decade later, Adelaide R. Hasse (1912) touted additional changes. Librarians were not clerks, retrieving and delivering books. "In these days the profession has grown much more complex,"

Hasse explains, "and there are endless openings for special work requiring special training and talents."

Over a hundred years after Hasse, librarianship continues to be a profession marked by constant evolution, the regular assumption of new duties, and the resulting scramble by everyone to keep up. This quality of our profession can be invigorating, but also daunting. For teaching librarians, particularly those teaching in academic libraries, the most recent shift in library instruction is away from skills-based training and toward conceptual learning. We (Amy, Silvia, and Lori) propose that, to meet this challenge, librarians can look to Jan Meyer and Ray Land's threshold concept model of teaching and learning as a way to transform their information literacy instruction.

Reactions to this suggestion have encompassed a wide spectrum, from "I've been doing that since before you were born" to "absolutely no way" and all points in between. Librarians have taken to Twitter, given conference presentations, written to professional listservs, and found myriad other ways to convey the message that threshold concepts are not for them. After reading some responses, we wanted to ask, "Other than that, how did you like our article?"

This is to say that while we publish in order to share our ideas, it's also terrifying to do so. With apologies to ABC-CLIO, there are days when we hope that this book will sink like a stone. Perhaps a few completist research libraries will buy a copy, adding it to the Zs in compact shelving on a basement level where most people don't go because it has a musty smell. Future researchers for the *Journal of Historical Footnotes in Library and Information Science* will have a glimpse, through a small window high up on the wall, of people's feet passing by on their way to toss sandwich wrappers and apple cores in a trash can after lunch on sunny afternoons.

Yet, we have continued to publish on threshold concepts for information literacy instruction because this approach has worked for us. The threshold concept model helped us redefine our teaching content and convey it to students with a new level of engagement, because we were working from a place of disciplinary expertise. Moreover, this approach has brought us into a community of practice where we try out new ideas, disagree, refine, and try again. Writing this book has given us a reason not only to explore some of the corners of library and information science that we don't feel expert in but also to collaborate in hammering out how we want to share the ideas that we spend so much time discussing among ourselves. It's wonderful to meet new colleagues who have also found ways to apply Meyer and Land's work to our field, and we hope that this book will help other librarians consider conceptual teaching content for information literacy.

Part I, "Introduction to Threshold Concepts for Information Literacy Instruction," provides background on the threshold concept model and its application to information literacy instruction. Chapter 1 covers the basics of threshold concepts and where this model fits in the information literacy instruction discourse, while Chapter 2, on identifying threshold concepts for information literacy, gets into the specific content that librarians might teach with this approach.

Part II, "Exploring Threshold Concepts for Information Literacy," takes a close look at five threshold concepts that we believe are useful in teaching information literacy content. We articulate content from our own discipline, information science, in order to connect the rules of the academic game with the underlying disciplinary concepts that put the rules in context. We lay out the basic and advanced topics that we teach relating to each threshold concept.

Chapter 3, on authority, considers the extent to which authority is both constructed and contextual. Chapter 4, on format, looks to genre theory and the way the information cycle has changed in the digital age to clarify the means by which information is produced, organized, and disseminated. Chapter 5 investigates the economic side of information and asks which academic practices might be better understood through the concepts of commodities and property. Chapter 6, on organizing systems, connects the structure and function of our information systems to the human efforts (and human bias) with which they were created. Last, Chapter 7 explores the research process as a process of inquiry.

Part III, "Threshold Concepts for Information Literacy in Practice," offers our take on some of the nuts and bolts of using threshold concepts in an information literacy course or program. Chapter 8 shows how a threshold concept approach to information literacy instruction fits in with existing approaches to assessment and accreditation. Chapter 9 suggests activities and assignments that we use to help students cross the learning thresholds discussed in this book.

We conclude in Chapter 10 with a case study that considers the problem of fake news (and other information crises) through the lens of three of the threshold concepts explored in Part II. Taken together, the threshold concepts introduce a distinct disciplinary perspective that librarians bring to instruction. Thinking about one topic from various angles shows how librarians can offer meaningful instruction that prepares students to bring deeper understandings about information into their academic context and beyond.

References

Hasse, A. R. (1912, December 1). What a girl should know who wants to be a librarian. *The New York Times*. Retrieved from https://www.nytimes.com/1912/12/01/archives/what-a-girl-should-know-who-wants-to-be-a-librarian.html

Horton, C. S. (1898, April 16). Library schools: The new profession for men and women. *The New York Times*. Retrieved from https://www.nytimes.com/1898/04/16/archives/library-schools-the-new-profession-for-men-and-women-what-new-york.html

PART I

Introduction to Threshold Concepts for Information Literacy Instruction

CHAPTER ONE

Threshold Concepts and Their Application to Information Literacy Instruction

We—Amy, Silvia, and Lori—became interested in threshold concepts because we needed an answer to a really basic, practical question. We had to stand up in front of a roomful of first-year students for 10 weeks in a row. What were we going to teach?

When we were starting our careers as instruction librarians, the Association of College & Research Libraries (ACRL) offered the *Information Literacy Competency Standards for Higher Education* to guide our information literacy instruction sessions. The multilevel *Standards* didn't represent a course or session outline exactly, but they articulated the many things that an information literate student would be able to do. We soon found that in spite of copious details, outcomes, and performance indicators, the *Standards* did not lend themselves to a coherent course plan.

Like many librarians, we found ourselves in a teaching role without having had any formal instruction on how to teach. Learning on the job means that we enter the profession not quite certain of our instructional content. For us, the threshold concept model helped answer the question of what to teach better than rereading the *Standards* did.

Introducing Threshold Concepts

Threshold concepts are an emerging theory that has generated a high degree of interest and excitement in many disciplines. As first articulated by Jan Meyer and Ray Land, they are the core ideas and processes in any discipline that define the discipline but are so ingrained that they often go unspoken or unrecognized by practitioners. They are the central concepts that students should understand and put into practice—those that encourage them to think and act like practitioners. Threshold concepts are the ideas that are often most difficult to grasp but that a student needs to understand in order to progress.

Threshold concepts are likely to be characterized by the following features (Meyer & Land, 2003):

- Transformative—They cause students to see the class material, and the discipline, and maybe themselves and the rest of the world in a different way. Students see the content through the lens of the practitioner community and adopt the ways of thinking and practicing common to the discipline.
- Integrative—Grasping a threshold concept helps students tie together facts and procedural information in order to make the connections that allow them to see the whole. They may also be able to apply this new understanding in other areas.
- Irreversible—Once students learn them, they don't unlearn them. This explains why teachers sometimes have trouble relating to where their students are. The experts have been on the other side of the threshold for so long that they may not remember what it was like before they got it.
- Bounded—They may help define the boundaries of a particular discipline and are perhaps unique to the discipline. This is a problematic criterion for librarians because information literacy is arguably not a discipline. However, librarians do share a common way of thinking and practicing that is acquired by crossing the thresholds of our discipline, information science.
- Troublesome—The trouble can come in different varieties, but threshold concepts often provoke anxiety and resistance because they are usually difficult or counterintuitive ideas that can cause students to hit a roadblock in their learning.

Meyer and Land extend the metaphor of the threshold to the idea of liminality and the liminal space, a concept borrowed from anthropology (*limen* is from the Latin word for "threshold"; e.g., Meyer & Land, 2005, 2006b). In this context, it is the space where the threshold comes into view for the learner, but the learner has not yet passed through it. The liminal space is an in-between, transitional place. It is typical to oscillate between states in this space, as the threshold seems near and then recedes once more. It can be exciting, terrifying, humbling, troubling, short, long, deeply alienating, and engaging. One thing it is not: comfortable. Learners will move through the liminal space in different ways and at different speeds, but they will not leave the space unchanged.

This change occurs in two broad ways. First, learners experience epistemological change. This is a cognitive shift, the extent to which the student understands a new concept. Second, learners undergo ontological change as well. This is the shift in identity they experience as they get an inkling of what it's like to look through a particular disciplinary lens. This means that threshold concepts engage learners both cognitively and affectively. Understanding the liminal space helps illuminate the troublesome nature of threshold concepts, because crossing a threshold can be both an intellectual and an emotional experience.

We agree with James Atherton, Peter Hadfield, and Renee Meyers that "the idea of a threshold concept is in itself a threshold concept" (2008, p. 4). If threshold concepts are new to you, you may find yourself in a liminal space, where one moment you grasp the theory and the next moment that understanding has fled.

On the other hand, many instruction librarians are already avid students of pedagogy and will recognize elements of other current educational theories in Meyer and Land's work. In a book chapter titled "Old Wine in New Bottles?" Glynis Cousin (2008) acknowledges the similarities. One differentiating factor, though, is that threshold concepts may provide an accessible on-ramp to educational theory for librarians and faculty who do not hold additional degrees in education (Meyer & Land, 2007). Further, the threshold concept model need not be the only tool in your pedagogical toolkit, as it has been demonstrated to work well in combination with other related approaches such as Decoding the Disciplines and backward design (e.g., Lundstrom, Fagerheim, & Benson, 2014; Miller, 2018).

We find that it is productive to consider threshold concepts alongside the "big ideas" that Grant Wiggins and Jay McTighe describe in their book on backward design:

> A big idea is not necessarily vast in the sense of a vague phrase covering lots of content. Nor is a big idea a "basic" idea. Rather, big ideas are at the "core" of the subject; they need to be uncovered; we have to dig deep until we get the core. Basic ideas, by contrast, are just what the term implies—the basis for further work; for example, definitions, building-block skills, and rules of thumb. Ideas at the core of the subject, however, are ideas that are the hard-won results of inquiry, ways of thinking and perceiving that are the province of the expert. (Wiggins & McTighe, 2005)

Threshold concepts are one way of getting at these big ideas.

Learning about the threshold concept model helps relate learning theory to classroom practice and is useful for clarifying which teaching content should be prioritized when curricula are often overstuffed. In our experience, it also promotes a reflective teaching practice, which Sheila Corrall (2017) traces from its origins with educators John Dewey and Paolo Freire and philosopher Donald Schön to the central role given to reflection by information literacy practitioners seeking to become more effective instructors today. Further, we have found that this approach encourages productive engagement with colleagues. This may be because threshold concepts prompt us to articulate a distinct disciplinary perspective that we bring to the conversation (Swanson, 2017), or because they help us identify areas of overlapping concern that provide entry points for collaboration (Fullard, 2016).

This way of seeing information literacy content—in its acknowledgment of both cognitive and affective transitions—stands in contrast to viewing information literacy solely as a set of skills to master. The skills approach, commonly associated with bibliographic instruction, certainly continues to meet a need for students who arrive in an academic library lacking a basic understanding of how to find information. The landscape, however, has shifted, and information literacy instruction must shift as well.

The How-To Approach

Do librarians really need a new way of handling our instruction sessions? Consider the how-to approach to teaching library skills, often called bibliographic instruction. Bibliographic instruction is arguably more useful and relevant to students than ever before.

This is because in the past, when college populations were more limited by race, gender, and class, most students came to college already prepared to learn how academia works. Students with professional, college-educated parents have a significant advantage. They seem to absorb the rules by osmosis—something many disciplinary faculty still seem to expect. However, student populations have shifted. And at the same time, the information landscape has grown increasingly complex and chaotic. Both of these factors mean that offering bibliographic instruction to students is immensely helpful and has the potential to impact retention and graduation rates.

That sounds like a big claim, but there is compelling research to back it up. A longitudinal study at the University of West Georgia analyzed 12 years of data on 15,000 students who could choose to take a library credit course as part of their core requirements. Students who chose to take the library course graduated at almost double the rates of students who didn't. There are limitations to the research—self-selected population, nonrandom sample, variables like race or gender not accounted for—and the data show a correlation rather than causation. However, the study is able to infer that "library instruction has a lasting and measurable impact on student graduation rates" (Cook, 2014, p. 282).

The University of West Georgia's course was based on the ACRL *Standards* (J. M. Cook, personal communication, June 5, 2014; see also American Library Association, 2000). Indeed, many library courses teach what could be called the rules of the academic game. Much like transitional courses offered by student services, or tutoring centers that teach study skills, when librarians teach students to use the library's resources, we give them time to learn about the intellectual rules of the game. Libraries house the products of academia, which can help students understand the way it functions and what is expected of them. They otherwise have to simply pick up these understandings during the course of their academic career. It's important to acknowledge that learning the how-to content enumerated in the *Standards*' performance indicators and outcomes can help students succeed in their academic careers.

Yet, there is a crucial limitation to this type of skills-based instruction: information no longer lives mostly in the library. It's out there roaming the wilds of the internet. Self-published novels sit next to authoritative blog entries from the *New York Times*, and the best evidence-based *Nature* article can be found alongside questionable academic journals produced by pharmaceutical companies. In this environment, how does the novice learner distinguish between the bad and the good, or even just the relevant and the irrelevant? Librarians have to venture beyond the details of database demos and citation tools and delve into the concepts that also make sense of information systems outside the library, where the majority of finding, using, and creating information actually happens.

Martin Shanahan and Jan Meyer (2006) find that if content is oversimplified in order to make it more accessible or palatable to students, there is a risk that students will settle for the simplified version and never progress to a more nuanced understanding. While students may be served by a credit course taught like an extended bibliographic instruction for specific skills (how to search a database, how to use a reference work, how to write citations, and so on from one week to the next), they can bring those skills more smoothly into the rest of their lives if they are also taught the underlying big ideas, because teaching conceptually helps make those skills transferable. By situating the content of information literacy squarely within the discipline of information science, a course can cover big and fascinating issues in information that put the how-tos in context and actually interest students—things like the filter bubble, net neutrality, or bias in search engines. This is a more engaging approach because while everyone needs to learn the rules of the game, playing the game is more fun (Hofer, Lin Hanick, & Townsend, 2015).

Librarians who have been working on the front lines since library school may need some review in order to do this, much as newly minted PhD students have to go back and relearn parts of the foundations of their discipline in order to teach a first-year course. We hope that the exploration of disciplinary content in Part II of this book will help readers find connections between conceptual content and the how-tos that students also need to learn.

Threshold Concepts and the Culture of Librarianship

There are a few points about threshold concepts that are uniquely noteworthy in the context of librarianship.

First, threshold concepts are unusually empowering for a profession that has at times struggled to find secure footing in the academy. Librarians sometimes seem to hesitate to own a piece of the college curriculum, due to institutional hierarchies between faculty and staff, working in a traditionally female field, or entrenched cultural stereotypes. We learned in library school that we shouldn't try to make "little librarians" out of our students—a powerful message that what we have to teach is so basic that if we go beyond linear directions on using various information systems, we are wasting students' time on too much minutia that's irrelevant outside the profession.

Threshold concepts, rather, treat students as potential disciplinary practitioners. In teaching with threshold concepts, we ask students to try seeing the world through our disciplinary lens. In other words, we ask them to try seeing information the way that a librarian does, with no apologies.

Threshold concepts validate the classroom observations of disciplinary experts as valuable in identifying students' "stuck places" and the underlying learning thresholds (Meyer & Land, 2005). There is plenty of advice out there that might be overextended into a suggestion that your students really know best what they need to learn about information seeking (often this comes out of otherwise useful approaches to student-centered pedagogy, as in Allen, 2008; Dunaway & Orblych, 2011). By contrast, Glynis Cousin writes that "the thrust of threshold concept research is to share an inquiry into the difficulty of their subject *with* the academics and the students. It is student-focused but not student-centered in ways that remove the academic from the stage" (2010, p. 7). There are teaching practices that honor student experience and prior knowledge without erasing the instructor's expertise. In fact, a years-long, multimodal study that attempted to use student perspectives to determine threshold concepts for a discipline ultimately concluded that it was far more useful to look to instructor expertise instead (Shinners-Kennedy & Fincher, 2013).

On a related note, others object to the notion of librarians' being the best qualified to determine what librarians should teach. This is a variant on the idea that students know best. In this case, faculty in other disciplines must be consulted in detail to validate the information literacy curriculum. Along these lines, our work has been critiqued on the grounds that we asked librarians to identify students' stuck places, and then we (also librarians) analyzed the data. This was dismissed as "collective navel-gazing" and "librarian-on-librarian metaanalysis" (Morgan, 2015, p. 186). This line of thought is an even more extreme example of abdicating our own expertise. If librarians are not to determine our teaching content, who is? Faculty from other departments? Even if librarians could possibly persuade those faculty to give up their own research agendas to pursue ours, librarians would then be left without a major research area, with our own scholarship of teaching and learning off-limits. Disciplinary faculty might help us articulate information literacy threshold concepts specific to their discipline, but ceding our own discipline entirely to others is waving the white flag before the battle. While approaches that include collaboration with students and faculty from other disciplines are worthwhile, the threshold concept model returns the expertise to librarians as subject specialists in our own right.

The second important point about threshold concepts as applied to information literacy is structural: you cannot rush a threshold concept. By nature, these are the concepts that students will need to revisit again and again before they can get across the threshold and stay on the other side. Then, once they are across, they will likely need to revisit earlier material as they integrate formerly disparate facts with their new understanding. If students aren't given adequate time with threshold concepts, the risk is that they will wind up with superficial knowledge that might be adequate to pass a test, but doesn't develop their true understanding of the material. Therefore, this approach is of limited use for teaching one-shots, which is the majority of instruction that librarians do (as documented, for example, by Owusu-Ansah, 2007).

Once it's established that librarians are subject matter experts with big ideas to teach, and that one instruction session may not be enough time to teach them, the implications for instruction programs loom into view. To work closely with students on advancing their conceptual understanding of information, there is simply no substitute for time on task. When you have a credit course and the ability to assign homework attached to a grade, that gives you a mandate to require that students put in the time. It's the only way to get beyond the surface.

Of course, librarians have known for a long time that a one-shot just isn't enough time with students, whether we're taking a conceptual or procedural teaching approach. What sometimes happens, though, is that somehow—through persistence, advocacy, and administrative alignment—librarians might get a credit course to teach. We're so used to being in "less is more" mode that we don't know what to do with all that time. Threshold concepts are helpful at this point because these complex understandings are a better fit for a credit course than the outcomes in the old *Standards* document are.

If you do need to design a credit course, reading a book about planning one-shot instruction sessions probably isn't going to help you very much—a course really isn't 10 one-shots in a row. However, diving into threshold concepts for information literacy is incredibly useful in the context of designing a credit course *and* can help with planning one-shots by zooming in on one part of a concept for a single session.

For librarians, the most ambitious extension of the threshold concept model is to acknowledge that more time is the best (most effective) way to help students cross learning thresholds. Radical change in your information literacy instruction program is not in the cards for everyone, but could be worth considering. Because information literacy threshold concepts are interdisciplinary, the content often productively overlaps with that of other disciplines (with a unique angle). Integrating information literacy into the curriculum with enough time to cover threshold concepts may therefore be possible through collaboration with other faculty.

Third, and close to the librarian's heart, threshold concepts don't readily lend themselves to collecting the type of data that are often required by institutional assessment programs (Hofer, Brunetti, & Townsend, 2013). If your primary goal is to fill in an accreditation form, you are probably reading the wrong book right now. In fact, trying to assess the crossing of thresholds may seem like an obvious task to take on but in practice is extremely difficult.

The culture of academic librarianship tends to emphasize finding ways to advance the value proposition for the library—understandable, since librarians often feel under siege with cuts to our budgets and lack of support from administrators who don't understand what libraries do (Oakleaf, 2010). What the existing research shows as of this writing is that threshold concepts are most useful in helping faculty reengage with a reflective teaching practice. What you already do with developing and assessing learning outcomes is probably not going to change drastically as a result of incorporating threshold concepts into your pedagogy (Chapter 8 covers assessment in more detail).

Some Critical Perspectives

Our group of coauthors—Amy, Silvia, and Lori, along with our colleague Korey Brunetti—began looking at threshold concepts because we wanted to improve our teaching in a required credit course. At the time, library-land was teeming with standards, guidelines, and advice, yet in practice we felt that our checklist approach to learning outcomes didn't feel very effective or engaging on our end, and worse, seemed to bore our students. From our perspective as early-career instruction librarians, we wrote that "for the librarian who wants to progress beyond teaching students how to use the library and address some of the more complex themes of information literacy, the question of what to teach and how to teach it can seem very complicated" (Townsend, Brunetti, & Hofer, 2011, p. 857).

Our work led us to pinpoint some problems with the ACRL *Standards* document and to suggest how learning theories such as threshold concepts could make a revised document more useful for practitioners wanting to get away from the how-tos (Hofer et al., 2013). Unexpectedly, the threshold concept model entered the conversation for academic librarians in a big way when the ACRL Task Force for Information Literacy used threshold concepts to inform the new *Framework for Information Literacy for Higher Education* (ACRL, 2014; coauthor Lori Townsend was a member of that task force). Yet from our perspective now, as midcareer librarians involved in an ongoing research project on an emerging theory, the use and implications of this model for information literacy instruction are far from settled.

Meanwhile, the new *Framework* has sparked a tremendous amount of discussion among librarians on the topic of threshold concepts. Naturally, critical voices have emerged. In some cases, librarians object to the use of an emerging theory to underpin a foundational document of a professional association; while these objections may be valid, they aren't relevant to the discussion in this book (since this isn't a book about the *Framework*). On the other hand, there are also arguments both against threshold concepts and against their use in information literacy instruction that are useful to look at.

If these objections speak to you, we sincerely encourage you to find a different learning theory that helps you feel confident about what you do in the classroom to help your students become information literate. Threshold concepts are certainly not supposed to be the only means to that end. Fortunately, the final draft of the ACRL *Framework* moved away from explicit mention of threshold concepts, which leaves room for more varied approaches without the distraction of a specific theoretical reference.

In the following section, the arguments against threshold concepts, unless otherwise noted, are drawn from the summary given in Lane Wilkinson's 2015 presentation at LOEX (Wilkinson, 2015). Our responses to these arguments first appeared in an *ACRLog* blog post (Townsend, Lu [now Lin Hanick], Hofer, & Brunetti, 2015).

To begin, some find the threshold concept model insufficiently rigorous. These arguments object to Meyer and Land's use of hedging qualifiers to define the five criteria (threshold concepts *may* be troublesome, *might* integrate disparate concepts, etc.). Does this mean that anything can be called a threshold concept, that is, that a concept could pass muster even if it meets none of the criteria? In our opinion, the answer is no—librarians are busy people and are not going to waste time on proposing irrelevant content. Meyer and Land's careful language is more likely intended to avoid ruling out something as a threshold concept just because it doesn't meet all five criteria.

Along similar lines, some object to a lack of empirical research to support the effectiveness of threshold concepts, which is true to a point. Although some disciplines have used them to great effect, threshold concepts research is still emerging in our field, and there's a lot of work to be done. But before threshold concepts are dismissed on these grounds, it's worth asking how much else of what librarians do in the classroom is supported by positivist proof. If your colleague showed up in the break room all excited about the class they just taught, would you reply, "That sounds pretty great—I can't wait for you to publish a double-blind peer-reviewed study on that so that I can try it myself"? Librarians certainly don't need threshold concepts to engage more deeply and meaningfully with our content and students, but if the model helps we can try it, even if it's unproven.

Citing a lack of this particular type of proof may, in fact, be an intellectual dead end. Elevating positivist ways of knowing above others has been discredited since sociologists, in the 19th century, began to suggest that the scientific goal of objective knowledge is a fallacy. More recently, research paradigms that understand all knowledge as socially constructed, often collected under the umbrella of critical theory, have called the positivist worldview very much into question (Schroeder, 2014). In short, positivism is as positivism does.

On a different note, some of the objections raised take issue with eliding the differences between individual learning experiences and differing perspectives on content within a discipline. On the one hand, who are we to say what is troublesome for all students approaching an information literacy threshold? On the other hand, who are we to say that information literacy has disciplinary content that everyone in the field agrees upon?

Threshold concepts are not monolithic dictates opposed to the diversity of human experience. Meyer and Land's work supports this view:

> It might easily be implied that there is then one definitive and total conceptual understanding available, to which the tutor aims to bring the learner in due course. This would imply an objectivist position which would be in contradiction to our earlier characterizing of threshold concepts as discursive in nature. (Meyer & Land, 2005, p. 383)

Threshold concept theory acknowledges that students come to us with varying levels of prior knowledge. It is possible to make observations and perform interventions at the places where students are likely to get stuck, without ignoring their differences.

Threshold concepts catalyze an ongoing conversation that gets us thinking about teaching content—a core set of understandings that librarians bring with us even when we disagree. Peter Davies (2006) normalizes the idea that colleagues can have heterogeneous perspectives on teaching content while still being able to all fit into the disciplinary minivan when he writes,

> Insofar as there are different schools of thought within disciplines, there will also be integrating "school threshold concepts" that *characterize* these schools as well as "discipline threshold concepts" that distinguish *all* members of a subject community from those in other communities. (Davies, 2006, p. 78)

Cousin (2009) also writes about differences within disciplines: "[Threshold concepts] are not fixed truths about a subject. What might be a threshold concept for economics in one phase or school of the discipline might be considered to be outmoded or erroneous by another" (p. 203). Threshold concepts, moreover, have been applied to disciplines far broader than library science—for example, biology, which encompasses a wide range of specialties, yet is still acknowledged to have common learning thresholds (Taylor, 2008).

Librarians don't all need to teach identical curricula in order to introduce students to the big ideas that enlarge their perspectives about the information landscape. To suggest that student experiences are so fundamentally different that there are no common points of confusion, or that experts disagree so profoundly that there are no common understandings or teaching topics in our field, calls into question the idea of learning in groups and dividing knowledge into disciplines at all.

Finally, some object to threshold concepts on the grounds that they reinforce hegemonic power structures. Certainly, by teaching with threshold concepts, librarians might acknowledge or examine power structures, but this is not at all the same as endorsing them. For example, there has been confusion over whether acknowledging the commodification of information is the same as an endorsement of this state of affairs. But students hit paywalls on Google Scholar, and they sometimes spend more than their tuition on textbooks; libraries exhaust their budgets buying back research that faculty conducted on university time. Information is, in fact, bought and sold, and this makes it a commodity. Why would librarians not teach students that these forces are in play, even if it is prefaced with "I hate that this is the way the world works, but . . . "? Librarians can teach a critical approach; emphasize the importance of open licensing and fair use; and share examples of alternative models, radical views, and critical resistance. But students don't get the chance to be critical of a thing unless they have a chance to understand it first.

Here is an analogy. It would be impossible to teach the history of the civil rights movement in the United States if you believed that it was racist to acknowledge the existence of racism. You just can't fully understand the civil rights movement if you don't have a chance to understand its context—and indeed, failing to teach the context inexplicably denies a shared reality.

The idea put forth by Ian Beilin that librarians shouldn't teach the existence of certain concepts on ideological grounds shades into a disturbing paternalism: "Teaching students how to function within an academic discourse can be perilously close to teaching students how to conform, how to get along, how to succeed" (Beilin, 2015). It is unconscionable that librarians would judge or undermine students' wish to succeed (especially at institutions serving traditionally underrepresented groups). Nicole Cooke writes powerfully of her experience on the tenure track and the impact of microaggressions and other forms of racism; she has worked to change her inner monologue from "***Do I want to be at this table?***" to "***I deserve to be at the table and I need to stay at this table. How do I make this happen?***" (2014, pp. 40, 45, emphasis in the original). Librarians must not cede the possibility of serving as the kind of supporter and mentor that Cooke describes as being essential to her decision to stay at the table.

Using the threshold concept approach doesn't force you to teach your content one way or another; it doesn't force you to agree with all the implications of a particular disciplinary lens. What threshold concepts do is acknowledge the existence of the lens. If we are going to ask students to look through a librarian lens—that is, help them become information literate—we should be able to articulate what that means. Threshold concepts can be used to encourage students to engage critically with our content in order to assist them in defying structural expectations. We believe that librarians should show students the lens and then let them make up their own minds what they think about it.

Threshold Concepts in Use for Information Literacy Instruction

While some have criticized threshold concepts as a pedagogical approach, others have embraced it and written about their successes in applying it for information literacy instruction. Craig Gibson and Trudi Jacobson, chairs of the ACRL Information Literacy Competency Standards for Higher Education Task Force, write,

> [Meyer and Land's] theory of threshold concepts has been accepted by academics in other disciplines as one way of thinking about the recurring difficulties experienced by students when faced with unfamiliar landscapes of learning . . . such understanding would facilitate [students'] navigation of the complex environment of academic research. (2014, pp. 251–252)

Gibson and Jacobson were instrumental in incorporating threshold concepts and other current learning theories into the revised *Framework* filed by ACRL in 2015 and adopted in 2016. This section looks at some ways that the threshold concept approach has been useful for information literacy instruction to date.

For some, threshold concepts have been a springboard to think about authentic assignments. Along these lines, Kevin Seeber (2014) suggests ways that the threshold concept Format as a Process might be taught through learning activities such as editing a wiki, creating a blog post, and publishing work in the institutional repository. As another example, Louise Fluk (2015) suggests that the research log or research journal may be a uniquely useful assessment for librarians teaching with threshold concepts: "The notion of learning as a journey which must cross multiple thresholds on the way to mastery of important concepts merges nicely with the view of research as a recursive process and the research log or journal as the story of that process" (p. 490). Lindsay Roberts (2017) offers evidence that a problem-based learning approach to conceptual information literacy instruction may be particularly effective when working with nontraditional learners; her students showed notable improvement in transferring new skills to personal information needs.

In other cases, using the threshold concept model has helped librarians shift their teaching of a specialized subset of a more general information literacy curriculum. For example, Rebecca Kuglitsch (2015) applies threshold concepts to teaching information literacy in the context of STEM (science, technology, engineering, and mathematics) disciplines and proposes a discipline-specific discussion of peer review, credentialing, predatory publishers, and retractions in order to explore the concept of authority:

> For example, the concept of how authority is constructed initially appears clear in science: experimental research is conducted and then peer-reviewed to ensure it is accurate and meaningful. But as more and more research has been called into question and found to be unreproducible, the question of authority becomes complicated. (Kuglitsch, 2015, p. 463)

Along similar lines, Megan Bresnahan and Andrew Johnson (2014) developed lesson plans that apply the new ACRL frames to a data literacy component of an information literacy program. For example, using the frame Scholarship Is a Conversation, they developed a lesson plan that asks students to analyze a retracted article from a data management perspective. To teach the Searching as Exploration frame, students use and evaluate citation and data management tools to organize and share their own research information.

Threshold concepts have been applied to graduate- and doctoral-level research in many disciplines, and the model has been useful in looking at information literacy concepts for advanced researchers as well. Nina Exner (2014), writing about the information literacy needs of faculty and graduate researchers in formulating and researching an original inquiry, explores the Research as Inquiry frame of the ACRL *Framework* and concludes that it may not fully cover the learning thresholds that need to be crossed for more advanced researchers. Her work is an example of the potential to identify new threshold concepts for information literacy topics not already covered by the existing literature. Marianne Buehler and Anne Zald (2013), similarly, identify the process of getting published as a learning threshold for graduate students entering the scholarly communication process. They suggest that librarians are uniquely positioned to contextualize new media in which scholarly conversations are taking place, such as open repositories, blogs, and other interactive venues, to offer a more nuanced view of scholarly communication.

Librarians are also making the case that the conceptual approach articulated in the new *Framework* helps them forge deeper connections with faculty in other disciplines. For example, William Badke (2015) argues that in order to use the *Framework*, librarians must "break free of the librarian silo and foster a strong discussion about student research and information use within academia as a whole . . . This means faculty and academic administrators must be on board" (p. 5). Illustrating this principle, Catherine Baird and Jonathan Howell (2017) describe a collaboration between a librarian and a linguist that resulted in an activity examining how different approaches to the phenomenon of "vocal fry" (as heard on *This American Life*) complicate the notion of authoritative information from both an information literacy perspective and a linguistics perspective. They write of this experience:

> We found that the language of threshold concepts significantly changed the tenor and substance of our collaboration, which was immediately reflected in the way we approached our teaching and had a direct impact on student learning. It also helped to mitigate some of the typical barriers to librarian-faculty collaboration. (Baird & Howell, 2017, pp. 48–49)

Finally, there are examples in the literature that show how libraries have begun to use the threshold concept model to rethink their instruction programs. Brandi Porter (2014) describes how Ferrum College used threshold concepts to redesign a scaffolded information literacy program away from bibliographic instruction and toward conceptual teaching. Along similar lines, Dan DeSanto and Susanmarie Harrington (2017) write about how the University of Vermont incorporated information literacy learning thresholds into their Writing in the Disciplines/Writing Across the Curriculum program and their revised general education requirement outcomes.

Examples of Threshold Concepts in Related Disciplines

Threshold concepts have been identified and used for teaching in a wide variety of disciplines, in addition to vocational and interdisciplinary settings. This section presents examples that have particular relevance in relation to information literacy.

As mentioned previously, there is a great deal of literature on threshold concepts for doctoral students learning a more advanced approach to research. Margaret Kiley and Gina Wisker look at interdisciplinary threshold concepts for graduate students learning to become researchers (e.g., Kiley & Wisker, 2009). They identify six threshold concepts for research and discuss how doctoral supervisors were able to perceive that a researcher has crossed a threshold. For example, they identify a threshold concept that they call Knowledge Creation, which relates to the information literacy concept Research Process: students demonstrate "contribution of new ideas and thought, and in self-motivated research that indicates not just a willingness to work but an engagement with the essential issues and the leading edge work on the field" (p. 438). Kiley's subsequent work (e.g., Kiley, 2015) continues to examine where students may become stuck in liminal spaces but also proposes strategies to help them become unstuck, such as peer discussion groups, frequent writing, and structured reading guided by the supervisor. Preliminary findings from librarians suggest that there may be information literacy threshold concepts specific to graduate research, so Kiley and Wisker's work may help with their identification.

When librarians do teach credit courses, they are often included in the General Education curriculum or first-year experience program (for better or worse). As such, it is useful to consider work such as that of Linda Adler-Kassner, John Majewski, and Damian Koshnick (2012), which looks at threshold concepts shared by English and history courses taught in a General Education curriculum. They present learning thresholds for composition that have to do with understanding writing as a practice related to communities of discourse involving genre, purpose, audience, and context. They find that these concepts are very closely related to those used by historians in analyzing primary documents and historical narratives. Yet, thresholds for writing in a history context remained tacit when "instructors missed the opportunity to relate *and* distinguish their discipline to others in the general education curriculum." The authors' conclusion may also provide a possible model for teaching information literacy within the disciplines:

> Working from this perspective enables us to consider, as we have done here, whether there are concepts that exist within specific disciplines, like composition and history, that then can also span *across* disciplines. This perspective positions these concepts not as all-purpose habits that exist within liberal learning, as in the distribution model, but as discipline-specific concepts that operate within . . . different contexts . . . Working together, instructors can help students to explicitly, consciously enact these shared threshold concepts, facilitating more effective transfer across both. (Adler-Kassner et al., 2012)

In a similar effort, Brittney Johnson and I. Moriah McCracken crosswalk the *Framework*'s six frames with complementary learning thresholds identified for composition in *Naming What We Know: Threshold Concepts of Writing Studies* (Adler-Kassner & Wardle, 2015). This work presented "an opportunity for rich, crossdisciplinary integration that could potentially empower teachers in two separate fields to advocate collectively against one-off, skills-focused writing and research instruction" (Johnson & McCracken, 2016, p. 180).

Librarians can also consider threshold concept research in our own discipline—information science—and consider whether there is a useful application in the teaching of information literacy. Chris Cope and Lorraine Staehr (2008), for example, propose a threshold concept of information systems as social systems. This notion is closely related to information literacy threshold concepts relating to deeper understandings of database structure and the information landscape that inform effective search technique. Our own research group extensively discussed "Searching Is Not Magic," proposed by a Delphi study participant, along with other ways to capture the concept that the algorithms and retrieval systems that govern search results, often reified, are in fact designed by people and are therefore predictably biased. "Recognizing that people are an integral part of [information systems] and understanding the process of attribution of meaning as a human activity are educationally critical aspects of [information systems] as social systems" (Cope & Staehr, p. 354). Cope and Staehr designed learning activities that problematize ideas of information systems as purely technical and introduce the role of people, meaning, and interpretation into data output and analysis.

Taking a bigger-picture look, Ian Kinchin and Norma Miller (2012) studied the possibility of threshold concepts for university teaching, which might be extrapolated from a U.S. perspective as learning thresholds for instructors in higher education settings. This topic is relevant for librarians who, as previously noted, may not have received formal instruction in learning theory before finding themselves in a teaching role. Understanding whether there may be learning thresholds for all teaching faculty can help librarians enter conversations with other disciplinary faculty with shared understandings. Additional research by Margaret Blackie, Jennifer Case, and Jeff Jawitz (2010) suggests that the broader notion of student-centeredness may also be a threshold concept for instructors in higher education.

In addition to the aforementioned examples, which directly bear on information literacy instruction, librarians might find resonance with disciplines not obviously connected to our content areas. For example, Lynn Clouder's (2005) work on caring in the context of professional nursing may offer interesting analogies for librarians at the reference desk since ours is a helping profession as well. Ursula Lucas and Rosina Mladenovic (2006) consider the ways in which accounting instructors tend to overfocus on rules-based procedures at the expense of conceptual knowledge in response to students' negative preconceptions of the subject, which resonates with our own experiences teaching information literacy in a required credit course. Carol Zander et al. (2008) describe impediments to using the curriculum standards defined for computer science and propose that threshold concepts might provide a more useful way to prioritize the same teaching content, mirroring the problem that the library profession had with the old *Standards* for information literacy.

Further Reading

In the years since the threshold concept model was first developed, there has been a tremendous amount of writing on the subject, while a biennial conference has served to further develop a community of practice. There are several edited, multiauthor books exploring the emerging threshold concept theory as well as its applications in a wide variety of disciplines and learning settings (Land, Meyer, & Smith, 2008; Meyer & Land, 2006a; Meyer, Land, & Baillie, 2010). Mick Flanagan maintains an invaluable bibliography on threshold concept publications (Flanagan, 2018). Not only that, but the library profession as a whole is in the midst of an explosion of papers and conference sessions as we grapple with the implications of turning toward conceptual teaching.

These resources not only are useful to read in their own right but also may help librarians connect with disciplinary faculty who are interested in teaching with threshold concepts. We encourage interested librarians to broaden their reading beyond this book.

Takeaways

- Threshold concepts help instructors understand why concepts that seem easy or straightforward can present real difficulty for students who lack a disciplinary perspective.
- The instructional content of information literacy is complex and may be troublesome for students.
- There is an extensive, international discourse around threshold concepts for teaching and learning that librarians can benefit from participating in.

For Further Consideration

- Can you remember an "aha" moment when you crossed a learning threshold for information literacy or information science? What changed for you? What new understandings came into view?
- Conceptual teaching is an uncomfortable fit with one-shot instruction sessions. What solutions might be effective at your institution to resolve these seemingly contradictory needs?

- How do you prioritize what to teach under the information literacy banner? What do you see as the ways of thinking and practicing that librarians can teach students? How do these align with disciplinary faculty expectations?

References

Adler-Kassner, L., Majewski, J., & Koshnick, D. (2012). The value of troublesome knowledge: Transfer and threshold concepts in writing and history. *Composition Forum, 26*. Retrieved from http://compositionforum.com/issue/26/troublesome-knowledge-threshold.php

Adler-Kassner, L., & Wardle, E. (Eds.). (2015). *Naming what we know: Threshold concepts of writing studies*. Boulder, CO: Utah State University Press.

Allen, M. (2008). Promoting critical thinking skills in online information literacy instruction using a constructivist approach. *College & Undergraduate Libraries, 15*(1–2), 21–38. doi:10.1080/10691310802176780

American Library Association. (2000). *Information literacy competency standards for higher education*. Retrieved from http://www.ala.org/acrl/standards/informationliteracycompetency

Association of College & Research Libraries. (2014). *Framework for information literacy for higher education*. Retrieved from http://www.ala.org/acrl/standards/ilframework

Atherton, J., Hadfield, P., & Meyers, R. (2008). *Threshold concepts in the wild*. Expanded paper presented at the Threshold Concepts: From Theory to Practice conference, Kingston, Ontario. Retrieved from https://www.researchgate.net/publication/228873314_Threshold_Concepts_in_the_Wild

Badke, W. B. (2015). Diktuon: The Framework for Information Literacy and theological education: Introduction to the ACRL Framework. *Theological Librarianship, 8*(2), 4–7. Retrieved from https://theolib.atla.com/theolib/article/download/385/1310

Baird, C., & Howell, J. (2017). Exploring authority in linguistics research: Who to trust when everyone's a language expert. In S. Godbey, S. B. Wainscott, & X. Goodman (Eds.), *Disciplinary applications of information literacy threshold concepts* (pp. 37–50). Chicago, IL: Association of College & Research Libraries. Retrieved from http://works.bepress.com/jonathan-howell/6/

Beilin, I. (2015). Beyond the threshold: Conformity, resistance, and the ACRL Information Literacy Framework for Higher Education. *In the Library with the Lead Pipe*. Retrieved from http://www.inthelibrarywiththeleadpipe.org/2015/beyond-the-threshold-conformity-resistance-and-the-aclr-information-literacy-framework-for-higher-education/

Blackie, M. A. L., Case, J. M., & Jawitz, J. (2010). Student-centredness: The link between transforming students and transforming ourselves. *Teaching in Higher Education, 15*(6), 637–646. doi:10.1080/13562517.2010.491910

Bresnahan, M., & Johnson, A. (2014). *Building a unified data and information literacy program: A collaborative approach to instruction*. Presented at

Library Instruction West. Retrieved from http://scholar.colorado.edu/libr_facpapers/8/

Buehler, M. A., & Zald, A. E. (2013). At the nexus of scholarly communication and information literacy. In S. Davis-Kahl & M. K. Hensley (Eds.), *Common ground at the nexus of information literacy and scholarly communication* (pp. 215–235). Chicago, IL: American Library Association. Retrieved from http://digitalscholarship.unlv.edu/lib_articles/421

Clouder, L. (2005). Caring as a "threshold concept": Transforming students in higher education into health(care) professionals. *Teaching in Higher Education, 10*(4), 505–517. doi:10.1080/13562510500239141

Cook, J. M. (2014). A library credit course and student success rates: A longitudinal study. *College & Research Libraries, 75*(3), 272–283. doi:10.5860/crl12-424

Cooke, N. A. (2014). Pushing back from the table. *Polymath: An Interdisciplinary Arts & Sciences Journal, 4*(2), 39–49. Retrieved from https://ojcs.siue.edu/ojs/index.php/polymath/article/view/2934/1000

Cope, C., & Staehr, L. (2008). Improving student learning about a threshold concept in the IS discipline. *Informing Science: The International Journal of an Emerging Transdiscipline, 11*, 349–364. Retrieved from http://www.inform.nu/Articles/Vol11/ISJv11p349-364Cope217.pdf

Corrall, S. (2017). Crossing the threshold: Reflective practice in information literacy development. *Journal of Information Literacy, 11*(1), 23–53. doi:10.11645/11.1.2241

Cousin, G. (2008). Threshold concepts: Old wine in new bottles or a new form of transactional curriculum inquiry? In R. Land, J. H. F. Meyer, & J. Smith (Eds.), *Threshold concepts within the disciplines* (pp. 261–272). Rotterdam, the Netherlands: Sense Publishers.

Cousin, G. (2009). *Researching learning in higher education*. New York, NY: Routledge.

Cousin, G. (2010). Neither teacher-centred nor student-centred: Threshold concepts and research partnerships. *Journal of Learning Development in Higher Education* (2), 1–9. Retrieved from http://journal.aldinhe.ac.uk/index.php/jldhe/article/viewFile/64/41

Davies, P. (2006). Threshold concepts: How can we recognise them? In J. H. F. Meyer & R. Land (Eds.), *Overcoming barriers to student understanding: Threshold concepts and troublesome knowledge* (pp. 70–84). New York, NY: Routledge.

DeSanto, D., & Harrington, S. (2017). Harnessing the intersections of writing and information literacy. In *At the helm: Leading transformation, conference proceedings of ACRL 2017*. Retrieved from http://www.ala.org/acrl/sites/ala.org.acrl/files/content/conferences/confsandpreconfs/2017/HarnessingtheIntersectionsofWritingandInformationLiteracy%20.pdf

Dunaway, M. K., & Orblych, M. T. (2011). Formative assessment: Transforming information literacy instruction. *Reference Services Review, 39*(1), 24–41. doi:10.1108/00907321111108097

Exner, N. (2014). Research information literacy: Addressing original researchers' needs. *Journal of Academic Librarianship, 40*(5), 460–466. doi:10.1016/j.acalib.2014.06.006

Flanagan, M. (2018). *Threshold concepts: Undergraduate teaching, postgraduate training, professional development and school education: A short introduction and bibliography*. Retrieved from http://www.ee.ucl.ac.uk/~mflanaga/thresholds.html

Fluk, L. R. (2015). Foregrounding the research log in information literacy instruction. *Journal of Academic Librarianship, 41*(4), 488–498. doi:10.1016/j.acalib.2015.06.010

Fullard, A. (2016). Using the ACRL Framework for Information Literacy to foster teaching and learning partnerships. *South African Journal of Libraries and Information Science, 82*(2), 46–56. doi:10.7553/82-2-1627

Gibson, C., & Jacobson, T. E. (2014). Informing and extending the draft ACRL Information Literacy Framework for Higher Education: An overview and avenues for research. *College & Research Libraries, 75*(3), 250–254. doi:10.5860/0750250

Hofer, A. R., Brunetti, K., & Townsend, L. (2013). A threshold concepts approach to the Standards revision. *Communications in Information Literacy, 7*(2), 108–113. Retrieved from http://www.comminfolit.org/index.php?journal=cil&page=article&op=view&path%5B%5D=v7i2p108&path%5B%5D=168

Hofer, A. R., Lin Hanick, S., & Townsend, L. (2015, April 10). *What's the big idea? Incorporating threshold concepts into your teaching practice*. Keynote at the Information Literacy Summit, Palos Hills, IL. Recording retrieved from https://youtu.be/OSahSjLBf-w?t=1s

Johnson, B., & McCracken, I. M. (2016). Reading for integration, identifying complementary threshold concepts: The ACRL Framework in conversation with *Naming What We Know: Threshold Concepts of Writing Studies*. *Communications in Information Literacy, 10*(2), 178–198. Retrieved from https://pdxscholar.library.pdx.edu/comminfolit/vol10/iss2/2/

Kiley, M. (2015). "I didn't have a clue what they were talking about": PhD candidates and theory. *Innovations in Education and Teaching International, 52*(1), 52–63. doi:10.1080/14703297.2014.981835

Kiley, M., & Wisker, G. (2009). Threshold concepts in research education and evidence of threshold crossing. *Higher Education Research & Development, 28*(4), 431–441. doi:10.1080/07294360903067930

Kinchin, I. M., & Miller, N. L. (2012). "Structural transformation" as a threshold concept in university teaching. *Innovations in Education and Teaching International, 49*(2), 207–222. doi:10.1080/14703297.2012.677655

Kuglitsch, R. (2015). Teaching for transfer: Reconciling the Framework with disciplinary information literacy. *portal: Libraries and the Academy, 15*(3), 457–470. doi:10.1353/pla.2015.0040

Land, R., Meyer, J. H. F., & Smith, J. (2008). *Threshold concepts within the disciplines.* Rotterdam, the Netherlands: Sense Publishers.

Lucas, U., & Mladenovic, R. (2006). Developing new "world views": Threshold concepts in introductory accounting. In J. H. F. Meyer & R. Land (Eds.), *Overcoming barriers to student understanding: Threshold concepts and troublesome knowledge* (pp. 148–159). New York, NY: Routledge.

Lundstrom, K., Fagerheim, B. A., & Benson, E. (2014). Librarians and instructors developing student learning outcomes: Using frameworks to lead the process. *Reference Services Review, 42*(3), 484–498. doi:10.1108/RSR-04-2014-0007

Meyer, J. H. F., & Land, R. (2003). *Threshold concepts and troublesome knowledge: Linkages to ways of thinking and practising within the disciplines.* ETL Project Occasional Report 4. Edinburgh, Scotland: Enhancing Teaching-Learning Environments in Undergraduate Courses Project. Retrieved from http://www.etl.tla.ed.ac.uk/docs/ETLreport4.pdf

Meyer, J. H. F., & Land, R. (2005). Threshold concepts and troublesome knowledge (2): Epistemological considerations and a conceptual framework for teaching and learning. *Higher Education: The International Journal of Higher Education and Educational Planning, 49*(3), 373–388. doi:10.1007/s10734-004-6779-5

Meyer, J. H. F., & Land, R. (2006a). *Overcoming barriers to student understanding: Threshold concepts and troublesome knowledge.* London, England: Routledge.

Meyer, J. H. F., & Land, R. (2006b). Threshold concepts and troublesome knowledge: Issues of liminality. In J. H. F. Meyer & R. Land (Eds.), *Overcoming barriers to student understanding: Threshold concepts and troublesome knowledge* (pp. 19–32). New York, NY: Routledge.

Meyer, J. H. F., & Land, R. (2007, August 17). Stop the conveyor belt, I want to get off. *Times Higher Education Supplement* (1807). Retrieved from http://www.timeshighereducation.co.uk/90288.article

Meyer, J. H. F., Land, R., & Baillie, C. (2010). *Threshold concepts and transformational learning.* Rotterdam, the Netherlands: Sense Publishers.

Miller, S. D. (2018). Diving deep: Reflective questions for identifying tacit disciplinary information literacy knowledge practices, dispositions, and values through the ACRL Framework for Information Literacy. *Journal of Academic Librarianship, 44*(3), 412–418. doi:10.1016/j.acalib.2018.02.014

Morgan, P. K. (2015). Pausing at the threshold. *portal: Libraries and the Academy, 15*(1), 183–195. doi:10.1353/pla.2015.0002

Oakleaf, M. (2010). *The value of academic libraries: A comprehensive research review and report.* Retrieved from http://www.ala.org/acrl/sites/ala.org.acrl/files/content/issues/value/val_report.pdf

Owusu-Ansah, E. K. (2007). Beyond collaboration: Seeking greater scope and centrality for library instruction. *portal: Libraries and the Academy, 7*(4), 415–429. doi:10.1353/pla.2007.0043

Porter, B. (2014). Designing a library information literacy program using threshold concepts, student learning theory, and millennial research in the development of information literacy sessions. *Internet Reference Services Quarterly, 19*(3–4), 233–244. doi:10.1080/10875301.2014.978928

Roberts, L. (2017). Research in the real world: Improving adult learners web search and evaluation skills through motivational design and problem-based learning. *College & Research Libraries, 78*(4), 527–551. Retrieved from https://crl.acrl.org/index.php/crl/article/view/16644

Schroeder, R. (2014). Exploring critical and indigenous research methods with a research community: Part II—The landing. *In the Library with the Lead Pipe*. Retrieved from http://www.inthelibrarywiththeleadpipe.org/2014/exploring-the-landing/

Seeber, K. P. (2014). Teaching "Format as a Process" in an era of web-scale discovery. *Reference Services Review, 43*(1), 19–30. doi:10.1108/RSR-07-2014-0023

Shanahan, M., & Meyer, J. H. F. (2006). The troublesome nature of a threshold concept in economics. In J. H. F. Meyer & R. Land (Eds.), *Overcoming barriers to student understanding: Threshold concepts and troublesome knowledge* (pp. 100–114). New York, NY: Routledge.

Shinners-Kennedy, D., & Fincher, S. A. (2013, August). Identifying threshold concepts: From dead end to a new direction. *Proceedings of the ninth annual international ACM conference on International Computing Education Research*. doi:10.1145/2493394.2493396

Swanson, T. (2017). Sharing the ACRL Framework with faculty: Opening campus conversations. *College & Research Libraries News, 78*(1), 12–48. doi:10.5860/crln.78.1.9600

Taylor, C. E. (2008). Threshold concepts, troublesome knowledge and ways of thinking and practising: Can we tell the difference in biology? In R. Land, J. H. F. Meyer, & J. Smith (Eds.), *Threshold concepts within the disciplines* (pp. 261–272). Rotterdam, the Netherlands: Sense Publishers.

Townsend, L., Brunetti, K., & Hofer, A. R. (2011). Threshold concepts and information literacy. *portal: Libraries and the Academy, 11*(3), 853–869. Retrieved from http://archives.pdx.edu/ds/psu/7417

Townsend, L., Lu, S., Hofer, A. R., & Brunetti, K. (2015). *What's the matter with threshold concepts?* Retrieved from http://acrlog.org/2015/01/30/whats-the-matter-with-threshold-concepts/

Wiggins, G., & McTighe, J. (2005). *Understanding by design*. Alexandria, VA: ACSD.

Wilkinson, L. (2015). *Reconsidering threshold concepts: A critical appraisal of the ACRL Framework for Information Literacy*. Presented at LOEX, Denver, CO. Slides and handout retrieved from http://www.loexconference.org/sessions.html

Zander, C., Boustedt, J., Eckerdal, A., McCartney, R., Mostrom, J. E., Ratcliffe, M., & Sanders, K. (2008). Threshold concepts in computer science: A multinational empirical investigation. In R. Land, J. H. F. Meyer, & J. Smith (Eds.), *Threshold concepts within the disciplines* (pp. 261–272). Rotterdam, the Netherlands: Sense Publishers.

CHAPTER TWO

Identifying Threshold Concepts for Information Literacy

The threshold concept model provides one way to prioritize our teaching content. The first step in applying the model is working through what we think the threshold concepts for our content are. Our group of researchers has considered many iterations and ideas, and we believe that our own list will continue to change over time. It has been productive to try out different ideas and see whether they work with the threshold concept criteria. Sometimes they do, and sometimes they don't.

For example, at one point Amy posited that "Let's go to the library" might be a threshold concept since library awareness was a major trouble spot for the students she was working with at the time. However, not all troublesome knowledge is a threshold concept, and we couldn't all agree that using the library is a transformative concept that lets students into a tacit understanding uniquely shared by librarians. Of course, our thinking continues to evolve, and we still go back and forth on this concept, but we haven't resolved the question in our own minds enough to include the concept in this book.

This chapter covers how our group of researchers has worked to identify threshold concepts for information literacy. Because the threshold concepts for information literacy are not settled, and need not ever be considered settled, the reader might also use this chapter to think about developing threshold concepts that are relevant to a specific setting, course, or topic within our field.

Identifying Threshold Concepts

One exciting aspect of the threshold concept model is that any instructor is in a position to theorize what the learning thresholds for their discipline may be. Looking at the places where students tend to struggle, through a lens of disciplinary expertise, can lead to insight into the underlying concepts that students need to grasp in order to cross a learning threshold. Herein lies the potential of threshold concepts to revitalize teaching and learning.

In an early work, Peter Davies (2006) theorizes several ways to identify threshold concepts. He suggests that researchers might compare how scholars from different disciplines analyze the same topic in order to pinpoint the differences in their ways of thinking and practicing. He also suggests that researchers might compare the ways that experts and novices analyze the same topic in order to differentiate the ways of thinking and practicing of those already within the community. Last, he proposes that analysis of students' metacognitive record, such as interviews or diaries, might elicit which thresholds were crossed in order to create an awareness of having joined a disciplinary community (the latter two approaches were put into practice and written up in Davies & Mangan, 2005).

Most importantly, Davies's work establishes identifying threshold concepts as something that occurs through conversation, discussion, comparison, or observation of student attitudes and work products. There are many references throughout the threshold concept literature to the importance of discussion among practitioners. For example, Glynis Cousin writes,

> In my experience, the very inquiry into threshold concepts creates lively debates among subject specialists about what is central to their curriculum ... Indeed one of the big advantages of threshold concept research is that it animates discussion and interest among academics in ways in which more generic educational issues do not. (Cousin, 2009, pp. 203, 206)

These statements mirror our experiences. Contrary to Patrick Morgan's assertion, threshold concepts are not " 'out there' to be 'discovered' " (2015, p. 7). We do the work of identifying threshold concepts for our teaching content in order to reflect on ways to help students grasp the ways of thinking and practicing of our discipline and decide whether to join that disciplinary community. This reflection both establishes and deepens communities of practice as we deeply consider our disciplinary content in detail.

Sarah Barradell (2013) wrote a very useful review of the methods that different researchers have used to identify threshold concepts in the years since Davies wrote his speculative piece. The methods vary widely: "informal, semi-structured, phenomenographic interviews . . . , questionnaires, surveys, short answer problems and review of old examination papers . . . , and observation of classroom behavior" (p. 269). The literature of threshold concepts as a whole suggests that there are many possible methods for conducting threshold concept research, and it may not be appropriate to establish fixed procedures (Cousin, 2009).

Should student perspectives be included in threshold concept research? Barradell (2013) argues strongly for the inclusion of students and other stakeholders, such as instructional designers, in the process of identifying threshold concepts. In a perhaps unique case, Marina Orsini-Jones (2008) based her threshold concept research entirely upon student perspectives (though still carried out the analysis of the student data herself). In other cases, students contribute to the process of compiling proposed threshold concepts, as in Harold Morales and Mark Barnes's (2018) religious studies course at Morgan State University, where students create a list of challenging concepts at the beginning of the course and are invited to revise their lists at the end of the term. Rachel Scott (2017) conducted a notable study that sought student input on whether the six concepts in the Association of College & Research Libraries' (ACRL) *Framework for Information Literacy for Higher Education* are transformative, integrative, and troublesome. A counter-perspective was presented in Chapter 1, where Dermot Shinners-Kennedy and Sally Fincher (2013) emphasize that the most productive place to start in determining threshold concepts for a discipline is with instructors. This is an empowering message for librarians, who may feel obligated to validate our curriculum with disciplinary faculty. However, it does not rule out the desirability of engaging both librarians and nonlibrarians (of various stripes) in threshold concept research for information literacy.

Barradell raises a concern about lack of rigor in the process of identifying threshold concepts in some of the work she reviews. This echoes the criticism of Darrell Rowbottom (2007) and Rod O'Donnell (2010), both of whom find the entire premise of threshold concept theory far too squishy to stand up to critical scrutiny. We argue, though, that threshold concepts are a model—no more and no less. To borrow an engineering perspective: "all models are wrong; the practical question is how wrong do they have to be not to be useful" (Box & Draper, 1987, p. 74). Models are not meant to be infallibly applicable to every real-world situation; in this case, they can provide a helpful experimental space.

Therefore, we can test the model and take away what is useful from it. Did you have an energizing discussion with a colleague? Did your students engage with your class session? Did you get a new idea about how to teach a lesson that had previously been a trouble spot for students? In a very practical and day-to-day sense, these outcomes should not be minimized, since they are the issues that truly have an impact on a frontline instruction librarian. If you can answer yes to those questions, then it's likely that the model was useful to you, and you should go ahead and continue using it if you like it. This perspective is supported by a concept from the literature of action research called "value-in-use" (e.g., as used by Elliott, 2007).

Both critics and proponents of the threshold concept approach caution against overprivileging the particular disciplinary lens being taught. For example, in an early paper, Jan Meyer and Ray Land (2003) wrote, "It might, of course, be argued, in a critical sense, that such transformed understanding leads to a privileged or dominant view and therefore a contestable way of understanding something" (p. 1). Yet, it is possible to teach that librarians have a common way of thinking and practicing *while at the same time* teaching that there are different schools of thought within the profession. Because librarians value critical thinking, we will encourage students to consider alternative perspectives—in fact, this is one of the cornerstones of information literacy. Threshold concepts don't aim to set up a false either-or dichotomy that shuts off conflicting viewpoints or eliminates ambiguity.

To summarize, there are many possible methods for identifying threshold concepts. Conversation with colleagues and others is essential. In addition, lack of rigor and unexamined ideologies have been flagged as potential pitfalls for this model. This helps us avoid them when we apply the model ourselves.

A Closer Look at the Definitional Criteria

Meyer and Land (2003) posit that threshold concepts are likely to meet the following definitional criteria:

- Transformative
- Integrative
- Irreversible
- Bounded
- Troublesome

Identifying threshold concepts is not the same as identifying learning objectives or the basic building blocks for a course or subject. Threshold concepts are interconnected, so while understanding one might help you progress with another, they are not meant to be tackled sequentially. These concepts are the ones that transform the learner and help integrate disciplinary information into a larger understanding.

It is an open question as to whether certain criteria are more important than others, whether certain criteria have a hierarchical or nested relationship to others, and whether all five criteria must be present for a concept to be considered a threshold concept. As Barradell (2013) points out, different researchers have used different interpretations of what threshold concepts are and have prioritized the definitional criteria in different ways. Certainly, the language that Meyer and Land use to talk about the criteria leaves room for threshold concepts that interpret the five definitional criteria loosely or that don't meet all five of the criteria.

The first three criteria are often grouped together. In fact, Peter Davies and Jean Mangan (2005) argue that the bounded and troublesome aspects of threshold concepts are a *result* of their being transformative, integrative, and irreversible: "A threshold concept helps delimit the boundaries of a subject because it integrates a particular set of concepts, beliefs and theories . . . The more transformative a concept, the more likely it is to be troublesome because it requires reconfiguration of previously acquired understanding" (p. 2). So let's look at these first three criteria in more detail.

Transformative, Integrative, Irreversible

Transformative: Davies (2006) points out that the "ways of thinking and practising" for a discipline cannot "simply be reduced to the acquisition of a set of distinct concepts or skills. It is the way in which such concepts are related, the deep-level structure of the subject which gives it coherence and creates a shared way of perceiving that can be left unspoken" (p. 71). Crucially, acquiring the ways of thinking and practicing for a discipline provides students with access to the community of the discipline. Joining a community transforms the students' perception of themselves and the subject matter. This transformation tends to tie in with the affective components of learning (Meyer & Land, 2003). This possibility for radical transformation represents one of the most exciting parts of teaching and learning.

In order to test whether a concept is transformative, ask whether a new understanding causes an ontological as well as a conceptual shift (i.e., a shift in the way of being, not only in the way of knowing; does it change the student's sense of self?). Why is this concept foundational to a grasp of information literacy?

Integrative: Threshold concepts are integrative precisely because experts see the building blocks of their discipline as integrated into their way of thinking and practicing. A novice who has not undergone this transformation will see a flow of disparate facts and ideas without understanding the concepts that connect them and therefore find them more difficult to grasp (Land, Cousin, Meyer, & Davies, 2005). Everyone has had an experience of a dawning understanding when something challenging that you were learning finally falls into place. You need to learn the concepts in order to integrate them, but they are hard to learn because you haven't integrated them, and then suddenly you are unstuck from this circular problem.

In order to test whether a concept is integrative, ask whether it not only pulls together procedural knowledge directly related to it but also sheds new light on adjacent concepts in the field. Another relevant question is how proposed threshold concepts relate to each other.

Irreversible: This criterion is one that our group of researchers struggled with quite a bit. We found ourselves arguing in a loop: a concept is irreversible because it is irreversible. The ur-example of irreversible knowledge is learning how to ride a bike, but Amy actually did have to relearn this (after a prolonged break). Perhaps the most salient point is that a transformative concept will be irreversible. Once you're transformed, you can't go back through the threshold you crossed. Learning the mechanics of bike riding is not the same as becoming a cyclist.

For experts identifying threshold concepts, this ties in with the idea that we identify with the perspective of the student who is still approaching that threshold and has not undergone the transformation. For this reason, the irreversible characteristic of threshold concepts provides the most obvious path into research that includes students in order to test the differences between novice and expert understandings.

Therefore, it is possible to approach this criterion not so much by looking for concepts that are irreversible, but by asking whether a concept is irreversible because it is truly transformative.

Troublesome

The troublesomeness of threshold concepts may be as important a factor as their transformativeness. Meyer and Land define troublesome knowledge as "knowledge that is 'alien', or counter-intuitive or even intellectually absurd at face value" (2003, p. 2). This section examines troublesome knowledge in detail.

In their very first paper on threshold concepts, Meyer and Land (2003) extensively cite the work of David Perkins. Perkins (1999) breaks down four different kinds of troublesome knowledge; Meyer and Land go on to identify two additional kinds of troublesome knowledge. Troublesome concepts are not necessarily threshold concepts, and threshold concepts will certainly cause varying degrees of difficulty from one student to the next. Still, it is worth looking closely at different kinds of troublesome knowledge because troublesomeness can help instructors theorize about the learning thresholds that students need to cross in order to get unstuck—that is, to leave the liminal state and proceed to the other side of the threshold.

1. *Ritual knowledge* seems meaningless because it is routine. The way that arithmetic operations are ritual might be analogous to the way that Boolean operators work in an advanced search. The default AND in the database interface can be given more meaning by contextualizing Boole's work with its application to telephone switches; by exploring the operators more playfully using, for example, ingredients in candy bars; or by inviting participation in a kinetic stand-up/sit-down lesson on the basis of what students are wearing (like jeans and glasses).

2. *Inert knowledge* is learned well enough to pass a quiz but is not operationalized—that is, it does not become integrated into the student's understanding of the discipline or worldview. To continue with the search example, a student might pass a posttest after sitting through a session on advanced keyword searching in CINAHL yet still enter a complete grammatical sentence into a Google search box and read the advice of WebMD the next time a personal health issue arises. The knowledge that there are authoritative voices in the health profession, that there are specific places to search for them, and that there is a specialized grammar to do so, is inert. The instructor's challenge is to identify strategies that help students make these connections.

When students handle troublesome knowledge by staying at the level of ritual or keeping it inert, they are resisting learning at a deeper level. There are certainly valid reasons for resistance, particularly if the ideology or worldview implied by the content is at odds with the student's identity. Acquiring this knowledge "requires the student to accept a transformation of their own understanding" (Land et al., 2005, p. 54). In order to integrate the troublesome content, that is, to learn at a deeper level than that required to pass a quiz and forget about it, the student will have to make an ontological change that may require severing ties with the old identity, family, community, religious beliefs, and so on.

3. *Conceptually difficult knowledge* is often counterintuitive and involves unlearning prior misunderstandings that seemed to be common sense. In the case of search, it is conceptually difficult to understand why the library doesn't—and in fact, can't—just have a single search box for everything. The everyday impression is that such a thing should be possible given the example of Google. A little bit of understanding of different database sources makes it seem simple to create a cross-platform search. It is counterintuitive that a more effective search may be less efficient until the user has a

clear mental model of why relevant information may be siloed in different platforms with incompatible indexing.

4. The perspective shift needed to acquire *foreign knowledge* is very much related to the overall project of teaching with threshold concepts. Continuing the search example, it may be foreign to think of an information search as an object of study at all. From the everyday perspective, search is a magical means to an end to be accomplished as quickly as possible. From the information professional's perspective, it is a series of informed choices that draws on extensive knowledge of what is being searched and how the search is carried out. This type of troublesome knowledge, again, may have an affective learning component. This is the kind of shift required to slow down and examine the process of retrieving information in detail.

Acquiring conceptually difficult or foreign knowledge can be connected to acquiring the ways of thinking and practicing of an expert in the field.

5. Meyer and Land (2003) go on to identify *tacit knowledge*. The following example from the epistolary memoir *Love, Nina* perfectly illustrates tacit knowledge:

> These are some of the things I've picked up so far at Thames Polytechnic.
> English Literature ignores most of its subject.
> It's not important for a thing to *be* true, but to *ring* true.
> Women have been ignored but have been their own worst enemy.
> You should give Thomas Hardy a chance . . .
> They don't *tell* you this stuff; you work it out for yourself. (Stibbe, 2013, p. 140)

An example of tacit knowledge, in the search scenario we have been using, would be the difficulty in accessing the library's resources. Tracking down information can, at times, take a tremendous amount of persistence and patience. Awareness of the library's resources, where to find them, how to get to the full text, and even whom to ask to speed the process along, all represent a tremendous amount of tacit knowledge about information systems that the expert has built up through practice and repetition.

6. Last, Meyer and Land (2003) discuss *troublesome language*. This is certainly present in the search example, where Boolean AND and OR mean the opposite of their everyday counterparts. At a picnic, asking for a hamburger AND a hot dog AND a vegetable kebab leads to a full plate, whereas OR will leave you with a much smaller portion. In a database, of course, a search for green energy AND net zero buildings AND solar panels leads to fewer results, while OR expands your search. Joining a community of practice in many ways means adopting a new language in order to participate fully through the

"discursive practices of a given community" (p. 9). Elsewhere, Meyer and Land (2005) have argued strongly that this adoption of the language of the community of practice is deeply connected to the transformative nature of crossing the thresholds for a discipline: "What is being emphasised here is the interrelatedness of the learner's identity with thinking and language. Threshold concepts lead not only to transformed thought but to a transfiguration of identity and adoption of an extended discourse" (p. 375).

Shinners-Kennedy (2008) notes that the characteristics of threshold concepts might seem to suggest that the researcher should look for especially big, advanced, important, or otherwise grandiose concepts to label as "threshold." In order to temper this lure, he advances the idea of "everydayness" (p. 120): everyday knowledge is often tacit or inert and therefore troublesome. Seemingly simple concepts might be the ones that in fact serve to integrate disciplinary knowledge.

In order to identify troublesome concepts, librarians can look at places where students get stuck. We can theorize about why students are getting stuck on that content—does the trouble seem to fit into one of the categories identified by Davies or Meyer and Land? These are the kinds of trouble that are often provoked when students are working through threshold concepts.

Bounded

The *bounded* criterion may be the most difficult to apply for information literacy, where the scope of our subject community is very broad and our content area is considered by many not to be a discipline at all. Indeed, Meyer and Land write that "threshold concepts would seem to be more readily identified within disciplinary contexts where there is a relatively greater degree of consensus on what constitutes a body of knowledge (for example, Mathematics, Physics, Medicine)" (2003, p. 9). Information literacy doesn't carry the academic cache of the hard sciences, and, in fact, on many campuses it is a struggle to have its existence recognized.

Positing that there are learning thresholds for information literacy, then, can be seen as an advocacy position. Reflecting upon an interdisciplinary threshold concept workshop, Naomi Irvine and Patrick Carmichael wrote,

> The "concept of threshold concepts" may not only function as a means of initiating and focusing practitioner enquiries . . . but also fulfil the dual role of stimulating reflection ("what is it we do?") and encouraging a self-conscious consideration of disciplinary distinctiveness ("how might others see us?"). (2009, p. 113)

Certainly, this observation holds true in the case of information literacy, which may be considered interdisciplinary, and which is connected with a profession highly sensitive to how it is viewed.

There is a debate among information literacy practitioners about whether the best approach is to embed information literacy into the disciplines or to teach it as a stand-alone topic. William Badke (2008) likens information literacy to ethics in suggesting that it is a discipline that finds multiple footholds within the curriculum:

> The discipline of ethics can form a good analogy [to information literacy] as it ranges through the academy as philosophical ethics, bioethics, business ethics, professional ethics, and so on. While the philosophical framework within which it operates has a strong consistency, it works out its methodology and application in different ways, depending on its subject matter. (Badke, 2008, p. 11)

By contrast, Bill Johnston and Sheila Webber (2006) argue for information literacy as a discipline that should have its own curriculum; they posit that an embedded approach to information literacy instruction "will tend to underplay the complexities . . . and be prone to compromise and dilution of effort" (p. 118). Whether or not information literacy is a stand-alone or an embedded discipline, it is the case that all disciplines interact with information in a variety of ways and that the librarian is the only role in academia positioned to observe all of these processes at work.

Korey Brunetti, Amy Hofer, and Lori Townsend (2014) wrote that librarianship is an interdisciplinary practice:

> Librarians are trained in information science, a field that sits at the intersection of the philosophy of knowledge, computer science, law, library science, communication, management and more. As opposed to professional training in librarianship, the typical information literacy curriculum is a sort of "information sciences lite," or basic applied information science. (p. 90)

Ray Land, on the other hand, suggests that information literacy may be "cross-disciplinary" rather than interdisciplinary (2015). Regardless of how this idea is formulated (inter-, cross-, trans-, multi-, etc.), it may be useful to consider that information literacy threshold concepts need to be grasped both in order to progress within a discipline and to become information literate. For example, a student needs to get the concept of primary sources in order to deeply understand information formats, but that knowledge must also reflect the way that primary sources are used in the student's chosen discipline.

James Atherton, Peter Hadfield, and Renee Meyers (2008) add that vocational or professional disciplines tend to teach affective knowledge that highlights ontological change rather than epistemological change (ways of being rather than ways of thinking). They offer the example of hospitality and catering instructors who suggest that "how to wash one's hands" is a threshold concept for their field. What seems at a first glance to be merely a rote skill to learn (i.e., a building block or foundational knowledge) is argued compellingly to be, in fact, a threshold into a new professional perspective on hygiene and risk: "Learning in this area was not merely 'additive' but in some measure transformative" (Atherton et al., 2008, p. 5). This example resonates for information literacy instruction because much of what librarians teach could be categorized as skills, yet the information professional will recognize the disciplinary frame of reference that differentiates skill acquisition from transformative learning.

All that said, some of the threshold concepts identified by our research group do not meet the bounded criteria, since they are not uniquely owned by information literacy or information science. Generally speaking, we recommend bracketing the debate about whether information literacy is a discipline by looking at information literacy as a body of knowledge for which there are learning thresholds that we can identify, debate, teach, and ultimately use to help our students become more information literate. It is possible to consider whether there is a unique way that librarians understand nonbounded content given our professional training. We can also ask whether a working list of proposed threshold concepts tells us something new about our discipline.

Identifying Threshold Concepts for Information Literacy

It is demonstrably useful to come to a broad agreement about the core concepts that our profession teaches, as articulated, for example, in ACRL's *Information Literacy Competency Standards for Higher Education* (American Library Association, 2000) or in widely used information literacy textbooks (e.g., Badke, 2014; Jacobson et al., 2014). On a purely pragmatic level, this kind of shared understanding enables efficient reuse of learning materials, assessment instruments, and programmatic documents. It allows for articulation and transferable learning outcomes between courses and institutions. It is how librarians orient new instructors about the expectations for the content they should cover and explain to other faculty and administrators what librarians do. It is very much the norm in academia, and for good reasons (Hofer, Brunetti, & Townsend, 2013).

On the other hand, while our group of coauthors has done research on identifying threshold concepts for information literacy, we don't propose a final list or exclude the possibility of new concepts being added. The threshold concept literature provides many examples of researchers arriving at complementary conclusions about the threshold concepts for a field. So while we are all for good standards documents, the research that we do is not intended to be used for that purpose. We continue to study threshold concepts for information literacy in order to better understand how to be more effective instructors. The work of formulating national standards (or frameworks for that matter) is a different endeavor.

The purpose of developing a list of threshold concepts is not to discover a radically new content area for information literacy. Part of the point of this model is that the learning thresholds represent the tacit knowledge of our discipline—the things that we have learned so well that they go without saying. This makes them difficult to pinpoint but not very surprising once they are articulated, though they may surface a different way of looking at our teaching content.

We were encouraged in our research process to find that we were not the first information literacy instructors to explore threshold concepts as a teaching approach. While some early publications considered information literacy to be a single learning threshold to be crossed, two Australian researchers, Margaret Blackmore (2010) and Virginia Tucker (2012), shared our perspective that there are many learning thresholds that can be crossed along the way to becoming information literate. This view has become the more widely accepted one, as reflected in ACRL's *Framework* (ACRL, 2014).

Blackmore developed learning thresholds for information literacy by enlisting the expertise of librarians at her institution to identify content that is troublesome for students. Participants agreed upon topics that consistently caused students to require help and then created categories for these troublesome topics. Last, smaller groups looked at each category and abstracted it in order to describe threshold concepts: a technology threshold concept that encourages systemic thinking; a words threshold concept that encourages an improvisatory or playful approach to language; a time threshold concept that encourages understanding of the balance between time invested and the outcome of research; a recognition threshold concept that develops pattern perception and interpretation skills; and an academic rules threshold concept that develops a cultural understanding of information engagement in academia (Blackmore, 2010).

Tucker's doctoral thesis work looks at the differences between expert and novice searchers using the threshold concept model as a theoretical framework. She found that four concepts emerged from her data analysis that had the characteristics of threshold concepts for expert searchers. Crucially, she points out that the concepts she identified "do not define search expertise; they are, instead, threshold concepts that must be grasped in order to move a learner forward in the direction of search expertise" (Tucker, 2012, p. 229). The threshold concepts that she identifies are the information environment; information structures; information vocabularies; and concept fusion, in which the three other threshold concepts are integrated into the practitioner's identity (Tucker, 2012).

Our group of coauthors began identifying threshold concepts for information literacy by taking walks, arguing, reading, writing, and presenting on this approach at information literacy conferences. The first structured research we conducted was a qualitative survey of information literacy practitioners in order to identify common stumbling blocks for students. We analyzed the survey responses and extrapolated threshold concepts—that is, concepts that students would need to grasp in order to get unstuck (Hofer, Townsend, & Brunetti, 2012).

One of the limitations of the qualitative survey was that all of our participants' thinking about information literacy was very much structured by the ACRL *Standards*. Granted, we couldn't expect a group of information literacy librarians to become familiar enough with a complex learning theory to be able to participate in a 15-minute online survey, so we let them bring the subject expertise, and we provided the familiarity with threshold concepts ourselves. Yet, we felt that we needed more confidence that there was some kind of consensus around the learning thresholds we had identified. Our next study, a Delphi study (Townsend, Hofer, Lin Hanick, & Brunetti, 2016), was designed to draw conclusions that we could rely on as a theoretical underpinning to the kinds of activities and assignments shared in Chapter 9.

Delphi studies seek the opinions of experts, which makes them a good fit for identifying threshold concepts (which, as we've seen, are effectively identified by subject matter experts). This method has been used to conduct information literacy research, to guide development of information literacy standards documents, and, in other fields, to identify threshold concepts. Barradell (2013), in her review of methods, supports the use of a consensus methodology such as Delphi as an effective way to structure a discussion about threshold concepts.

Delphi Study Method and Results

A Delphi study is a *qualitative* research method in which a small group of experts is asked to anonymously answer questions about a topic in writing. The answers are collected and summarized by a moderator and then sent back to the experts. This process is called a round. In each round, the experts read the responses of their peers, potentially make adjustments to their own answers, and address questions raised during the previous round. Sometimes, when a group of experts gathers in one room, one person's reputation or demeanor might have a great deal of influence on the conversation. The Delphi method removes this influence, so the best ideas rise to the top.

Delphi studies represent a significant commitment for participants. Our study ran for a year and took four rounds to complete. We are grateful to the participants for contributing so much time to the study.

We chose to use a qualitative research method because the aim of our study was not to prove or disprove the threshold concept theory itself, or generate quantitative data that would let us back up our claims numerically. Rather, the Delphi method enabled us to enlist the help of respected experts in our field in garnering consensus around the use of the model and its application to our teaching content. Our analysis remains just that—our own analysis—but we now have the benefit of thoughtful contributions to further inform our experience and judgment.

Of course, as with any research method, there are limitations to the Delphi method. In particular, the choice of experts included can affect the outcome of the study, and the experts are also fallible. Keep in mind, too, that this study began before the ACRL *Standards* revision committee started working and ended after two drafts of the new *Framework* had been released; this was a major upheaval for many North American librarians (not all participants were North American, however). Please take our results, then, with a grain of salt. You can read in much more detail about our methodology and its limitations in Townsend et al. (2016). The complete data from the study can be found online at https://sites.google.com/site/thresholdconceptsdelphistudy/home.

We asked our participants three questions:

1. The authors posit that threshold concepts are a useful way to prioritize teaching content for information literacy instruction. Do you agree that this approach holds promise for our field?
2. The authors propose seven information-related threshold concepts. For each proposed threshold concept, please answer the following question: Is this an information literacy threshold concept? Why or why not?
3. On the basis of your expertise with information literacy instruction, do you have any additional threshold concepts to propose?

The answer to our first and most general question—"Do threshold concepts have potential for information literacy instruction?"—was resolved after Round 1. The answer was a resounding YES.

However, the "yes" came with much discussion. While participants were intrigued by the threshold concept approach, there was also recognition that the approach is challenging—to students, to faculty, to our institutions, and to us, as librarians. Three major themes emerged in the discussion of Question 1.

The first theme can be summarized by the question "What do we teach when we teach information literacy?" The debate about how to define it and even what to call it is still going strong. Participants disagreed sharply over whether the ACRL *Standards* were an adequate representation of information literacy, with one participant saying, "I've given up on the standards long ago," and another proposing that threshold concepts could be used in conjunction with them. Participants engaged with the question of whether the bounded criteria can be applied to information literacy given the ongoing question of whether information literacy is a discipline.

Our takeaway from the discussion on this topic is that on the one hand, we can understand information literacy as something that is open to ongoing discussion (including the term "information literacy" itself: one participant wrote, "I hate, hate, hate with the heat of one thousand suns this phrase"). On the other hand, because threshold concepts spark in-depth examination of our teaching content, they offer us greater clarity about our understanding of information literacy. Because threshold concepts are bounded by a discipline, this can create an opportunity to step back and ask whether the list of proposed threshold concepts adds up to a new or revised understanding of information literacy.

The second theme was pedagogy. Though today pedagogy is offered as an elective in some programs, it has yet to make its way into the library school core curriculum; you can graduate from most library programs without ever taking a course on instruction (Hensley, 2015). Many practicing instruction librarians learn on the job, without the benefit of receiving any workplace training either (Farkas, 2017). Our participants drew a very helpful distinction between training and teaching. *Training* is showing people how to do specific tasks and skills. It's an important part of library instruction and relates back to what used to be called bibliographic instruction. *Teaching*, as opposed to training, requires a different skill set—one that librarians may not have had a chance to develop. An information literacy instruction program comprised solely of one-shots does not allow room for teaching conceptual knowledge, which means that many librarians don't often get the opportunity to focus on the big ideas of our discipline, unless we happen to teach in a library school or credit-bearing information literacy program.

Many respondents posited that engaging with threshold concepts would result in more intentional, reflective, critical teaching. This process can also reveal the underlying complexity of information literacy content. What librarians teach is not simple. Working to identify and define these areas is part of the teaching process.

Closely related to pedagogy is the question of assessment. In Round 1, one of the participants asked about how to tell if a student has crossed a threshold. Does crossing a threshold always make a difference in behavior? This led to a lively discussion in Rounds 2 and 3 about assessment and the potential challenges involved in assessing student progress with threshold concepts. It was acknowledged that threshold concepts would be difficult to assess.

Our takeaway from the pedagogy discussion is that on the one hand, our profession may feel unprepared to teach conceptual content. We have a lot of resources at our disposal for strengthening our teaching practice, but we are talking about more than teaching technique for improved one-shots. On the other hand, engaging with threshold concepts can, potentially, make us better teachers. Even if we teach only one-shots, the leap to reflective teaching, to interrogating our current practices and what we teach, can help us improve.

The third theme that emerged from Question 1 had to do with implementation. Several respondents pointed to curriculum mapping as a way forward. If you ever tried curriculum mapping with the *Standards*, you know that it is frustrating because the standards are a laundry list of skills, competencies, and knowledge, making it difficult to know what to prioritize or what is beginner/intermediate/advanced. Curriculum mapping with threshold concepts may offer an alternative way of categorizing our learning objectives because crossing one threshold helps shed light on others. Some of our respondents also suggested that threshold concepts offer a potential way to connect with faculty in the disciplines who are used to thinking about their content conceptually. They saw the potential to get away from an "inoculation" or "checklist" approach to information literacy instruction.

Our takeaway from the discussion on this topic is that on the one hand, the one-shot session doesn't meet librarians' needs because you can't get a complex, difficult concept across in one instruction session. On the other hand, threshold concepts may represent an exciting and potentially unifying way forward because they do not require that we try to integrate information literacy with a host of other literacies, but ask us to focus on the content that is unique to our discipline and represents our perspective.

Developing Threshold Concepts Using the Delphi Method

In each round, Questions 2 and 3 asked participants to evaluate the current drafted list of information literacy threshold concepts presented in that round and then propose new threshold concepts not yet represented in the list.

In order to show what this process looked like, this section will provide an example by following the development of a single threshold concept throughout the study. The Research Process threshold concept was contentious and underwent significant revision over the course of the study. Let's look at how it took shape.

The concept that came out of the 2012 qualitative survey, and was presented to participants in Round 1, read as follows:

> Research Solves Problems
>
> That research has a purpose beyond the compilation of information seems obvious to librarians and academics, but beginning scholars struggle to see the point of the generic "research" paper because it is removed from their real-world context of information retrieval and use. Understanding the role of research in academia helps students understand research as a nonlinear, integrative process of finding and using information.

In answering Question 2, Delphi study participants commented on this proposed threshold concept, as in the following examples:

> The description conflates the literature review with research . . . the important info is that knowing what is already known on a topic and questions that are out there is key to framing inquiry and building knowledge.

> Not all research solves problems, but research does always ask questions. I would reframe this as Research Answers Questions . . . Research Solves Problems strikes me as overly simplistic and, well, not quite troublesome enough ;)

> When you say research solves a problem, it implies that there is a final answer and a resolution . . . Research is a way to enter a conversation.

In Question 3 of Round 1, participants proposed new threshold concepts that related to the research process:

> Research Answers Questions
>
> I would also add to the threshold concept Research Solves Problems the idea that Research Answers Questions . . . the student should begin with the inquiry and then develop a thesis and an argument based on the answers uncovered in the course of research.

> Research Is a Process
>
> Starting and conceptualizing a research project is incredibly difficult for students. If students could realize that research is more than finding papers, or borrowing books, I think it could actually transform student behaviors and approaches to [information literacy].

In Round 2, we presented a list of all 38 proposed threshold concepts generated by our first study and responses from Round 1. We asked participants to each make a list of the strongest threshold concepts along with comments on the proposed concepts. Regarding the concepts relating to the research process, participants wrote,

> Research Is a Process gets to the iterative nature of research; that research will never be a "once and done" process, that it involves multiple steps including discovery, analyzing/synthesizing, reconsidering the topic and approach, with potentially multiple rounds of this before producing their own content, followed by more rounds of review and revision.
>
> Research as Inquiry can be combined with Research Solves Problems and Research Answers Questions. The ideas are the same—what do we do with information as researchers?

Participants also suggested new ways to frame the threshold concept relating to the research process, as in this example:

> Maybe Research Solves Problems and Research Answers Questions can come together under the encompassing Research Facilitates Inquiry heading? I think they are two distinct but important sides of a similar coin.

In Round 3, we used the ranked lists and analysis of the discussion so far to consolidate down to nine proposed threshold concepts. The research process threshold concept was proposed as follows:

> Research Is a Process of Inquiry and Creates New Knowledge
>
> That research has a purpose beyond the compilation of information seems obvious to librarians and academics, but beginning scholars struggle to see the point of the generic "research" paper because it is removed from their real-world context of information retrieval and use. The minute an inquiry is formed in a student's mind, new knowledge is created as connections are made and this iterative process, from inquiry, to databases query, to the selection of relevant information, to the development and testing of a thesis/hypothesis and subsequent analysis and synthesis of the results, is the same one that experts engage with in the creation of new knowledge.

This title and description combined ideas from the following previously proposed threshold concepts:

- Academic Libraries Are in the Knowledge Creation Business
- Research Solves Problems

- Research Answers Questions
- Research Is a Process
- Research Facilitates Inquiry

In response, participants commented,

> I support the working title but some parts of the definition are troubling. The image of the student as a "beginning scholar" is narrow and does not reflect the reality for many students ... Perhaps the problem here is how the word "research" is being used.

> I think that Research Is a Process of Inquiry and this TC [Scholarship as a Conversation] could be combined.

Part of our analysis of the Round 3 responses included making a Venn diagram to check on what was distinct about the research process and scholarship as conversation threshold concepts. This helped us to clarify that two separate concepts were indeed needed to cover the intellectual territory.

Before we tell you about Round 4, we need to explain why there is no "Scholarship as a Conversation" chapter in this book. Since the completion and publication of the Delphi study, our stance on the Scholarship as a Conversation threshold concept has changed; we now think that Scholarship as a Conversation should not stand alone as a threshold concept.

First, Scholarship as a Conversation is a metaphor for how we interact with one specific type of information rather than an abstract, conceptual disciplinary idea. The metaphor explains the kind of interaction that scholars have with the literature, but it does not function the same way that other information literacy threshold concepts do: no other threshold concept we've proposed relies on a metaphor. Relying on figurative language invites more comparisons. Scholarship may be a conversation, but it could also be climbing a mountain, building a house, or surviving a battle. The conversation metaphor could be applied to scholarship, but it could also be applied to peer review or active reading. Characterizing scholarship as a conversation may help us describe some functions of scholarship, but it doesn't pin down the concept of scholarship for us.

Second, as we zoomed out from the classroom to find connections between our lived experiences and the proposed threshold concepts, focusing on scholarly conversations and scholarly communities felt increasingly limited. Inquiries are developed and information is sought in academia, to be sure, but information literate individuals should be able to take their skills into the real world. Communities are built, uphold standards, and create systems of apprenticeship; their inquiries need not be produced by, nor reside within, academia in order to be valuable. These insights should persist and transfer outside of the academic context.

Third, while we agree that it is important for students to begin seeing scholars as people asking questions and seeing research as a social endeavor, these understandings are relevant to *all* of the threshold concepts that we consider in this book. Even though threshold concepts are, as Craig Gibson once said, "a network of interconnected understandings," this concept was too close to the other proposed concepts to offer a distinct transformation for students. The Delphi methodology brought the idea *scholarship as a conversation is a threshold concept for information literacy* to the top of the pile, but the threshold concept approach encourages and allows for rethinking previous positions. That's what we are doing in this book. Okay, back to Round 4.

In Round 4, the proposed concept read as follows:

> Inquiry Creates Knowledge
>
> The research process is characterized by iterative inquiry. Its practical purpose is to solve problems or answer questions. Identifying and articulating useful questions requires an existing foundation of knowledge and is difficult intellectual work. However, the moment an inquiry is formed, new knowledge is created as connections are made and the process from inquiry, to database query, to the selection of relevant information, to the development and testing of a thesis/hypothesis and subsequent analysis and synthesis of the results, is the same one that experts engage with in the creation of new knowledge.

This was one of six proposed threshold concepts sent out in the final round, which was understood to be a last check that we were all on the same page. Some participants responded critically:

> I feel that the revisions to this threshold concept lessened the relevance of this concept and made it more ambiguous . . . I appreciated the prior focus on research as a process, specifically that research is an iterative, ongoing process, and throughout the research process knowledge is created.
>
> Inquiry Creates Knowledge is very closely related to Scholarship Is a Conversation, in my mind, so close that I support the suggestion that they be combined. Both describe the research process and rely on experienced researchers and disciplinary experts to serve as models for the novice.

The majority of comments, however, concluded that the list of threshold concepts was useful and represented some important understandings in information literacy. We used the Round 4 feedback to come up with the final draft of the threshold concept, including the new name:

> Research Process
>
> Identifying and articulating useful research questions requires an existing foundation of knowledge and is difficult intellectual work. Applying information to a problem, or using it as evidence in an argument, or for inspiration in a creative endeavor, requires that the researcher understand what will qualify as disciplinary evidence. This process of inquiry, research, and use is one of iterative inquiry, allowing for mistakes and correction of earlier misapprehensions. This process—from inquiry, to seeking out existing knowledge, to the selection of relevant information, to the development and testing of a thesis/hypothesis and subsequent analysis and synthesis of the results—results in the creation of new knowledge. Engaging in the information creation process is an extension of the thinking process, and therefore "research" may be understood as a broadly encompassing term though some forms of research may be more or less valued in academia.

Theory to Practice

At the beginning of this chapter, we mentioned that the reader might consider developing new threshold concepts for information literacy that have particular relevance to your setting or teaching content. Unpacking the process of completing a lengthy Delphi study hardly constitutes practical advice for the busy practitioner. Yet, once you learn about threshold concepts, it's nearly irresistible to try to figure out new ones for yourself. What do you need to know if you want to apply this model?

On the basis of the reading we've done, along with our research, we feel comfortable saying that you don't necessarily need a fancy methodology to identify threshold concepts. What you do need is a community of practice in which to bounce ideas around and work through several iterations of drafts. This is because threshold concepts pinpoint disciplinary knowledge that exists in precisely the kind of scholarly communities we're trying to introduce our students to.

You should also get familiar and comfortable with Meyer and Land's criteria. The purpose of identifying threshold concepts is to engage in a reflective teaching practice. Figuring out why your proposed concept meets the criteria—or doesn't meet all the criteria, but may be useful to think of as a threshold concept anyway—is part of the process. You can start by looking at places where students get stuck, but then take a step back: Can you put your concept through its paces using Meyer and Land's model?

Last, keep in mind that identifying threshold concepts isn't the end goal. It serves a wonderful purpose in reconnecting to the student mind-set and reenergizing your approach to your content. At the end of the day, however, the point is to improve the design of delivery and assessments so that students have a better experience learning from you. We love Anne-Marie Deitering's (2015) metaphor of providing students with a balance bike instead of training wheels. Learning how to pedal is the easy part of riding a bike, and that's all that training wheels teach you to do. Learning how to balance is the hard part, and that's what a balance bike teaches you. Students need assignments that give them practice with the difficult parts of information literacy so that when they are assigned a major research project or have an important information need, they will have transferable skills.

The next section of this book, Chapters 3–7, does just that. We will explore the threshold concepts identified by the Delphi study described here and consider how they can be integrated into a curriculum in order to support students in mastery of the concepts.

Takeaways

- Threshold concepts for information literacy are not out there to be discovered, but rather are the result of productive discussion among colleagues.
- The threshold concepts for information literacy are not settled, and need not ever be considered settled.
- This model can be applied by any practitioner: get familiar with the threshold concept criteria, and start discussing ideas about learning thresholds with your colleagues. Avoid the potential pitfalls: lack of rigor and unexamined ideologies.

For Further Consideration

- Where do you stand on "Let's go to the library"—threshold concept or not? Why?
- What would you propose as a threshold concept unique to your population or teaching specialty?
- How would you design a study to identify new threshold concepts for information literacy?

References

American Library Association. (2000). *Information literacy competency standards for higher education*. Retrieved from http://www.ala.org/acrl/standards/informationliteracycompetency

Association of College & Research Libraries. (2014). *Framework for information literacy for higher education*. Retrieved from http://www.ala.org/acrl/standards/ilframework

Atherton, J., Hadfield, P., & Meyers, R. (2008). *Threshold concepts in the wild*. Expanded paper presented at the Threshold Concepts: From Theory to Practice conference, Kingston, Ontario. Retrieved from www.doceo.org.uk/tools/Threshold_Concepts_Wild_expanded_70.pdf

Badke, W. B. (2008). A rationale for information literacy as a credit-bearing discipline. *Journal of Information Literacy, 2*(1), 1–22. doi:10.11645/2.1.42

Badke, W. B. (2014). *Research strategies: Finding your way through the information fog* (5th ed.). Bloomington, IN: iUniverse.

Barradell, S. (2013). The identification of threshold concepts: A review of theoretical complexities and methodological challenges. *Higher Education: The International Journal of Higher Education Research, 65*(2), 265–276. doi:10.1007/s10734-012-9542-3

Blackmore, M. (2010, July). *Student engagement with information: Applying a threshold concept approach to information literacy development*. Paper presented at the Third Biennial Threshold Concepts Symposium, Sydney, Australia. Retrieved from http://unsworks.unsw.edu.au/fapi/datastream/unsworks:8914/SOURCE01

Box, G. E. P., and Draper, N. R. (1987). *Empirical model building and response surfaces*. New York, NY: John Wiley & Sons.

Brunetti, K., Hofer, A. R., & Townsend, L. (2014). Interdisciplinarity and information literacy instruction: A threshold concepts approach. In C. O'Mahony, A. Buchanan, M. O'Rourke, & B. Higgs (Eds.), *Threshold concepts: From personal practice to communities of practice. Proceedings of the National Academy's Sixth Annual Conference and the Fourth Biennial Threshold Concepts Conference* (pp. 89–93). Cork, Ireland: NAIRTL.

Cousin, G. (2009). *Researching learning in higher education*. New York, NY: Routledge.

Davies, P. (2006). Threshold concepts: How can we recognise them? In J. H. F. Meyer & R. Land (Eds.), *Overcoming barriers to student understanding: Threshold concepts and troublesome knowledge* (pp. 70–84). New York, NY: Routledge.

Davies, P., & Mangan, J. (2005). *Recognising threshold concepts: An exploration of different approaches*. Paper presented at the European Association in Learning and Instruction (EARLI) Conference, Nicosia, Cyprus. Retrieved from http://www.researchgate.net/profile/Jean_Mangan/publication/228377119_Recognising_Threshold_Concepts_an_exploration_of_different_approaches/links/02e7e51fb9189eb947000000.pdf

Deitering, A. M. (2015). *No training wheels, revised*. Retrieved from http://info-fetishist.org/2015/06/03/no-training-wheels-revised/

Elliott, J. (2007). Assessing the quality of action research. *Research Papers in Education, 22*(2), 229–246. doi:10.1080/02671520701296205

Farkas, M. (2017, October 11). The ballad of the sad instruction librarian [Web log post]. Retrieved from https://meredith.wolfwater.com/wordpress/2017/10/11/the-ballad-of-the-sad-instruction-librarian/

Hensley, M. K. (2015). Improving LIS education in teaching librarians to teach. In *ACRL 2015 Proceedings*. Paper presented at ACRL 2015, Portland, OR. Chicago, IL: American Library Association. Retrieved from https://www.ideals.illinois.edu/handle/2142/73412

Hofer, A. R., Brunetti, K., & Townsend, L. (2013). A threshold concepts approach to the Standards revision. *Communications in Information Literacy, 7*(2), 108–113. Retrieved from http://www.comminfolit.org/index.php?journal=cil&page=article&op=view&path%5B%5D=v7i2p108&path%5B%5D=168

Hofer, A. R., Townsend, L., & Brunetti, K. (2012). Troublesome concepts: Investigating threshold concepts for information literacy instruction. *portal: Libraries and the Academy, 12*(4), 387–405. doi:10.1353/pla.2012.0039

Irvine, N., & Carmichael, P. (2009). Threshold concepts: A point of focus for practitioner research. *Active Learning in Higher Education, 10*(2), 103–119. doi:10.1177/1469787409104785

Jacobson, T., Bobish, G., Bernnard, D., Bullis, D., Hecker, J., Holden, I., . . . Loney, T. (2014). *The information literacy user's guide: An open, online textbook*. Retrieved from http://textbooks.opensuny.org/the-information-literacy-users-guide-an-open-online-textbook/

Johnston, B., & Webber, S. (2006). As we may think: Information literacy as a discipline for the information age. *Research Strategies, 20*(3), 108–121. doi:10.1016/j.resstr.2006.06.005

Land, R. (2015). *"There could be trouble ahead": Threshold concepts, troublesome knowledge and information literacy—A current debate*. Presentation at the meeting of the Librarians' Information Literacy Annual Conference, Newcastle, UK. Slides retrieved from http://www.slideshare.net/infolit_group/ray-land

Land, R., Cousin, G., Meyer, J. H. F., & Davies, P. (2005). Threshold concepts and troublesome knowledge (3): Implications for course design and evaluation. In C. Rust (Ed.), *Improving student learning: Diversity and inclusivity* (pp. 53–64). Oxford, England: Oxford Centre for Staff and Learning Development. Retrieved from http://www.ee.ucl.ac.uk/~mflanaga/ISL04-pp53-64-Land-et-al.pdf

Meyer, J. H. F., & Land, R. (2003). *Threshold concepts and troublesome knowledge: Linkages to ways of thinking and practising within the disciplines*. ETL Project Occasional Report 4. Edinburgh, Scotland: Enhancing Teaching-Learning Environments in Undergraduate Courses Project. Retrieved from http://www.etl.tla.ed.ac.uk/docs/ETLreport4.pdf

Meyer, J. H. F., & Land, R. (2005). Threshold concepts and troublesome knowledge (2): Epistemological considerations and a conceptual framework for teaching and learning. *Higher Education: The International Journal of Higher*

Education and Educational Planning, 49(3), 373–388. doi:10.1007/s10734-004-6779-5

Morales, H., & Barnes, M. (2018). The Baltimore Mural Project: An approach to threshold concepts in religious studies. *Teaching Theology & Religion, 21* (3), 185–196. doi:10.1111/teth.12440

Morgan, P. K. (2015). Pausing at the threshold. *portal: Libraries and the Academy, 15*(1), 183–195. doi:10.1353/pla.2015.0002

O'Donnell, R. (2010). *A critique of the threshold concept hypothesis and an application in economics* (Working Paper No. 164). Retrieved from https://ideas.repec.org/p/uts/wpaper/164.html

Orsini-Jones, M. (2008). Troublesome language knowledge: Identifying threshold concepts in grammar learning. In R. Land, J. H. F. Meyer, & J. Smith (Eds.), *Threshold concepts within the disciplines* (pp. 261–272). Rotterdam, the Netherlands: Sense Publishers.

Perkins, D. (1999). The many faces of constructivism. *Educational Leadership, 57*(3), 6–11.

Rowbottom, D. P. (2007). Demystifying threshold concepts. *Journal of Philosophy of Education, 41*(2), 263–270. doi:10.1111/j.1467-9752.2007.00554.x

Scott, R. E. (2017). Transformative? Integrative? Troublesome? Undergraduate honors student reflections on information literacy threshold concepts. *Communications in Information Literacy, 11*(2), 283–301. Retrieved from https://doi.org/10.15760/comminfolit.2017.11.2.3

Shinners-Kennedy, D. (2008). The everydayness of threshold concepts: State as an example from computer science. In R. Land, J. H. F. Meyer, & J. Smith (Eds.), *Threshold concepts within the disciplines* (pp. 261–272). Rotterdam, the Netherlands: Sense Publishers.

Shinners-Kennedy, D., & Fincher, S. A. (2013, August). Identifying threshold concepts: From dead end to a new direction. *Proceedings of the ninth annual international ACM conference on International Computing Education Research.* doi:10.1145/2493394.2493396

Stibbe, N. (2013). *Love, Nina: A nanny writes home.* New York, NY: Little, Brown and Company.

Townsend, L., Hofer, A. R., Lin Hanick, S., & Brunetti, K. (2016). Identifying threshold concepts for information literacy: A Delphi study. *Communications in Information Literacy, 10*(1), 23–49. Retrieved from http://www.comminfolit.org/index.php?journal=cil&page=article&op=view&path%5B%5D=v10i1p23

Tucker, V. M. (2012). *Acquiring search expertise: Learning experiences and threshold concepts* (Doctoral dissertation). Queensland University of Technology, Brisbane, Australia. Retrieved from http://eprints.qut.edu.au/63652/

PART II

Exploring Threshold Concepts for Information Literacy

CHAPTER THREE

Authority

Johannes Guttenberg did not invent the printing press, Charles Darrow was not the creator of the Monopoly board game, and Christopher Columbus definitely didn't discover America. Columbus was far from the first explorer to reach the continent, and his arrival marked the beginning of centuries of genocide, enslavement, and oppression for Native Americans. More importantly, can one really discover an entire continent, full of complex cultures, established nations, and distinct identities? No, of course not. Still, imbued with the authority of the Spanish Crown, and elevated by Eurocentrism, Columbus became the trustworthy source on the (not so) New World.

Today, his name is used as a verb to describe "the art of discovering something that isn't new" ("Columbusing," 2014). This term was deployed when a luxury apartment building in the Bushwick neighborhood of Brooklyn was named "Colony 1209" and solicited new "settlers" in its marketing materials, implying that the majority-Hispanic, longtime residents in the area didn't exist (Whitford, 2015). Likewise, the *New York Times* had to apologize for Columbusing bubble tea, a Taiwanese beverage that has been popular in the United States for decades (Kaufman, 2017). In these two instances, the apartment building developers and the *New York Times* positioned themselves as the authority on an unknown territory, even though the territories were unknown only to those who shared a similar socioeconomic, ethnic, or racial context.

Within the classroom, authority can be freighted with similar complications. Authority can become a tautology; this author is authoritative because they are in this anthology, and this anthology is authoritative because it includes this author. Students may also consider the authority of information sources as something that has already been settled when they are handed a syllabus at the start of the semester, given a list of publications deemed acceptable for their paper, and encouraged to limit results to peer-reviewed, scholarly articles in a database search. There is nothing nefarious about these educational practices; for the most part, they are intended to introduce students to foundational texts and key disciplinary ideas so that they may eventually be able to find and use trustworthy information on their own. Still, many practices in higher education replicate existing structures of authority in ways that can be as problematic as they are beneficial. Examining and challenging these practices can be one way to understand the authority threshold concept.

This chapter will explore the authority threshold concept by reviewing concepts from the library and information science literature and then examining the characteristics of authoritative evidence in specific contexts. Controlled vocabularies and maps are instances that illustrate how authority is both constructed and contextual (Townsend, Brunetti, & Hofer, 2011). This learning threshold can help students develop a productive relationship with authority and authoritative sources by making clear when to trust the experts and when to mount a challenge.

Authority Defined

Our understanding of authority threshold concept begins with the work of Patrick Wilson, a University of California, Berkeley philosopher and librarian who is credited with developing the concepts of *cognitive authority* and *second-hand knowledge*. People can acquire a limited amount of knowledge first-hand, through direct observation and experience, but the vast majority of what we know must be learned second-hand from others. Yet, not all second-hand knowledge is credible. "Cognitive authority" is the term that Wilson developed to describe the sources of information we are willing to be influenced by because we trust their credibility: "Some people know what they are talking about, others do not" (Wilson, 1983, p. 13). Wilson points out that "second-hand knowledge" suggests "second-best" (1983, p. 10). We can think of many instances where being told about something is completely inferior to experiencing it: listening to a piece of music, falling in love, climbing a mountain. Yet, we receive most of our information second-hand and therefore must employ some means of deciding whether or not to believe that information.

In Wilson's conceptualization, "authority is a relationship involving at least two people. No one can be an authority all by himself; there has to be someone else for whom he is an authority" (1983, p. 13). In other words, cognitive authority isn't a characteristic inherent to a source but rather is conferred by the information user upon the information source. As a result, cognitive authority is a type of trust. When we do not possess personal expertise on a subject, we often decide whether to grant a source cognitive authority by checking for credibility, which Wilson defines as being composed of two primary elements: competence and trustworthiness (1983). Competence means that an information source possesses the expertise to get things right. Trustworthiness means the source intends to be accurate and objective, and their practices align with reliable information production.

Cognitive authority is subjective. People establish cognitive authorities throughout our lives, but early authorities help shape our worldview. This means that we often imbue sources of information with authority subconsciously, without closely examining our own reasoning. We may then experience strong negative affect when that trust is threatened or violated. Because cognitive authority often functions as a kind of tacit knowledge steeped in emotion, we may believe a cognitive authority simply because it just feels right to believe them.

Pamela McKenzie (2003) extends Wilson's work to suggest that information seekers' decisions about cognitive authority are not just the result of beliefs developed independently by individuals but are also influenced by unconsciously absorbed norms, beliefs, and ideology. Individuals are members of communities that have already built up hierarchies of knowledge about the varying degrees of legitimacy granted certain sources. Community members can resist or redefine which knowledge is authoritative in their context, but they are likely to face an uphill battle against the received justifications of the decisions that came before. These feelings can lead us to the mistaken conclusion that authority, rather than being composed of elements we can assess, simply exists outside of our control. We may not agree with these authorities, but the power of widespread belief in a cognitive authority may impose beliefs upon us. This can make the concept of cognitive authority feel weighted with inevitability, as though we have little choice in the matter.

We propose two additional ways to unpack authority for information literacy instruction. The first is to investigate the way that authority is *constructed*. Authority is built up over time; you can't simply declare yourself an expert, and it is not enough to earn a degree. This idea fits with commonsense understandings that cognitive authority requires substantive expertise. Additionally, we can consider the purpose/process/product model of information formats (described in Chapter 4) and recognize that cognitive authority is established in both the purpose and the process of information creation. The purpose of a piece of information, and who is responsible for creating it, speaks to its credibility: the intent (trustworthiness) and whether the creator or author is qualified to speak on that topic (competence). The process of creation—in particular, the processes associated with quality control—helps confirm the accuracy of the information and further build its authority.

Second, we look to the ways authority is *contextual*. Librarians often act as envoys between students and a variety of disciplines; the typical in-depth reference question represents a need to consciously seek second-hand knowledge, since most patrons ask questions outside of our own field of expertise. Therefore each proxy search also involves evaluation of whether sources are authoritative within a discipline, by someone outside of the discipline. Sydney Pierce argues that in order to understand the meaning of authority, librarians need to carefully examine the nature and boundaries of academic disciplines: "agreement on what constitutes expertise in a subject area does not take place in a vacuum" (1991, p. 22). Disciplines themselves are not abstract categories of knowledge but are groups of practitioners, with unique cultures, and specific ways of establishing who is a member and who is not. Communities create a meaningful context for insiders but inevitably create outsiders as well. Thus, authority is also *contextual*, because it is based in social relationships and communities of practice. This context creates realms of knowledge and specific cognitive authorities that reside therein.

Bringing together these threads, we propose the information literacy threshold concept *authority*, defined as follows:

> Authority is a form of intellectual trust granted by an individual or community to an information source. It is both constructed, built through expertise and persistent reliability, and contextual, limited to certain knowledge domains or situations and shaped by community norms.

Part of what librarians do, then, is teach students to choose their own authorities with care. Students can learn about the established rules and systems that build authority, and they can also question existing structures from a more informed standpoint. Librarians can help students use a broad range of evaluative criteria in order to meet their information needs with authoritative evidence.

Trust and Markers of Authority

For many years, Silvia's mother, Sue, worked in quality control for the textile industry. Sue worked for a company we'll call Acme Shorts. When a brand, like Nike, asked Acme Shorts to produce 5,000 pairs of running shorts, Acme Shorts would assign five factories to each make 1,000 pairs of running shorts. Before the running shorts were shipped to stores under the Nike brand, Sue would visit the factories and randomly pull pairs of running shorts in each size, checking for specific markers—in this case, that the running shorts were made to the specifications of the size chart, that seams were stitched neatly, and that tags or labels were correctly attached. Since it would be impossible to individually check all 5,000 pairs of running shorts, Sue and Acme Shorts had to trust that these randomly selected running shorts represented the quality standard of the entire shipment.

Quality control in a mass production setting has two elements: recognizable markers of quality and trust in the methods of production. This model can extend to apply to the evaluation of information in the case where the user of that information does not possess enough expertise to accurately evaluate the content. In deciding whether or not to grant a source cognitive authority, in other words to trust a source, we often check for credibility using markers that act as heuristics (rules of thumb). These markers include qualifications like degrees, years of experience, reputation, and indications of quality control processes such as editorial and peer review. From these markers, we discern whether the source intends to tell the truth, is concerned with being accurate, and possesses the necessary expertise to do so. Additionally, we attempt to evaluate the content of a source (even in the absence of personal expertise) to discern whether the information makes sense and seems convincing. Markers of authority, which Wilson refers to as "indirect tests," are an imperfect means to judge the information content of a source but often do signal a certain level of expected credibility or quality, much like name brands do for consumer goods like the previously mentioned Acme Shorts (1983, p. 166).

Librarians are very comfortable with markers of authority, as evidenced by tools like the CRAAP test (Currency, Relevance, Authority, Accuracy, and Purpose) for evaluating sources (Meriam Library, 2017). It's harder to handle the implications of trust being a crucial piece of the equation, but it undoubtedly is. Pierce points out, aptly: "We know the limits of our own knowledge, but not those of the experts upon whom we must rely" (1991, p. 31). We cannot check each pair of running shorts, nor can we replicate every research study, though most scholarly work goes through peer review, in addition to editorial processes. Ultimately, these judgments are "subjective, relative, and situational rather than objective, absolute, and universally recognizable" (Rieh, 2005, p. 4). While the phrase "quality control" seems to imply precision, and much as we may wish to have objective measures of authority, there will always be a leap of faith involved.

Michael Buckland's writing on the relationship between trust and truth emphasizes the practical side of the need for trust:

> In our daily lives, the presumption that all information is, by definition, true has no basis in common sense or personal experience. We may want to know if a statement is true, and we may well be doubtful, but in practice we usually end up trusting the evidence, an expert, a wise person, or a friend. Without trust, we would be paralyzed. (Buckland, 2017, p. 17)

Certainly, it is not a conscious choice for most people to decide to drive on freeway overpasses designed by engineers or to wash our hands with soap on the advice of epidemiologists, and both of these scenarios involve trust. But taking a step back, how do people decide who, or what, tells us the truth? This question was as relevant when Wilson wrote his book as it is today. Are subjective decisions about trust in academic sources simply a difference of degree from the student who insists that all perspectives are equally valid, including ones that reject a shared evidence-based reality or that justify intolerance? Or is there a bright line dividing the two?

Stefanie Bluemle writes that facts have come to seem mutable, or worse, irrelevant, with emotion taking the upper hand to undermine the cognitive authority of formerly trusted sources of second-hand knowledge. This feels vertiginous because so many public voices are rejecting received wisdom about which sources are legitimately authoritative, dismissing them as just another opinion that the public can choose to believe or not. At the same time, "post-facts politics are often contrary, and even openly hostile, to the aims and values of social justice" (Bluemle, 2018, p. 278). Perhaps the clearest example to date is the U.S. president Donald J. Trump's remark, after a counterprotester was killed at a white nationalist rally in Charlottesville, that there are "very fine people on both sides" (Gray, 2017). Librarians have to find a way out of this intellectual cul-de-sac if we are to talk about cognitive authority without enabling the position that some of the people in our classrooms should be enslaved or dead.

The current post-truth moment had its antecedents, of course. William Badke's work suggests that it arrived on a wave of democratization of knowledge that included the wisdom of the crowds, as in the example of *Wikipedia*; critical approaches to the concepts of authority and expertise by postmodern theorists; and student-centered educational models reaching back to Freirean pedagogy. Badke summarizes the problem for academic librarians thus:

> For many of our students, knowledge is flat, with none of it having more inherent authority than any other. This, of course, is an illusion, because none of us

> know enough not to need the guidance of those who know more than us. For academia, the exercise of cognitive authority is foundational. Our students need to acknowledge that reality but must also understand both how to discern it and when to challenge it. This is a difficult prospect for the average student who lacks deep subject knowledge and thus possesses neither the criteria nor the skills to evaluate it effectively. (2015, pp. 203–204)

Badke advises that librarians should not back away from asserting that some information is better than other information for certain purposes. Rather than worrying, as critical librarianship does, that this stance will "induct students into an existing system of authority, that is, academic culture" (Bluemle, 2018, p. 10), librarians must offer to students the belief that they should seek out cognitive authorities recognized by academia as such—because the information from those sources has the distinctive qualities of being accurate or correct for the purpose at hand. Librarians can help students understand both why this particular belief is privileged in academia and why this belief, like all beliefs about authority, is constructed as well as contextual.

Why do we take Badke's word for it? Amy, Silvia, and Lori have all found Badke's writing on information literacy instruction to be useful over many years. The teaching approach that he shares in his textbooks has worked with our students in various settings. Put another way, we have spot-checked so many pairs of running shorts from the Badke box that we are confident in the credibility of his authority. We believe him—and in the context of this discussion, that will never be satisfying, but it will be true. Badke is a cognitive authority for us, one that validates the notion that even if truth within a discipline continues to be negotiated, there are agreed-upon standards of evidence and discourse that separate academically acceptable information from misinformation or lies.

Reevaluating Academic Authority

Understanding the concept of authority as both constructed and contextual highlights how critical evaluation skills are in some ways more important than knowledge of specific and trusted sources in the current information landscape. Just as a cynical view of authority can lead to all knowledge being reduced to equally valid beliefs, a rigid view of authority may exclude potentially helpful sources of information that are not generally recognized by the structures that confer authority.

A more flexible understanding acknowledges that information considered unreliable in one context may be used to effectively answer questions in another; not all circumstances call for the same evaluative criteria. For example, though one might not look to online comments on election results for factual or objective information, a political scientist might monitor such responses when studying public perception of a political party or the political orientation of readers of certain publications. Voters might identify *Wikipedia* as an authoritative source for information about their congressional district and the incumbent candidate's stance on education funding, but they understand that the site is not an acceptable source when writing a political science paper about current trends in education policy.

A researcher—that is, a person in possession of a research question or basis for inquiry—may find that their information need is not met by existing evidence that is available. In this case the researcher must not only consider what will constitute authoritative evidence but also then design a process that generates new authoritative evidence. The validity of the author's methods and analysis must stand up to the same sort of evaluation that is brought to bear on any other evidence used for any of the aforementioned purposes. As James Elmborg (2006) points out, when it comes to academic information, students must learn how "academics validate information through complex peer review processes in ways that may seem obsessive, even paranoid, to outsiders" (p. 196).

Academic evidence is entwined with the scientific method. The Age of Enlightenment was marked by the popularization of scientific authority as an alternative to religious authority. The observable, methodological, and empirical stood in opposition to miracles, alchemy, and the supernatural. Scientific authority was defined by that which could be proven to be objectively true. As we briefly discussed in Chapter 1, though, the notion of objectivity has been upended in the centuries since the Enlightenment. Scientific objectivity has been called into question as well. For example, the finding of biotech firm Amgen, published in *Nature*, that only 6 out of 53 landmark papers in the areas of cancer research and blood biology could be validated and their original results replicated led its authors to conclude that "the academic system and peer-review process tolerates and perhaps even inadvertently encourages" authors to prioritize quantity of publications over quality of scientific rigor (Begley & Ellis, 2012). Such pressures complicate the authority of seemingly unassailable sources.

Given the varied treatments of authority from one discipline to another, it is useful to specify that in most academic contexts, authority should refer to thoughtful curation, subject expertise, and reliable methods of funding and dissemination. An authoritative text is likely to contain the sound scholarship and methods upon which researchers should rely. Barbara Fister asks how librarians can talk about problems with academic research in the classroom—they bring drama and humanity to high-level research, which might otherwise be just a checkbox—without turning students into cynics (2015a). She beautifully summarizes the qualities of a trustworthy source:

> Whatever method is used to conduct research, it cannot be driven by self-interest. One might question whether objectivity is possible, but it is generally an ideal that guides researchers' behavior. Research begins with a question or hypotheses, not with a foregone conclusion. Evidence matters, but it has to be handled fairly. Cherry-picking material that suits an argument while ignoring evidence that doesn't is conduct unbecoming of a scholar. Research is conversational, but it would be unethical to fail to cite the person who expressed an idea first. Other people's contributions to the conversation must not be misrepresented. Peer review is flawed; it can let bad research slip through, or it can be too conservative, suppressing research that challenges the status quo. Yet because originality is so highly valued among scholars, there are incentives for dissent. (Fister, 2015b, p. 97)

Fister's description points to an ethics of authority—ethics that are perhaps seldom upheld, but that we want our students to understand and practice. In a sense, giving students a checklist to evaluate for quality really represents a hope that they will recognize the markers of ethical authority in academic sources.

The emergence of ethical and functional problems in academic publishing points to another seismic shift in systems of authority. Just as scientific authority replaced religious authority, it now appears that new authorities are emerging that prioritize a wider range of voices and identities, exemplified by alt-metrics, open peer review, the #ownvoices movement, and the like. When these voices align with the ethics that academics recognize, it broadens the scope of available evidence. That is why these movements are not the same as asserting that every point of view is equally valid.

All sources are not created equal, and authoritative voices do exist for specific categories of knowledge. Indicators of authority, such as academic credentials, name recognition, journal titles, and governmental affiliation, often serve as useful shortcuts for the beginner when evaluating the accuracy and quality of information. On the other hand, authority is a reflection of power structures produced through established systems and institutions (peer review, editorial processes, scholarly presses, institutions of higher education). By passively conforming to dominant authorities, students lose the chance to uncover meaningful alternatives that are no less valuable or reliable.

An understanding of the authority threshold concept enables experts to critically examine all evidence—be it a *Wikipedia* article or a peer-reviewed conference proceeding—and ask relevant questions about origins, context, and suitability for the information need of the moment. By examining the characteristics of authoritative evidence in specific contexts, learners must confront the power structures that grant authority, including their faults, and consider when, where, and why these structures are in place. Thus, the expert respects the expertise that authority represents and remains skeptical of the systems which have elevated that authority and the information created by it.

The Trouble with Authority

Authority is closely associated with domination and power; along these lines, sociologist Max Weber defined authority as "the probability that certain specific commands (or all commands) will be obeyed by a given group of persons" (1978, p. 212). Put another way, authority is held by those who have the power to control decisions. Bluemle makes the helpful distinction that "cognitive authority, unlike political authority, cannot command or shape people's external behavior; it can only influence their thoughts" (2018, p. 273)—and the trouble is that the everyday understanding of authority is as political authority.

Consider the troublesome nature of political authority as it affects students. For many populations in the United States, the authorities have become synonymous with deportation officers from Immigration and Customs Enforcement, police officers acquitted for murdering unarmed black Americans, or countless managers and executives willing to ignore sexual harassment and assault. Students may carry negative political connotations of the word "authority," only to have their librarian come along and insist that authority is necessary for a successful essay. Librarians need to acknowledge the cognitive dissonance college students might experience in this moment and recognize that political authority does have bearing on information literacy instruction.

We can see Weber's type of political authority at work in the Library of Congress Subject Headings, which are routinely debated and sometimes changed. Sanford Berman's (1971/1993) classic work on racial bias in the Library of Congress Subject Headings drew attention to a problem that remains a major issue for an internationally dominant controlled vocabulary. Controlled vocabularies are how librarians manage and provide access to vast amounts of information, and they work extremely well for this purpose; moreover, before catalogs lived in computers, any changes represented a steep labor cost. Yet, the Library of Congress Subject Headings are an attempt to assign uniform terms to a universe of knowledge that can be subjective and may impose a norm that is alienating, offensive, disrespectful, or simply inaccurate to many library users (Cho, 2016).

Steven Knowlton's (2005) analysis found that of the changes Berman originally proposed, about a third had been made, with other changes at least reflecting his suggestions. This represents a partial win for social justice in librarianship, yet nearly 50 years on, Emily Drabinski points out that controlled vocabularies are on the one hand "remarkably resistant to change" (2013, p. 94) and on the other hand, inevitably, still in need of change. Drabinski uses the theoretical framework of queer theory to suggest that

> [c]orrections are always contingent and never final, shifting in response to discursive and political and social change. Just as Negro women could make political sense in 1972 but not in 2012, the corrections suggested by Berman, Freedman, and Roberto today are just as subject to the contingent vagaries of history and standpoint. (2013, p. 100)

Even when librarians are willing to slough off the assumptions that centered white, male, heterosexual, Christian (and so on) library users as the norm, outside forces sometimes provide the resistance to change. In March 2016, for example, the Library of Congress announced that it would remove *illegal alien* as a subject heading, with *noncitizen* and *unauthorized immigration* offered as alternatives. By June 2016, a resolution was passed in the House of Representatives to restrict the Library of Congress from making the proposed language change (Peet, 2016). Though the resolution did not appear in the final appropriations bill passed by the Senate, the process was illustrative of the back-and-forth inherent in the struggle for control. Continued change and resistance to change in the Library of Congress Subject Headings are inevitable. What librarians *can* teach students is not that someday a future librarian will at last log the final correction to the catalog's subject headings but rather that the catalog is an authority that, like any other, can be viewed critically.

In fact, questioning controlled vocabularies is one example of working with students to better understand how cognitive authority relates to political authority. Examining the characteristics of authoritative evidence in specific contexts turns a critical lens on the systems that grant authority, including their faults, along with considerations of when, where, and why these systems are used. For example, Amelia Koford (2014) found that disabilities studies scholars—whose focus is a marginalized community that is underrepresented or poorly represented in classification systems—tended not to use subject headings to find their research materials, preferring search work-arounds that enabled them to respond to the issue of encountering nonpreferred terms (which, she points out, "can vary with time, geography, culture, and individual preference"; p. 20). Understood in this way, authority is a reflection of societal structures of power. Our postmodern comfort with academic skepticism creates room to question existing power structures, structures largely built by wealthy white men in a heteronormative, ableist context.

Librarians can teach students that a single voice is rarely sufficient to support a claim, refute an argument, make a decision, inspire creativity, inform an opinion, or generate a new inquiry. Students can establish their own cognitive authorities in addition to learning to locate and recognize canonical or traditional authorities. In the present information landscape, information literate students need to know when to acknowledge, question, challenge, or reject political and cognitive authority.

Are Librarians Authorities?

While Weber's definition of authority is closely connected with authoritarianism, and Wilson's cognitive authority is about influencing how people think, practical authority influences other people's actions. Borrowed from the discipline of philosophy, the idea of practical authority considers how authority can help someone act more reasonably, as when a child wears a seat belt at their parent's insistence or when an employee arrives at work on time as instructed by a supervisor. Legal, moral, and political philosopher Joseph Raz offers an interpretation of this dynamic. Authoritative norms control actions using what he calls "protected reasons" (1979, p. 29). A protected reason encourages someone to do something while also giving them a way to ignore the reasons why they *shouldn't* do something.

For example, if a Master Gardener tells a new garden volunteer to use ladybugs to combat aphids, the volunteer is likely to use the recommended method. They are also likely to use ladybugs without considering a powerful but dangerous pesticide or a less effective method, like sprinkling flour onto affected leaves. These methods can be disregarded because the Master Gardener's ladybug endorsement makes other options less appealing. Authority has value, Raz argues, when "those subject to it act better on their other reasons for action under authority than they would in the absence of authority" (Murphy, 2006). Accepting this type of authority can be challenging, however, as when working with a physical trainer or a financial planner. It requires maintaining control and resisting temptation, neither of which comes easily without the influence of a recognized source of authority.

It is not much of a stretch to think about librarians wielding practical authority at the reference desk. We can nudge students to act in their own best interest. Start your research now instead of procrastinating; use academic sources instead of CliffsNotes; write your own paper instead of buying one from a paper mill. So why do we—Amy, Silvia, and Lori—feel a little queasy about telling people what they should do or should not do, even under the auspices of a benign type of authority?

We think this may be in part because of our profession's ingrained underdog status. It's the rare librarian who has not been asked some variation on the question, "What do librarians do all day now that everyone just Googles stuff?" Within academic librarianship, we aren't always sure where we stand, as evidenced by the ongoing debates about faculty status for librarians. There is an equal lack of consensus about the extent to which the Master of Library Science (MLS) is the appropriate entry into the profession; some universities now accept a PhD in a relevant area in lieu of the terminal degree for librarianship. Likewise, school and public libraries have seen an increase in the use of paraprofessionals, with staff or clerks replacing librarians with the MLS at storytime or reference desks. Librarians can be cognitive authorities on authority while simultaneously occupying precarious or ambiguous spaces with respect to our own professional authority.

While those debates are ongoing and contribute to varying degrees of imposter syndrome, it may help differentiate between authority in general and the practical authority that comes with our disciplinary expertise as librarians. An early-career librarian may not feel confident in their position or feel that they have clout in their department, but they still have a grasp on disciplinary content and know more than their students do. Even if it's not possible to know what others should do, in a larger sense, librarians still possess the expertise and experience to be considered trustworthy when it comes to finding, choosing, and using information.

Librarians use their practical authority when they encourage students to call upon authoritative evidence in different ways depending on the information need of the moment. It is easier to quote an article that confirms your stance without fact-checking its claims. It is quicker to write a paper using the first results from a search on the open web than it is to find and read carefully selected results from a credible think tank. Writing accurate citations to give proper attribution is time consuming. Librarians can exercise our practical authority to guide students toward more ethical, and more successful, research practices.

Maps and Authority

After turning off the congested interstate and onto a series of quiet suburban streets, Silvia's mother asked her, "Why are we here?" Silvia shrugged and said, "The app said this was the better route." Google Maps, the globe in an elementary school classroom, the colorful map of the London

Underground, and the badly folded road map lingering in your glove compartment are all classic exemplars of Wilson's second-hand knowledge. In order to use a map, you must trust that it was produced by credentialed experts who rely on authoritative evidence to provide accurate information. Taiwan is an island south of Japan and north of the Philippines. The Albuquerque Museum of Art and History is on Mountain Road NW. You take the 210 W to 57 S to get from the Inland Empire to Disneyland. It is because maps are so very authoritative that they present an entry point to explore how authority is constructed and contextual.

Consider the map in the glove compartment. Chances are that it's a Rand McNally *Road Atlas*; founded in 1856, Rand McNally produced its first road maps in 1904. Along with suggestions for road trip routes, most Rand McNally atlases also include landmarks, tourism information, and campsites. As far as texts go, it's about as authoritative as you can get. Or, perhaps it is the ever so slightly more modern American Automobile Association (AAA) road map, first published in 1905, known for its ranked lists of hotels, restaurants, and nearby attractions. If your cultural identity and context is that of a white American, either map likely meets your information needs and has met your information needs for the last century.

If, however, you are a black American planning a road trip during the Jim Crow era, these maps are much less useful. Writing for the Smithsonian National Museum of American History, historian Jay Driskell (2015) describes how black families "stuffed the trunks of their automobiles with food, blankets and pillows, even an old coffee can for those times when black motorists were denied the use of a bathroom." As road trips gained popularity after World War II, and after the building of the new interstate system, black motorists also had to contend with the possibility of property damage and physical harm as they traveled through unfamiliar cities "partitioned by segregation and scarred by lynching" (Driskell, 2015). For black motorists, relying on a Rand McNally or AAA map for information about the next rest stop was not enough; the prevailing authoritative text did not account for the fact that black Americans lived in a profoundly different country than white Americans. To use Wilson's terms again, black users of these maps discovered that there was an assumed first-hand experience embedded in the maps' recommendations that didn't line up with their needs.

In response to these dangers, Victor H. Green, a Harlem postal employee, used his contacts in the Postal Workers Union to compile *The Negro Motorist Green Book: An International Travel Guide*. Inspired by similar publications for Jewish travelers (Library of Congress, n.d.), Green published the guide to help black motorists identify hotels, restaurants, service stations, or other businesses where they could be served without fear of discrimination (Conan, 2010). The guide was not a map, exactly, but it served as a necessary filter through which a road map could be made useful. While the scope of the first guide was limited to New York City and its immediate surroundings, the final issues of the guide offered endorsements of airlines, European hotels, beaches in St. Lucia, listings for all 50 states, and an overview of each state's current statutes regarding legal segregation.

As the guide grew, so, too, did its influence over readers. It highlighted black-owned businesses in both listings and advertisements, campaigned for black politicians, and raised money for black causes; the 1947 edition included information about a United Negro College Fund campaign and a suggestion that travelers visit one of the listed college campuses as they traveled the country. In a letter to the editor published in the 1940 edition of the guide, Wm. Smith is effusive about the value of *The Negro Motorist Green Book*. Smith writes, "We earnestly believe 'The Negro Motorist Green Book' will mean as much if not more to us as the A. A. A. means to the White race" (Schomburg, 1940, p. 2). Users could trust the second-hand knowledge that had accrued in the guide over the years; it offered an alternative cognitive authority when the dominant culture's documentation simply didn't work.

The introduction to the 1949 edition reads,

> There will be a day sometime in the near future when this guide will not have to be published. That is when we as a race will have equal opportunities and privileges in the United States. It will be a great day for us to suspend this publication for then we can go wherever we please, and without embarrassment. But until that time comes we shall continue to publish this information for your convenience each year. (Schomburg, 1949, p. 1)

Green held true to his promise. In 1964, the Civil Rights Act passed, and the last issue of the guide was published. Lonnie Bunch, the director of the Smithsonian National Museum of African American History and Culture, saw the cessation of the guide as a celebration of sorts. "As segregation ended, people put such things away," he said, "they felt they didn't need them anymore. It brought a sense of psychological liberation" (McGee, 2010).

The story of the *Green Book* illustrates that second-hand knowledge is not neutral; the exact same data points have very different meanings from two different perspectives. Other maps are challenged on the basis that they reinforce power structures while misrepresenting scale or fostering misunderstanding. For example, one common criticism of the most recognizable world map is that it makes North America and Europe seem more prominent while minimizing the true size of the African continent and countries along the equator. Advocates of a south-up map orientation argue that a north-oriented map leads to the conflation of north with goodness, modernity, and wealth, and south with badness, regression, and poverty. There are many other possibilities that emphasize different aspects of representing geography. The Dymaxion map projects the world map onto an icosahedron (a polyhedron with 20 faces) to better represent the relative shape of countries and does not specify any point as the "top" of the map. Architect and artist Hajime Narukawa designed the award-winning AuthaGraph World Map, which is a proportionally accurate two-dimensional map based on a tetrahedron. Rather than orienting the map around a land mass, the AuthaGraph has the ocean at its center in order to foreground concerns about the impact of global warming on the planet's bodies of water (AuthaGraph, n.d.).

Even when an alternative map is unlikely to ever be adopted, it can still be a worthwhile thought exercise. Molly Roy's clever reinterpretation of the iconic New York City subway map (*City of Women*) confronts the systemic erasure of contributions by the city's women to art, politics, philanthropy, and beyond. Essayist Rebecca Solnit (2016) uses Roy's map to imagine a city landscape dominated by women: "I can't imagine how I might have conceived of myself and my possibilities if, in my formative years, I had moved through a city where most things were named after women and many or most of the monuments were of powerful, successful, honored women," Solnit writes, while conceding that "most American cities are, by their nomenclature, mostly white as well as mostly male. Still, you can imagine." By calling attention to the arbitrariness of excluding women from authority, Roy offers a what-if where women's names might take on cognitive authority as they become very recognizable as place-names.

Maps document and determine our geographic realities, but their authority is constructed and contextual. Their trustworthiness is built up over time and through use, yet they reflect the views and ideologies of their makers. Put another way, you can use your phone's GPS to find your way to the park, or you can follow your own internal compass, take the scenic route, or ask a local for directions—depending on your priorities for the day, one path may be more suitable than the other.

Applying the Threshold Concepts Criteria

Authority may seem like a good joke—innate, universal, and obvious. In fact, authority, like a good joke, is constructed and contextual. This understanding is transformative, at once complicating and clarifying the rules for trustworthy information. Textbooks are an immediate example of a source of presumed authority. Assigned at the start of each year, the covers of textbooks serve as physical boundaries that confine all of the information to be known on a given topic. This type of authoritative source has a whiff of other unhelpful binary thinking: credible/crappy, scholarly/popular. Research shows that equipped with just checklist-level knowledge, students are probably going to be able to determine whether an article is scholarly or not, but they are likely to stay at surface-level knowledge, unable to transfer those markers of authority to other types of evidence (Jankowski, Russo, & Townsend, 2018). From the other side of the threshold, textbooks represent a series of choices made by the authors on the basis of accrued expertise and community understanding; the credibility of sources is determined through in-depth reasoning rather than rules of thumb. For example, Judith Butler's theory of gender performativity as presented in *Gender Trouble* is not important because it was selected by a professor and placed on a syllabus. Instead, it was selected by a professor because it marked a shift away from conventional gender politics, influencing subsequent decades of literary and critical theory.

Once authority is understood to be constructed and contextual, this understanding is irreversible. It becomes clear why relying on just a few sources of information is problematic, giving novice researchers a way to reconsider their personal information-seeking behavior: How do you react when facts contradict your long-held beliefs? Do you limit yourself to media that reinforces your stance on issues? Can you disagree with a trusted source without rejecting all information from that source? This understanding positions the novice researcher as someone who builds their own expertise in order to make informed determinations about cognitive authority.

This threshold concept integrates information evaluation into the decision-making processes that define our experiences. Working with this concept requires students to accept that authority is a moving target; there may be an exception to every source of authoritative evidence, and criteria that work for one source of information may be irrelevant for another. At the same time that these good critical thinking skills are being instilled, though, students also learn that some authoritative sources are better than others. Even as students are encouraged to see the library as a place to find authoritative information, they encounter a series of exceptions. "You can trust the information you find in the library," an assignment prompt will say, "but don't use encyclopedia entries, book reviews, or dissertations in your research paper." Moreover, the authority threshold concept can help explain how power is maintained and replicated via the dissemination and restriction of information, pulling in conversations about the freedom of speech, the importance of a free press, propaganda, and dissent. The integrative function of this threshold concept pulls these disparate and seemingly contradictory elements together.

As previously discussed, authority as a concept is not unique to information science, but it is bounded by the field of information science when it is applied to the evaluation and use of information sources (*cognitive authority*). This concept has its own literature and its own ethics. Academics in other disciplines are not necessarily in possession of information literacy expertise, as illustrated by Silvia's experience compiling an annual list of faculty scholarship for her college. Each year, she invariably discovers a handful of articles that were published in predatory journals; at first glance, the journals seem valid, but closer examination reveals hidden publishing fees, questionable indexing practices, and editorial boards that associate her colleagues with the wrong institution. Assuming that faculty members published in these journals in good faith, we can conclude that expertise in their field did not extend to the darker corners of scholarly communication. Librarians can help users navigate these areas, which, in this case, overlap with our expertise.

Authority is troublesome, first, because of its close associations with power, domination, and authoritarianism. This example of troublesome language may cause users to take a too-critical approach to authority. It is also troublesome because of the affective elements of trust and belief that are associated with determining the legitimacy of a cognitive authority. For example, librarians sometimes encourage students to brainstorm areas of knowledge where they possess some expertise, where they can serve as legitimate sources of authority, in order to make the concept more accessible. While this exercise might seem to apply better to older students, still, traditional undergraduates might credibly lay claim to authority on a variety of subjects, including their own identity as it relates to dominant culture. In academia, this type of personal expertise has a very specific place (e.g., autoethnography) but does not relate to the expertise needed to evaluate sources in a discipline, with its own culture, language, history, and markers of authority. Students will need much more context before they arrive at a position to reinforce or dismantle existing power structures, though this is certainly attainable.

Teaching Authority

Basic

Authority and Bias

A basic entry point into the concept of authority can be a conversation about the idea of objectivity. On the one hand, objectivity is a myth, but on the other hand, ethical and accurate sources do exist, which is pretty close to what we mean by objectivity. Authoritative evidence should come from a source that we can trust, and objectivity is a crucial component of trust. Can a lawmaker supported by the National Rifle Association advocate for meaningful gun control? Do we trust a judge to maintain impartiality when deciding a case that may benefit them financially? Should we believe you when you say that your mom makes the best apple pie in the entire world? The answer to each of these questions could easily be "yes, of course," but the authority threshold concept helps highlight the ways that ideological, financial, or emotional bias can cloud objectivity. Uncovering bias can be one way of evaluating the authority of an information source.

Authority and Context

Using the authority threshold concept means letting go of a master list of good and bad sources of information. Instead, information evaluation should focus on the information need in context. Students should be encouraged to ask, "Is this source of information the best fit for my current information need?" Beyoncé's song lyrics may not be the best support for your essay on how Dorothy Parker basically always twirled on her haters by being quoteworthy, but they could easily support your thesis that *Lemonade* mirrors the way 19th-century women's novels disguised subversive feminism as entertainment. Alternatively, it can be useful to consider how context can complicate an authoritative source, even temporarily. Breaking news, for example, is notorious for being misreported, especially when it comes to mass shootings and terrorist attacks. WNYC's *On the Media* (2013) created *The Breaking News Consumer's Handbook* to help readers evaluate information after a tragedy, when even the most trustworthy news sources might be less authoritative than usual. As a result, we have to do more work to ensure that the information we get is reliable; we can't use the usual checklists as a shortcut. Instruction in this area could focus on retractions related to previous breaking news events ranging from 9/11 to the sinking of the *Titanic*.

Finding Authoritative Information

Students working with the authority threshold concept at the basic level should be reminded that authority is a slippery, complex, ever-shifting monster of an idea. Confusion and uncertainty are natural reactions when evaluating authority. Struggling with this threshold concept does not speak to a student's academic competence or aptitude. Instead, much of finding authoritative information has to do with experience. The more they read, the more classes they take in their discipline, the more they practice, the easier it will be. In the meantime, as librarians are the authorities on authority, asking a librarian can be a powerful shortcut.

Choosing and Becoming Cognitive Authorities

Wilson's cognitive authority model and the authority threshold concept offer us a chance to reframe authority for our students. Authority in this context is subjective: a choice and a relationship. Authority no longer has to come down on them from the powerful but is something they can define for themselves. Librarians can help students develop the metacognitive skills needed to recognize their current cognitive authorities and what criteria they are using in granting those authorities influence over their thinking. We can expose students to new criteria from different contexts and different markers for quality and reliability. Students should be encouraged to be deliberate when granting someone cognitive authority; they should understand the value of their own belief and be stingy with it. Students can also reflect on who they are cognitive authorities for and learn to regard that as a responsibility, an honor, and an encouragement toward developing expertise.

Advanced

Authority and Editions

More advanced studies of authority can explore the nuanced differences between editions of a text. *Hamlet* is easily and freely available as a PDF online, as a paperback in used bookstores, and in dozens of editions on most library shelves. What qualities make one edition more authoritative than the other? While a novice might prefer the No Fear Shakespeare edition, which places the original text next to plain English translations, more advanced researchers are likely to look to the Norton Critical Editions instead, and a scholar might travel to study archival texts in the British Library. Annotations, appendices, and editing choices all change the extent to which a text is authoritative.

Authority and Academia

Moving through the ranks of academia requires advanced students to develop an understanding of how perceived authority can impact their professional success. Is there a link between the competitiveness of a journal and its authority in the discipline? What about impact factor? Champions of the open access movement often hear from faculty that while they support open access in theory, they must continue to follow traditional publishing practices in order for their publications to count toward promotion and tenure. Yet, open journals increase accessibility and visibility, reaching a broader, possibly nonacademic audience. Which is more advantageous?

Authority as Trust, Not Truth

At the most advanced level, students should start to link authority to questions of trust and concrete facts rather than truth. In doing so, it is helpful to contrast the qualities of first-hand and second-hand knowledge. For example, it could be unquestionably true for some people that British Marmite, Icelandic hákarl, or Japanese natto are disgusting. For others, they are truly delicious. These describe subjective experiences. Marmite is made from yeast extract, hákarl from fermented shark, and natto from fermented soybeans. These are facts. At the advanced level, students should be able to work with facts to understand how truth shifts for individuals or groups of individuals. Authority should be granted to sources that present, analyze, or otherwise use factual evidence, like a food history article about how natto came to prominence in Japanese cuisine, rather than to sources that appeal to what feels true, like an American game show where contestants participate in a blind taste test of international food items and react to the taste of natto with shock and revulsion. Advanced students know that not all facts are accurate, but they should also recognize that it would be impossible to independently verify each fact they encounter. How is trust built? What makes a source trustworthy? At this level, authority is about trust, not truth.

Takeaways

- Authority as a concept is not unique to information science, but it is bounded by the field of information science when it is applied to the evaluation and use of information sources (*cognitive authority*).
- Authority is constructed because it is built through expertise and persistent reliability. Authority is contextual because it is limited to certain knowledge domains or situations and shaped by community norms.
- Markers of authority, such as academic credentials, name recognition, journal titles, and governmental affiliation, often serve as useful shortcuts for the beginner when evaluating the accuracy and quality of information. Yet, a critical information user will be skeptical of power structures produced through established systems and institutions.

For Further Consideration

- How can you incorporate critical evaluation skills, as opposed to reliance on shortcut indicators of authority, into database demonstrations or overviews of your library's collections?
- In your area of librarianship, do you feel like an authority on authority? Why or why not?
- How would you explain how we decide who, or what, to trust?
- Maps are an information source that users place great trust in, but there are cross-currents of perspective and identity under the seemingly factual surface. What's another example of an information source that can be looked at this way?

References

AuthaGraph World Map. (n.d.). Retrieved from http://www.authagraph.com/top/?lang=en

Badke, W. B. (2015). Expertise and authority in an age of crowdsourcing. In T. A. Swanson & H. Jagman (Eds.), *Not just where to click: Teaching students how to think about information* (pp. 191–215). Chicago, IL: Association of College & Research Libraries. Retrieved from https://www.researchgate.net/profile/William_Badke/publication/289504599_Expertise_and_Authority_in_an_Age_of_Crowdsourcing/links/568d404708aeaa1481ae44d0.pdf

Begley, C. G., & Ellis, L. M. (2012). Drug development: Raise standards for preclinical cancer research. *Nature, 483*(7391), 531–533. doi:10.1038/483531a

Berman, S. (1993). *Prejudices and antipathies: A tract on the LC subject heads concerning people*. Jefferson, NC: McFarland and Co. (Original work published 1971)

Bluemle, S. R. (2018). Post-facts: Information literacy and authority after the 2016 election. *portal: Libraries and the Academy, 18*(2), 265–282. Retrieved from https://digitalcommons.augustana.edu/cgi/viewcontent.cgi?article=1009&context=libscifaculty

Buckland, M. (2017). *Information and society*. Cambridge, MA: MIT Press.

Cho, J. S. (2016). *Producing discursive change: From "illegal aliens" to "unauthorized immigration" in library catalogs*. Retrieved from https://academicworks.cuny.edu/gc_etds/1559

Columbusing. (2014). In *Urban dictionary*. Retrieved from https://www.urbandictionary.com/define.php?term=Columbusing

Conan, N. (Host). (2010, September 15). "Green Book" helped African-Americans travel safely. In *Talk of the Nation*. Washington, DC: National Public Radio. Radio broadcast retrieved from https://www.npr.org/templates/story/story.php?storyId=129885990

Drabinski, E. (2013). Queering the catalog: Queer theory and the politics of correction. *Library Quarterly: Information, Community, Policy, 83*(2), 94–111.

Retrieved from https://digitalcommons.liu.edu/cgi/viewcontent.cgi?referer=https://scholar.google.com/&httpsredir=1&article=1007&context=brooklyn_libfacpubs

Driskell, J. (2015, July 30). An atlas of self-reliance: The Negro Motorist's Green Book (1937–1964) [Web log post]. Retrieved from http://americanhistory.si.edu/blog/negro-motorists-green-book

Elmborg, J. (2006). Critical information literacy: Implications for instructional practice. *Journal of Academic Librarianship, 32*(2), 192–199. doi:10.1016/j.acalib.2005.12.004

Fister, B. (2015a). Schooling for scandal [Web log post]. Retrieved from https://www.insidehighered.com/blogs/library-babel-fish/schooling-scandal

Fister, B. (2015b). The social life of knowledge: Faculty epistemologies. In T. A. Swanson & H. Jagman (Eds.), *Not just where to click: Teaching students how to think about information* (pp. 87–104). Chicago, IL: Association of College & Research Libraries. Retrieved from https://barbarafister.net/SocialLife.pdf

Gray, R. (2017, August 15). Trump defends white-nationalist protesters: "Some very fine people on both sides." *The Atlantic*. Retrieved from https://www.theatlantic.com/politics/archive/2017/08/trump-defends-white-nationalist-protesters-some-very-fine-people-on-both-sides/537012/

Jankowski, A., Russo, A. & Townsend, L. (2018). "It was information based": Student reasoning when distinguishing between scholarly and popular sources. *In the Library with the Lead Pipe*. Retrieved from http://www.inthelibrarywiththeleadpipe.org/2018/it-was-information-based/

Kaufman, J. (2017). Bubble tea purveyors continue to grow along with drink's popularity. *The New York Times*. Retrieved from https://nyti.ms/2v5yCUE

Knowlton, S. A. (2005). Three decades since *Prejudices and Antipathies*: A study of changes in the Library of Congress Subject Headings. *Cataloging & Classification Quarterly, 40*(2), 123–145. Retrieved from http://www.sanfordberman.org/biblinks/knowlton.pdf

Koford, A. (2014). How disability studies scholars interact with subject headings. *Cataloging & Classification Quarterly, 52*(4), 388–411. doi:10.1080/01639374.2014.891288

Library of Congress. (n.d.). *From haven to home: 350 years of Jewish life in America.* Retrieved from http://www.loc.gov/exhibits/haventohome/haven-century.html#obj0

McGee, C. (2010, August 22). The open road wasn't quite open to all. *The New York Times*. Retrieved from http://www.nytimes.com/2010/08/23/books/23green.html?_r=4

McKenzie, P. J. (2003). Justifying cognitive authority decisions: Discursive strategies of information seekers. *Library Quarterly, 73*(3), 261–288. Retrieved from http://publish.uwo.ca/~pmckenzi/McKenzie_LQ.pdf

Meriam Library, California State University, Chico. (2017, September 17). Evaluating information—Applying the CRAAP test [Assessment Instrument]. Retrieved from https://www.csuchico.edu/lins/handouts/eval_websites.pdf

Murphy, M. C. (2006). Authority. In D. M. Borchert (Ed.), *Encyclopedia of philosophy* (pp. 412–418). New York, NY: Macmillan Reference USA.

Peet, L. (2016, June 13). *Library of Congress drops illegal alien subject heading, provokes backlash legislation*. Retrieved from http://lj.libraryjournal.com/2016/06/legislation/library-of-congress-drops-illegal-alien-subject-heading-provokes-backlash-legislation/#_

Pierce, S. J. (1991). Subject areas, disciplines, and the concept of authority. *Library and Information Science Research, 13*(1), 21–35.

Raz, J. (1979). *The authority of law: Essays on law and morality*. Oxford, England: Clarendon Press.

Rieh, S. Y. (2005). Cognitive authority. In K. E. Fisher, S. Erdelez, & E. F. McKechnie (Eds.), *Theories of information behavior: A researcher's guide* (pp. 83–87). Medford, NJ: Information Today. Retrieved from https://web.archive.org/web/20080512170752/http://newweb2.si.umich.edu/rieh/papers/rieh_IBTheory.pdf

Schomburg Center for Research in Black Culture, Jean Blackwell Hutson Research and Reference Division, The New York Public Library. (1940). *The Negro motorist green-book: 1940*. Retrieved from http://digitalcollections.nypl.org/items/dc858e50-83d3-0132-2266-58d385a7b928

Schomburg Center for Research in Black Culture, Jean Blackwell Hutson Research and Reference Division, The New York Public Library. (1949). *The Negro motorist green-book: 1949*. Retrieved from http://digitalcollections.nypl.org/items/9dc3ff40-8df4-0132-fd57-58d385a7b928

Solnit, R. (2016, October 11). City of women. *The New Yorker*. Retrieved from https://www.newyorker.com/books/page-turner/city-of-women

Swanson, T. A., & Jagman, H. (2015). *Not just where to click: Teaching students how to think about information*. Chicago, IL: Association of College & Research Libraries.

Townsend, L., Brunetti, K., & Hofer, A. R. (2011). Threshold concepts and information literacy. *portal: Libraries and the Academy, 11*(3), 853–869. Retrieved from http://archives.pdx.edu/ds/psu/7417

Weber, M. (1978). *Economy and society: An outline of interpretive sociology*. Berkeley, CA: University of California Press.

Whitford, E. (2015). "Our home is not a new frontier": Bushwick locals fight new luxury development. Retrieved from Gothamist website: http://gothamist.com/2015/04/22/bushwick_colony_gentrification.php

Wilson, P. (1983). *Second-hand knowledge: An inquiry into cognitive authority*. Westport, CT: Greenwood Press.

WNYC. On the Media. (2013, September 20). *The breaking news consumer's handbook*. Retrieved from https://www.wnyc.org/story/breaking-news-consumers-handbook-pdf/

CHAPTER FOUR

Format

The format threshold concept was first suggested by a student's question: "What is the difference between a journal article and a website?" The student asked Lori this question near the end of a quarter-long Introduction to Information Literacy class, as he was working on his final project. The project required students to use a variety of sources and identify the format of each source.

His question prompted a sigh of teacherly frustration. All the more so because it came from a diligent student—he had completed all of the assignments, attended all of the classes, and appeared to be paying attention. The answer seemed obvious until Lori sat down to write an explanation of the difference between a journal article and a website. Here is the "short" answer Lori emailed to the student:

> A journal article is published in a journal (it can be online or in print)—usually you find journal articles in the databases available from the library's A–Z List of Databases. However, you might run across one online when using a search engine. The thing is, a journal article can exist as a part of a website. But journal articles are distinct because of their position in the "information cycle" or the production of knowledge within a discipline. They are published periodically (like a newspaper or magazine). They often report the results of academic research in a variety of fields and serve as one of the primary forms of scholarly communication. Scholarly journals are peer-reviewed (usually through some sort of editorial board or jury process) and the articles always cite their sources. A website is always published online (obviously) and ISN'T an online journal (or newspaper or magazine) or online book. Just about any other relevant and authoritative website is fair game for the purposes of this project.

Much of this material was covered in class: the information cycle, peer review, scholarly communication, finding journal articles in databases, different types of websites, and different types of sources. But the answer is so packed with complex terms and concepts that it's no wonder the student was confused. Bringing all of those various facets of class together to answer that one seemingly straightforward question begged another question: Is there a better way to cover format?

This chapter will explore the format threshold concept by defining format and articulating why it's important for students to learn how librarians view this concept. We borrow a concept from the field of rhetoric, genre theory, to consider new ways of looking at formats for communicating information in the digital age.

Format Defined

The concept "format as a process" was first proposed in the paper "Threshold Concepts and Information Literacy" (Townsend, Brunetti, & Hofer, 2011). The wording was intentionally ungrammatical in order to complicate the use of the word "format." Was format the best word? How was it being defined and used? Was a format a print book or print article? How about a website? Or was it a type of digital form like .mp3 or .doc? Could the concept of format be used as a productive shorthand for these questions in a teaching context?

The word "format" is undoubtedly troublesome language. Looking at the definitions of "format" that are available via a simple Google search, one finds a wide variance depending on the context. For example, from Wiktionary:

> The layout of a publication or document.
> The form of presentation of something.
> A file type.
> The radio station changed the format of its evening program. ("Format," 2016b)

Or how about a definition for "format" from one of the profession's most widely used dictionaries, the *Online Dictionary of Library and Information Science (ODLIS)*?

> A general indication of the size of a book, based on the number of times the printed sheets are folded in binding to make the leaves (folio, quarto, octavo, duodecimo, sextodecimo, etc.).

> Also refers to the particular physical presentation of a bibliographic item (AACR2). For printed publications, format includes size, proportions, quality of paper, typeface, illustration, layout, and style of binding. Synonymous in American usage with get up (books). In a more general sense, the physical medium in which information is recorded, including print and nonprint documents.
>
> In data processing, the manner in which data is arranged in a medium of input, output, or storage, including the code and instructions determining the arrangement (see file type). Also, to prepare a floppy disk for the recording of data (most floppies are sold preformatted) and to arrange text on a computer screen in the form in which it will be printed on paper (font, margins, alignment, type size, italic, boldface, etc.).
>
> Also used in reference to the physical characteristics of photographic and motion picture film (size, aspect ratio, etc.). ("Format," 2016a)

The *ODLIS* definition is lengthier and more detailed in comparison to common definitions, yet it still misses the purposes behind the various formats: *Why* is a scholarly journal article a scholarly journal article? What kind of information does it contain, and how does its structure facilitate the transmission, dissemination, and use of that information? Nor is there any consideration of the digital equivalent of "physical presentation" (e.g., a scanned PDF of a book, or a born-digital ebook), though "nonprint documents" are mentioned.

We found it helpful to consult Michael Buckland's classic article "Information as Thing" (1991). In it, Buckland identifies three types of information: information as process, information as knowledge, and information as thing. Information as process is the "act of informing"—one of the core functions of education and communication broadly. Information as knowledge is that which is communicated—the content of the message that is received. Information as thing refers to objects that "are referred to as 'information' because they are regarded as being informative" (p. 351). Librarians largely work with information as thing, that is, information embodied in objects or documents: books, photographs, artifacts, and so on. Librarians also organize and make accessible information as thing using systems of classification that attempt to catalog and logically arrange information as knowledge. Formats are categories of information things.

Robert Glushko, professor at the University of California, Berkeley School of Information, offers this definition of format in *Discipline of Organizing*:

> Information resources can exist in numerous formats with the most basic format distinction being whether the resource is physical or digital. (2013, p. 491)

Here an information resource is roughly equivalent to Buckland's information as thing, with the useful distinction that an information resource is created in order to "support goal-oriented activity." Though information things may support "goal-oriented activity," they aren't necessarily created with that intention.

Building on Glushko and Buckland, we can say that a given instance of a format is not only informative but also *intentionally* informative. This means that a format has a communicative purpose and is created by humans to serve that purpose. Moreover, a format serves a specific purpose in a particular context, and in order to be efficient and successful in carrying out that purpose, instances of a format will look a lot like each other. This line of thinking might prompt the question, what information thing isn't a format? A quick example may help clarify this: A leaf of a given plant is an information thing and is informative. It can tell us about that plant's interaction with various insects and animals, whether the weather this year has been favorable or unfavorable to that plant, what kind of climate that plant thrives in, and so on. A leaf housed in a specimen collection might even be considered a document, on the basis of its informative characteristics. However, a leaf wouldn't be considered an instance of a format—even though it possesses a set of common features and a purpose and is informative—because it isn't created by humans to serve a specific communicative purpose.

Therefore, we propose the following definition of formats for information literacy instruction:

> Each instance of a format shares a common intellectual and physical structure with others like it, and is intentionally produced to support or effect action. Intellectual structure refers to the textual and visual content of a format. Physical structure refers to the organization, design, and medium of a format. These categories are not strict and may overlap.

A format for information can manifest in the world digitally or physically, but it is fixed or recorded in some way. With this definition, format becomes the common way that information is produced and shared, and also how people often encounter information. A particular format is most effective once its primary features are ubiquitous and can be recognized and evaluated almost subconsciously, as with receipts, emails, newspaper articles, and menus. However, near-instantaneous digital publishing has caused new formats to proliferate so rapidly that it has undermined traditional notions of format, based as they were in formats produced and perfected over centuries, or at least decades. The information landscape is now filled with tweets, streams, blogs, and pins. In such a landscape, an abstract understanding of format is a tool for organizing and making sense of our rapidly changing information landscape.

Why Format Matters

Format is the way tangible knowledge has traditionally been disseminated. For a print source, this can mean its physical structure (e.g., binding, size, number of pages) as well as its intellectual structure (e.g., table of contents, index, references). For a digital source, this means its presentation, intellectual structure, and physical/technical structure (e.g., file format). Whatever the medium, the substance of format lies in the communicative purpose and the processes of information creation, production, and dissemination that are often distinct from the tangible or visible structures of the product. Crucially, focusing on purpose and process de-emphasizes the increasingly irrelevant dichotomy between print and online sources by examining content creation rather than how that content is delivered or experienced, which will always be in flux. Thinking of a format creation cycle beginning with its *purpose* (why it exists and who creates for whom), continuing through its *process* (how it is created and shared, including quality control processes), and concluding with the final *product* (what elements are expected or required and how are they arranged for efficient communication) can help students look more deeply at the product to discern and understand the purpose and the process.

Experts understand that the way in which information moves through an information cycle is affected by its purpose and final physical or digital manifestation. When presented with information in a given format, print or online, a librarian uses professional knowledge of these processes to inform an evaluation of the information contained within that particular resource and its potential as evidence. The expert both considers the wrapping and looks underneath the wrapping to ask critical questions about the content that are informed by an understanding of how and why it was produced. The expert is also aware of the influence of long-established formats on information production and dissemination, while understanding the enormous changes these cycles are undergoing.

By contrast, beginners often see a flat world of cut-and-paste information served up in a browser window. Without physical format to rely on, the beginner uses other means to evaluate information, such as website design, domain extension, language, and length. The beginner is not familiar with the common formats in a particular discipline and may not even be able to spot formats with which they are familiar in one medium if that medium shifts (print to digital, textual to audio).

Beginning researchers are frequently stymied by assignments that call for specific formats. Why is the news report on a promising new Alzheimer's drug reported on nytimes.com not an acceptable source, as opposed to the *Journal of the American Medical Association* (*JAMA*) article where the research was originally published? Why are there no books available about the #metoo movement in social media when that has been one of the biggest stories of the last year? What makes an online book a "book" and not a "website"? Why is a review of that book in a peer-reviewed journal not considered a peer-reviewed journal article? Why is the *Wall Street Journal* not a journal and the *Huffington Post* not a newspaper?

In many cases, the way that information is presented obscures not just the format but also the purpose and process of production that need to be understood in order to complete the picture. Understanding what distinguishes one format from another and why it matters requires a thorough understanding of the information cycle, communication in the disciplines, common publishing practices, and other information literacy–related competencies, especially for learners who have never experienced the print version of formats.

Learners who understand concepts around information production will be able to differentiate what may at first glance seem to be micro-formats. For example, one of Silvia's male friends once picked up an issue of *Marie Claire* (a women's lifestyle magazine) and asked in frustration, "How do you tell what is an advertisement and what is an actual article?" After decades of reading women's magazines, the differences between an advertisement, a styled editorial shoot, or a paid advertorial insert seemed obvious to Silvia. She pointed out the way advertisements appeared without introduction or commentary, the sources and prices for each item of clothing in fine print at the margins of styled shoots, and the way advertorials mimicked the tone of magazine while only endorsing one product. While it could also be argued that, really, the *entire* magazine was a commercial, styled shoots strive to inspire, provoke, and capture a trend or perspective with an editorial authority that is absent from advertisements. Though the distinction between the two might be subtle, once readers are familiar with the function and value of a fashion editorial, they could not look at even the most imaginative advertisement and mistake it for the former.

Further, a great deal about power in societies is revealed by understanding who has access to publishing via different formats and which voices are heard or silenced in different communication channels. Recognizing which scholarly information is in the peer-reviewed literature and which will be found in the gray literature is a sign of an advanced understanding of how information moves through a particular discipline. Likewise, in the news media, a nuanced understanding is needed to consider the persistence of placing women's health articles in the style section or the implications of alt-right (i.e., white supremacist) activists creating hashtags that percolate into traditional news media stories. In the popular media, one can look at perspectives to be found through user-generated content that aren't represented by traditional channels. From the role of social media during the Arab Spring to the use of Periscope to stream a congressional sit-in on gun control when C-SPAN was turned off, format can provide information to the careful observer at the meta-level as well as the level of the content conveyed.

In the context of a digital information explosion, it is more important than ever to articulate the issues and concepts that librarians teach when we deal with the purpose, process, and product of an information format.

Genre Theory

Librarians' understanding of format is illuminated by exploring a similar concept from the field of rhetoric: genre theory. Genre theory was developed to classify and analyze communicative actions in specific contexts. Though originally concerned primarily with text (written or verbal), the study of genre has expanded to more types of information and can offer another perspective on format in the digital age. Because threshold concepts, per Meyer and Land's criteria, are bounded by a discipline, contrasting the understanding of similar intellectual territory in a different discipline can clarify how the concept of format is particularly understood by librarians.

Rhetorician Carolyn Miller, in her seminal article "Genre as Social Action," states that "genre can be said to represent typified rhetorical action" (1984, p. 151). JoAnne Yates and Wanda Orlikowski followed with an expanded definition several years later:

> Genres (e.g., the memo, the proposal, and the meeting) are typified communicative actions characterized by similar substance and form and taken in response to recurrent situations. (1992, p. 300)

Genres represent common forms of communication, traditionally textual, written, or spoken. Each instance of a genre is created in context as a way to act; genre theory explores how communication works as action. The term "action" is purposefully chosen and appears repeatedly in the literature on genre. A genre is a text with a purpose.

For example, saying "I do" is a verbal vow that's legally binding. That statement is in the genre of a legal signature, whether written or spoken.

This type of genre is perfectly illustrated at the end of *The Princess Bride* when it turns out that Buttercup didn't really marry Humperdinck because she never said "I do."

LibGuides are an example of a new digital genre used by librarians. Though the name *LibGuide* originally referred to a platform created by Springhare, it has come to mean a certain kind of online document created to help library users with their research. LibGuides come in different flavors (one might call them subgenres), such as the course LibGuide, the disciplinary area LibGuide, and the single-topic LibGuide. However, all LibGuides serve the same general goal of research help and share common design features such as small boxes of content, lists of links, tabs, and librarian profiles. LibGuides are a wholly online genre, though they have a print relation in the pathfinder. LibGuides are not without their detractors in the community (Hicks, 2015), and the development of the LibGuide genre is also a good example of how community values and norms—such as ease of sharing and content curation (in the case of librarians)—influence genres.

The way that "genre" is used in the field of rhetoric can be considered troublesome language from the point of view of those outside the discipline, including librarians, because it is used to convey a specific meaning that is not captured by the common understanding of genres as broad categories for content, like fiction or nonfiction, tragedy, romance, science fiction, jazz, reggae, and classical. As used by librarians, these labels are applied to books, television, music, movies, and other media.

The more specific meaning of the term "genre" makes clear that the rules commonly used to classify types of content also work when thinking even of quotidian genres such as email and text messages. These rules or conventions help people quickly make sense of what they are reading, hearing, or seeing. Like formats, genres create shortcuts in communication because they signify through their structure as well as their content—as long as the audience is equipped to decode the communication. As with any social conventions, the rules are established and enforced in ways both overt and implied. To return to Yates and Orlikowski:

> Genre rules may operate tacitly, through socialized or habitual use of communicative form and substance, or they may be codified by an individual or body into specific standards designed to regulate the form and substance of communication. (1992, p. 304)

Rules and shared understandings can both strengthen ties within communities and also establish who is in and who is out.

Genre theory is especially concerned with the particular situation that gives rise to a specific genre, and how that situation shapes the genre. The theory thus examines the social context—the creator of the message and their audience or community—in addition to the explicit purpose of the communication. This perspective highlights processes for the creation of a genre and tends to de-emphasize its consumption. For example, genre studies will often examine a particular profession and what genres a professional in that field produces. An accountant might produce a variety of genres, including budgets, memos, and tax documents, and taken together, this production is referred to as a genre set. Students of accounting, then, must take on the genre set of their discipline and learn how to work within it as creators.

The scholarly journal article is a classic example of a genre, and can be unpacked from the point of view of the creator in the context of a community. It evolved from informal communication between individual researchers into a formal publication system with strict standards for quality control. A scholarly journal article has a predictable intellectual structure, depending on the discipline: an abstract, introduction, literature review, methods, results, and conclusions. Each section serves the purpose of communicating the results of original research in a concise but complete fashion. This particular genre has persisted, while the channels of dissemination have shifted from personal or small-group communication to public communication, albeit often accessed via subscription. The basic purpose of the scholarly journal article has not changed: to communicate the results of original research. The social context for that communication has shifted with the professionalization of research and the growth of university systems, and, as a result, the sharing and evaluation of such communication have also modified into the existing peer-review system.

New technologies are enabling further changes in scholarly communication, such as the rise of communities like arXiv where prepublication research is posted and discussed within an online community of experts. However, even with new technologies and digital formats, change to the genre of the scholarly journal article is limited by the sociocultural context. arXiv and traditional scholarly journals are dealing with the same type of rhetorical act, but the new digital medium offers a kind of flexibility that changes the format in significant ways. In this example we can say that while the format may change, the genre stays constant.

The intersection between format and genre is one instance where library and information science brings a unique disciplinary perspective to a concept that is also shared with other disciplines. Threshold concepts in different disciplines can be complementary, while also underlining the unique approach of each discipline; for example, format might be a productive concept to explore in the disciplines of computer science or journalism. Where there is overlap, librarians may find a new entry point for talking with faculty in other disciplines, in addition to new understandings of threshold concepts for information literacy.

Genre Theory and the Format Threshold Concept

Genre theory emphasizes the content of a particular genre, which is shaped by purpose and process, rather than the form that genre takes and how it is decoded by the recipient of the communication. The practical emphasis from a student's perspective is on how to craft functional and effective communication, that is, products, in the modes of the discipline.

By contrast, an instruction librarian begins a lesson at the opposite side of the information cycle—with the finished product that needs to be decoded. Often, the first step in doing so is to determine what the format of the information thing is in order to evaluate, use, or classify it. That is, the librarian starts with a product, evaluating it with a tacit understanding of its purpose and how it was created. Librarians use a conceptual understanding of format in a pragmatic and largely concrete way where information is a thing (embodied knowledge) created for a purpose. Yet, looking at similar intellectual content from the point of view of a related discipline can illuminate new ways of helping students cross the learning threshold. This is what happens when the emphasis with format is shifted from the finished product to the purpose and process of its creation.

Librarians have traditionally taught about formats by starting with the finished product and working backward to understand the thing—as if we had a dish of food in front of us and were looking for indicators of familiar ingredients and processes. For example, if it's a cookie, we know that it has been baked in an oven and likely contains flour, sugar, and butter among its ingredients. We know this on the basis of experience making cookies in the past. However, if you've never made a cookie before, the end product may only tell you a few things about how it was made, what it is made of, and how it got to you in its present form. It's not too difficult to understand the purpose of a cookie—eating and enjoyment—but it may not be apparent whether or not the cookie has special meaning within certain culinary traditions.

Information literacy is less concerned with teaching students to become members of disciplinary communities who can effectively craft specific genres than with helping them understand the systems of information that move those formats around and what those formats represent. Librarians are less likely to introduce students to the particulars of a specific disciplinary genre in order for them to reproduce it and more likely to ask students to understand a format produced by a community that they may never join. Yet, to be prepared for today's information environment, students should understand that information is packaged in formats for a purpose, be equipped to contend with unfamiliar formats, and use the concept of format to help them evaluate the information they come across in everyday life. If our focus in the past was on the product, librarians can serve students now with a both/and approach that includes also the purpose and process as informed by genre theory.

Digital genres offer a particularly vivid example of the format threshold concept for information literacy intersecting with genre theory. Both genre and format have radically changed in the age of ubiquitous digital information because of the much-shortened production cycle. From the librarian's perspective, this shorter cycle has altered the way that librarians work with information as thing and make it accessible through classification systems. Genre theory's focus on purpose and process may in fact make better sense of online formats that defy conventions. In a way, students are correct when they classify everything online as "it's a website." In order to differentiate online content, the user needs a new understanding that includes the purpose and process of creation.

Likewise, digital genres have altered the conception of genre, as Inger Askehave and Anne Ellerup Nielsen assert:

> We cannot really account for the characteristics of genres mediated on the net (for example a corporate profile) if we simply analyse "print-outs" of the web profile and treat them as static products and, thereby, neglect the fact that the internet as a medium have a number of characteristics which significantly influence and contribute to the way the web-mediated genres look and are used. (2005, p. 121)

Genre theory researchers have usually drawn a bright line between the substance of a genre (its content) and the physical form it takes. They have perceived genres as constructed of a physical form, substance (content), and a method of dissemination (medium). The medium and form are separate but related because the substance of the communication influences the physical form it takes, which likewise influences how that form is shared and spread. This makes sense in the print world.

However, digital formats challenge this traditional view of genre because the form and the medium now overlap significantly—the journal article in the browser being both a unique format and existing as part of a web page (a broad and uniquely flexible format-medium hybrid). For example, communities like arXiv make use of the online environment to conduct a rigorous peer-review process outside of traditional scholarly publishing routines. By the time the articles reviewed are eventually published, most of the community has already absorbed and begun to make use of the content. As form and medium collapse together into a different type of category, the way that content is received and understood changes as well.

Before the rise of digital networked information, genre theory may not have been particularly useful to librarians. Because content, medium, and form are intertwined in a new way, however, and no longer make sense without each other anymore, librarians can look to genre theory to think about the purpose and process of information creation. Traditionally, librarians have focused on physical formats—organizing them both intellectually and physically. The published form was little changed for hundreds of years, and it represented the content contained therein quite well. Yet, librarians have had a real reckoning when it comes to understanding and teaching digital information, and it's productive to consider why the web has presented so much difficulty. We—Amy, Silvia, and Lori—have definitely tried to teach students how to understand what they see in a browser by wheeling in carts of bound journals and reference works or offering the CRAAP test for website evaluation (a memorable acronym for Currency, Relevance, Authority, Accuracy, and Purpose; Meriam Library, 2017). Bound journals do tell you something about the format, but they don't completely explain what articles do. The CRAAP test can be useful, but it treats each piece of information as a world unto itself, rather than embedded in existing systems of information production and dissemination. How can we make sense of the mess?

Our current media environment has released the constraints on the publication process, once very tightly controlled by publishers who exercised editorial control and directed the dissemination of the final information product. The web, combined with access to personal computers with a variety of word processing and desktop publishing software, and various online content distribution platforms like Twitter, Instagram, Tumblr, WordPress, Medium, and YouTube, lowered the bar on publication. To return to the food metaphor, it's as though you only ever consumed professionally made bread in the past, and then someone gave you a bread machine. You might think that you now know how a professional baker makes bread on the basis of your experience with the bread machine, but you've only gotten a glimpse of the process. Students now understand how to easily create and share digital content, but it doesn't make clear the complexity of the long-standing processes already in place to create published formats. Nor does it clarify the value of those processes.

The sweeping changes to format, the proliferation of new formats, and the new systems of dissemination for those formats all raise an important point for instruction librarians. Yates suggests that genre rules may operate on a tacit level, through the "socialized or habitual use of communicative form and substance" (Yates & Orlikowski, 1992, p. 304). Format has always been tacit knowledge, but the current environment leads students into misunderstandings that were previously unlikely. The shift to the web as the primary point of mediation for textual genres has altered the information landscape to such a degree that librarians really do have to teach the tacit knowledge of genre that informs information production.

Applying the Threshold Concepts Criteria

We didn't realize how troublesome format was until that long-ago student asked what he perceived to be a minor clarifying question ("What's the difference between a journal article and a website?"). At the time, it seemed like a very odd misunderstanding. However, it went a long way toward elucidating how the librarian's understanding of the structure of information sources differed radically from that of the student.

To offer a classic example of students finding the concept of format troublesome, consider the perennial reference requests for peer-reviewed articles. Students love it when they find out that there is a checkbox in library databases for that. However, if students are asked to find original research articles, the communication of which is the reason peer-reviewed journals exist in the first place, they struggle. When asked what makes Google Scholar different from the vanilla version of Google, students will often answer "peer-reviewed" or "credible" as opposed to "scholarly literature" or "original research." They confuse the purpose of the format with the quality control process. This is simply the confusion engendered by one format, delivered in physical and digital form—a format that forms the backbone of scholarly communication and is the focus of much academic activity but is nonetheless only one format. What about all of the other formats rising and falling out there on the open web? What about the various formats sitting on the shelves (digital and virtual) in libraries?

Librarians regularly examine and analyze the essential features of both familiar and unfamiliar formats, with an eye toward the purpose of the formats in question—and how that purpose interacts with questions of trust (authority) and how it was accessed (organizing systems). Moreover, this examination and analysis is often a tacit process, rarely communicated to students beyond a superficial list of common format characteristics. A deeper engagement with the concept of format can give students a structure for making sense of the information they find both in print and in their browser, even absent the traditional print format markers. Instruction librarians are more familiar with teaching about types of information or evidence, and may doubt the existence of a potentially larger conceptual frame in the modern chaotic information environment. However, clarifying and making explicit the way librarians have traditionally used the term can offer a useful conceptual tool for students as they select and critically evaluate information.

How is an understanding of format transformative? Format, as librarians understand and use it, makes sense of the world of tangible knowledge. Format organizes the record of human knowledge and our everyday informational transactions. A well-defined or long-standing format comes to represent qualities independent of its actual embodiment or manifestation. For example, journal articles are published periodically because the results of many kinds of research can be communicated in a few pages that can be sent out more often and with less hassle than books. The volume and issue format arises out of the periodic publication. The structure of a scientific research article is the most efficient method of communicating the results of original research. But the form itself has come to signify a host of qualities like credibility and expertise.

An understanding of format allows a person to come into an entirely new information context or environment and make sense of it quickly. It allows a librarian to make choices about preserving the record of human knowledge while providing access to that record. Understanding format imposes a layer of order, even in the midst of real chaos, on information in the digital age. That is a transformative understanding.

Is an understanding of format irreversible? In order to demonstrate why we believe that it is, we've created two illustrations. The first, Figure 4.1, shows how students tend to view a list of Google search results.

Librarians, on the other hand, typically see the results of a Google search as a list of formats, as shown in Figure 4.2.

Libraries are organized on the basis of physical formats that have come to embody the purpose and process of the information they contain (e.g., journals, books, newspapers). In fact, this understanding of formats has sometimes hindered the ability of librarians to make collections accessible. Formats in online library catalogs are labeled in ways that assume library users already possess a working knowledge of format, yet reference and

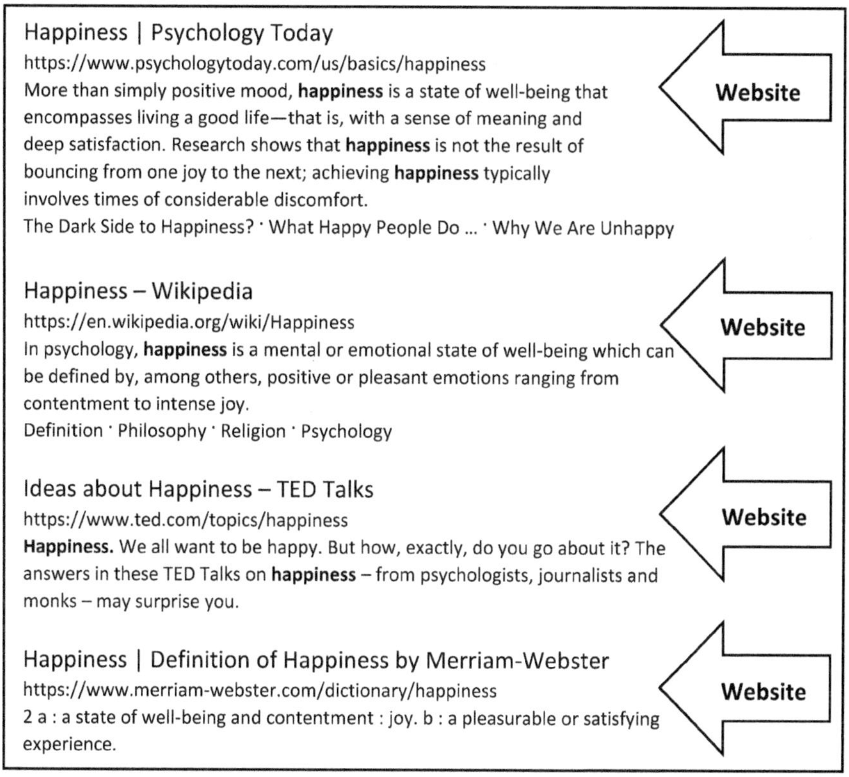

Figure 4.1 Google search results: Student perspective.

instruction librarians regularly encounter students who explain the difference between a scholarly book and a scholarly journal article solely in terms of length. Some librarians hold fast to print-era mental models, for instance by preferring journal article .pdfs that reproduce the print versions. Librarians can see information without taking format into consideration, but it takes real effort. Students, on the other hand, may not be bound by the same considerations because they often do not look past the medium to identify the format.

With respect to whether format is bounded by information literacy, we assert that this concept offers a unique library and information science perspective on the world of information and knowledge organization. Librarians have traditionally been tasked with the preservation of the record of human knowledge. More recently, librarians have tried to increase access to that knowledge through advocacy, education, and support of various open movements (open access, open data, open education, etc.). However, librarians see format differently than just about

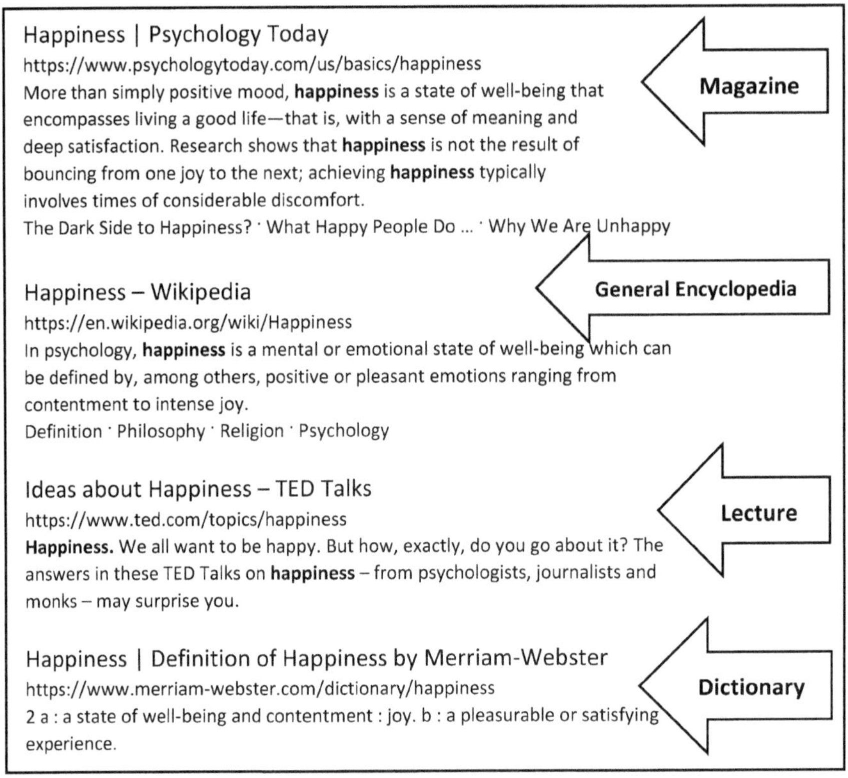

Figure 4.2 Google search results: Librarian perspective.

everyone else. The concept of format as defined by librarians reflects an orientation toward organizing, disseminating, and preserving knowledge. Format must be taken into consideration when building a library, whether digital or physical. Formats are products that librarians organize and make accessible. Format reflects both the intellectual and the physical spaces that define a particular type or source of information, as well as the process that went into creating it. In these respects, this concept is bounded by our discipline.

Finally, and perhaps most importantly, format is integrative. Returning to that confused student, Lori's response email refers to a whole host of ideas and concepts that populate the academic information landscape. Format brings together concepts related to authority and how it is constructed and represented, information cycles and how they create new knowledge, the elements of citation, how to structure an academic paper, and more. This is potentially the greatest power of the format threshold concept.

Teaching Format

Basic

Information Formats Exist, to a Purpose

Making the connection between communicative action (i.e., sharing information) and format is key. Students should understand that information arrives packaged in a certain way in order to facilitate a specific purpose—though the packaging sometimes obscures both the purpose and the process by which it was created and shared. The concept of genre is useful here in helping students understand the commonplace nature of a variety of formats that they regularly produce and use. Introducing students to format through the menu or the ticket or the text message as opposed to common, published formats can help them begin to understand an abstract and complex concept. The goal is for students to see formats as the results of differing processes with varying, but intentional, purposes. Format is a purpose, a process, and a product. Students will first encounter formats as information products, but they can be taught to ask questions that help reveal the purpose behind the product and the process that went into creating it.

Common Academic Formats

Students should already be familiar with some published formats, like news, movies, television, and books (and various genres for each of these). However, they should begin to learn about common formats created and published in the scholarly context: conference papers, peer-reviewed journal articles, scholarly monographs, lab manuals, and so on. Of particular importance at this level is emphasizing the purpose of various formats, as well as the processes for creation and sharing. It's also important for students to become aware of the publishing process and how it has been affected by digital formats. Students at this stage should focus on learning to recognize disciplinary formats and use them as evidence, rather than on attempting to create disciplinary formats (e.g., legal briefs, scholarly research papers, and design specifications).

Common Student-Authored Formats

Understanding how the formats that they commonly produce for school (papers, notes, reports, presentations) connect to published, workplace, and other common formats can help students make the transition from consumers to creators of information. Realizing that they produce work in recognizable, standard formats on a regular basis can demystify the processes by which published work is created while also increasing awareness of the quality standards and complexity involved when creating professional quality formats, published or unpublished. Recognizing that they are already content creators, but drawing a distinction between common student-authored formats and published formats, can help transition students after college into the workplace or graduate school, where they are expected to develop into independent researchers.

Scholarly Formats and Credibility

Students often arrive at university with a linear understanding of credibility (related to the authority threshold concept) that they apply to the evaluation of information in various formats. The key in understanding scholarly formats is to move them away from characterizing the difference as primarily one of quality information versus bad information. Here instructors should emphasize the purpose of scholarly publishing (to communicate the results of original research between scholars) and the purpose of the academy. Certainly, indicators such as bibliographies, author credentials, technical language, and the like can be taught as markers to aid in identifying scholarly work. However, given the ease with which one can limit to scholarly or peer-reviewed articles in library databases and using Google Scholar, students need another context for evaluating scholarly work that moves beyond a basic binary.

Characteristics and Interactions of Medium, Form, and Substance

By nature, the web is dynamic and interactive. The web also has the ability to act as both a method of dissemination (medium) and a container of information (form). These factors have a direct impact on the content (substance) of formats available via the internet. Consider, for example, our ability to see election results presented alongside demographic information updated in real time by clicking on a map of a state, rather than hearing updates on counties in the order decided by a news anchor or by reading about results in the newspaper the next day. By making clear distinctions between medium, form, and substance, students will be able to see these characteristics and interactions in areas outside the web. We can then introduce questions like "What makes a book a book? Is it its medium, form, or substance?" and "How does this format change when it's on the web versus when it's sitting on my desk?"

Information Cycles

The information cycle is often narrowly characterized in information literacy instruction as either the scientific information cycle or the news-driven social sciences information cycle. However, each product of a given format represents the culmination of an information cycle—some smaller, some massive—and can serve as evidence or inspiration for the start of a new information cycle. Information cycles often begin with an information need and vary depending upon the professional or disciplinary context. In order to understand how and why information is created and spread, students should also understand some basic (though not necessarily easy) concepts about the definition of information and knowledge. Basic information cycles are often prompted by simple information needs and relatively concrete purposes, such as directions to a location, going out to eat, registering for classes, doing laundry, and any number of commonplace tasks. Examples of more complex information cycles include scientific research, journalistic coverage of a major event, large creative works, and the production of professional-level formats.

Advanced

Information Cycles in Context: Professional and Disciplinary

More advanced study of information cycles explores the work done in the disciplines to communicate the results of inquiry as practitioners apply new knowledge to real-world problems. Here students will be working in a particular disciplinary context. Students will be able to create formats in a given context, such as a thesis for a degree, a syllabus to teach a class, a presentation for a city council meeting, and so on. It is expected that experts in that context, whether academic, professional, or personal, will provide the best instruction and training in the production and dissemination of particular formats. For example, librarians-in-training learn to create and manage a variety of formats such as catalog records, LibGuides and other web pages, finding aids, digital learning objects, and various types of social media, under the guidance of professional librarians.

Formats as Evidence in Context

Formats can be used as evidence in a variety of academic, professional, and personal contexts. Formats can broadly be characterized as primary or secondary, depending upon how close to the original activity or communicative actions the researcher and the format sit. Primary sources are the direct result of communicative action or observation. Secondary sources make use of primary sources as evidence in creating and communicating new knowledge. Each discipline uses a specific set of primary and secondary sources as evidence when creating new information and knowledge. For example, an artist uses a variety of primary and secondary sources as inspiration and materials for creating a new primary source—a work of art like choreography or a piece of music. Likewise, a scientist collects data (a primary source) in the pursuit of solving a scientific problem, which is published in a scholarly journal article (technically a secondary source, but often containing primary research).

Social Context of Format/Genre

Because formats are developed and maintained by communities, the same social and power structures that manifest in communities are reflected in formats. The expert understands that power influences both who can access specific formats and who can create specific formats. One does not have to be a member of a given community to make use of information produced by that community, but one should understand that power dynamics influence what gets produced and evaluate that information accordingly. The web upended traditional power dynamics through providing a widely accessible platform for publishing information without oversight from established authorities. Less powerful individuals and marginalized communities have made good use of online platforms. The democratizing influence of digital networked information is well documented; however, traditional formats are still largely controlled by powerful stakeholders, and this influences what gets published, how it is shared, and who has access to it.

Formats Are a Moving Target

Formats are created, managed, and used by communities in specific contexts. As communities and their needs change over time, so do formats. New technologies have the potential to greatly impact the development of formats, as when the web and digital networked information led to new formats such as blogs and tweets, and the revision of older formats such as those associated with news. The business letter became the memo that developed into the email, which, in the business context, can arguably have led to productivity apps like Slack and its ilk. Digital information is also more easily manipulated and changed. Its flexibility has led to the development of ephemeral formats, such as Vine, which lasted for a few years before losing relevance and eventually being shut down by Twitter. But while it lasted, a passionate user community developed Vine into a unique format and genre—with its own conventions, innovations, and even star creators.

Takeaways

- An abstract understanding of format is a tool for organizing and making meaning of our rapidly changing information landscape.
- Genre theory, a concept from the field of rhetoric, can help librarians define and differentiate our disciplinary understanding of format. Genre theory emphasizes the production of information, where librarians have traditionally focused on information products.
- The format creation cycle begins with purpose (why it exists and who creates for whom), continues with its process (how it is created and shared, including quality control processes), and concludes with the final product (what elements are expected or required and how are they arranged for efficient communication).

For Further Consideration

- The format threshold concept was first suggested by a student's question: "What is the difference between a journal article and a website?" Can you think of a question you've been asked that has revealed a very deep misunderstanding of information literacy content?
- Pick a format—the newer and more novel, the better. What is its process of creation, production, and dissemination? How would you describe the information cycle for this format?
- What are the genres in the library profession's genre set? What formats do we use to communicate them?

References

Askehave, I., & Ellerup Nielsen, A. (2005). Digital genres: A challenge to traditional genre theory. *Information Technology & People, 18*(2), 120–141. doi:10.1108/09593840510601504

Buckland, M. K. (1991). Information as thing. *Journal of the American Society for Information Science, 42*(5), 351–360. Retrieved from https://pdfs.semanticscholar.org/b3d4/d7980d6a628b503003ef4e7763a93544508e.pdf

Format. (2016a). In *Online dictionary of library and information science.* Retrieved from http://www.abc-clio.com/ODLIS/odlis_f.aspx#format

Format. (2016b). In Wikitionary.com. Retrieved from https://en.wiktionary.org/wiki/format

Glushko, R. J. (2013). *The discipline of organizing*. Cambridge, MA: MIT Press.

Hicks, A. (2015, April 16). LibGuides: Pedagogy to oppress? Retrieved from Hybrid Pedagogy website: http://hybridpedagogy.org/libguides-pedagogy-to-oppress/

Meriam Library, California State University, Chico. (2017, September 17). Evaluating information—Applying the CRAAP test [Assessment Instrument]. Retrieved from https://www.csuchico.edu/lins/handouts/eval_websites.pdf

Miller, C. R. (1984). Genre as social action. *Quarterly Journal of Speech, 70*(2), 151–167. doi:10.1080/00335638409383686

Townsend, L., Brunetti, K., & Hofer, A. R. (2011). Threshold concepts and information literacy. *portal: Libraries and the Academy, 11*(3), 853–869. Retrieved from http://archives.pdx.edu/ds/psu/7417

Yates, J., & Orlikowski, W. J. (1992). Genres of organizational communication: A structurational approach to studying communication and media. *Academy of Management Review, 17*(2), 299–326. doi:10.2307/258774

CHAPTER FIVE

Information Commodities

"Information wants to be free" is an expression that is typically credited to the counterculture stalwart Stewart Brand. It has also been adopted as a rallying cry by hackers, activists, and some librarians. Information may *want* to be free, and it may *seem* to be free, but this chapter will explore why students can understand information better by knowing when it's *not* free. To start, we'll use an example from the world of stand-up comedy.

Since 2009, Marc Maron has used his weekly podcast, *WTF with Marc Maron*, to take listeners behind the scenes with comedians. Ali Wong appeared on Maron's show right before the release of her lauded Netflix special, *Baby Cobra*, which deftly balances comedy conventions with innovation. Wong's stand-up comedy is in the tradition of the kind of crass observational humor that may be familiar to fans of Chris Rock or Hannibal Buress, but her content is distinct for its fearless examination of interracial dating, miscarriage, HPV, and breast-feeding; Wong was also seven and a half months pregnant during the filming of her special. These topics, Wong explains, "make men uncomfortable" and also make "women uncomfortable, but they're so happy that there's a revelation. Like you literally do stuff, in depth, that women do not f—g talk about in public" (Wong & Maron, 2016). In terms of content creation, Wong's jokes fall into the most unambiguous category: she is the first person to tell *this* joke in *this* way, and she gets credit for it.

Often, however, the origins of a joke are much more difficult to trace. Joke theft is a recurring topic on Maron's podcast, and two of the best-known episodes have Maron investigating and then confronting Carlos Mencia with accusations from other comedians. In conversation with Steve Trevino (2010), one of Mencia's former friends, Maron says, "I really think that there is a difference between being you know, derivative, or using stock premises, and actually lifting someone's joke." Trevino agrees, contrasting jokes about Latino food culture with the fact that Mencia repeated fellow comedian Freddy Soto's bits, verbatim, within a week of Soto's death. Even in the face of clear evidence to the contrary, however, Maron observes that "no one admits to stealing. They'll all say maybe it's similar."

Such distinctions also apply to the information commodities threshold concept—after all, it's the rare student who would admit to intentional dishonesty when neglecting to cite their sources. Some jokes, like the one about a chicken crossing the road, are so generic that they can be told by anyone and belong to everyone. Other jokes, like Jim Gaffigan's tribute to Hot Pockets, belong to their creator, and to repeat it without attribution constitutes theft. The information commodities threshold concept clarifies that creation takes effort, and that effort should be acknowledged—things that seem to be free may not actually be free.

This chapter will define the information commodities threshold concept and examine the way that the information economy shapes student access to information in general, and textbooks in particular. We explore the economic concepts of public and private property and Marx's definition of a commodity. This discussion leads to issues of privacy, rights, and the economic context of this very book.

Information Commodities Defined

Librarians sometimes find themselves in the unfortunate position of policing the use of information. This tendency toward restriction was clearly stated in Standard 5 of the Association of College & Research Libraries' (ACRL) *Information Literacy Competency Standards for Higher Education*:

> *Performance Indicator 2:* The information literate student follows laws, regulations, institutional policies, and etiquette related to the access and use of information resources. (American Library Association, 2000, p. 14)

The *Framework for Information Literacy for Higher Education*'s Information Has Value frame takes a more conceptual approach, hoping that students will adopt a critical stance toward information rights and responsibilities:

> Experts also understand that the individual is responsible for making deliberate and informed choices about when to comply with and when to contest current legal and socioeconomic practices concerning the value of information. (ACRL, 2014, p. 6)

Still, what this usually looks like in the classroom is training about what you either can't or shouldn't do with information: students must learn to respect copyright, avoid plagiarism, use a variety of citation styles, and lock down personal data. The reason for the disconnect is simple: most people don't take a deep dive into the economics of information on their way to getting a degree in a different field. Kevin Seeber suggests that this restrictive orientation to the content results in a "pedagogy of punishment over meaningful instruction" (2016, p. 133). It falls to librarians to lay out, if not enforce, the rules, but there doesn't seem to be a place in the curriculum where students have the opportunity to gain a deeper understanding of the reasons for the rules.

We posit that if students can understand information as a commodity, they will better understand the reasons for the wide-ranging, apparently arbitrary, and internally inconsistent practices that they encounter in academia (Townsend, Brunetti, & Hofer, 2011). It can be eye-opening to see information as a thing that is bought and sold, while in everyday use it is usually accessed for free and given away unknowingly. Though this threshold concept may seem to be axiomatic to librarians, students often struggle to understand the economic side of information, especially information that seems to be free.

In Karl Marx's seminal critique of political economy, *Capital*, commodities are defined as goods and services with use value or exchange value, produced by human labor (1967, p. 38). Marx's model of commodities can be applied to information in order to explore how economic forces influence our decisions. To clarify, the model contains three parts:

- Goods or services
- Value
- Labor

When one or more of the three elements in the model are not apparent, users' ability to evaluate the commodity as such is compromised, and they are less able to understand the economic influences driving the production and dissemination of information. Teaching information commodities as a threshold concept enables students to rid themselves of some of the misconceptions that happen when one or more characteristics of commodities are hidden.

As a brief example of applying Marx's model to an information commodity, consider newspapers as *goods*, with *value*, produced through *labor*. Their status as *goods* might be compromised by an online interface that blurs the line between news content and other content around the web. Their *value* may be undermined by the availability of identical content posted for free online. The *labor* of journalism, research, fact-checking, and the editorial process may no longer seem necessary in an environment of user-generated content.

The term "commodity" is relatively simple to understand when it is applied to tangible goods (newspapers, or the kinds of things you trade in the board game Settlers of Catan: grain, lumber, brick). Information is different from other types of commodities in a crucial way, though: using information does not use it up. Because information, and digital information in particular, is intangible, it can be consumed by any number of users without having to be divided or becoming depleted. Further, because infinite copies can be made, it is impossible to protect information commodities from being widely shared by anybody who has a copy. These two distinctions make it seem as if information commodities belong in the commons, even when they are privately owned (we are using the term "commons" to refer to "cultural and natural resources accessible to all members of a society"; Wikipedia, 2018).

It's obvious that you would need to ask permission before borrowing a lawn mower from a neighbor's front lawn—to do otherwise would look to the neighbor like stealing, even if the intention is to return the tool. The lawn mower is clearly private property owned by the neighbor. By contrast, there is no need to ask, and no obvious person to ask, before drinking from a public water fountain. Public property belongs to everybody. Information, especially online, seems to be water in the water fountain, because it's free to access and hard to figure out whom to ask permission for use. It's more difficult to see when information belongs, like a lawn mower, to someone else.

Commodities, then, matter in the context of information literacy because they are widely understood to be owned as property, and this understanding can be extended to information. Information in the commons is publicly available (via the public domain and open license permissions). However, in an academic setting, a very high premium is placed on ownership of intellectual property, whether that manifests in holding patents to new discoveries, retaining copyright of original works, or giving credit to the intellectual contributions of others in the field. We—Amy, Silvia, and Lori—do not mean to say that the current information economy is our favorite model or the one we would choose if we could design things from scratch. Yet, in order to successfully navigate their academic careers, students should understand that in addition to fitting Marx's model of commodities, information, though intangible, is treated like property:

something that is either privately owned or publicly available in the commons.

For the purposes of this chapter, here is the definition we'll use for information commodities:

> Information is a commodity because it can be described by Marx's model: it is a good or service, has value, and is produced by human labor. Like other commodities that can be bought and sold, information is property that can be either privately owned or publicly available in the commons.

As with other information literacy threshold concepts, oversimplifying a concept leaves students on the surface of understanding, without making a deeper shift in thinking. These shallow understandings create conceptual problems around a number of information functions and practices, both inside and outside the library.

Is Information Really Intangible?

Bear with us while we take a very oversimplified tour through thousands of years of economic history in the next paragraph.

Some of the very first written documents were cuneiform tablets that contained business records—accounts of sales and debts. Over time, information sources developed into things that were themselves bought and sold as commodities. Consider the moment, impossible to precisely identify, when the critical mass of information was treated as a commodity but still existed in the physical world rather than online. These tangible information sources could be understood as commodities somewhat like coffee or sugar. You had to borrow materials from the library. If you lost a textbook you had to buy another copy. If you didn't want anyone to ever see your prom photos, you tore them up.

The difference now is that a critical mass of information is available digitally, with the two key implications mentioned earlier: it can be infinitely used without being used up, and it is impossible to protect from infinite copies being made. Gatekeepers can monetize the new model by charging over and over for the same information, but only if they can keep unauthorized copies from undermining their stake. It's no wonder that "information wants to be free" has stuck as a catchphrase.

There is a problem, however, with thinking of information as an intangible commodity: it is conditional upon having access to the mode of communication. The digital divide remains a problem for low-income, rural, disabled, and other marginalized populations. In the United States, according to the Pew Research Center, 20 percent of adults own a smartphone and do not have broadband service; percentages are higher for younger adults, people of color, those with less educational attainment, and lower earners (2018). For those whose sole device is a phone, this is simply how you apply for jobs, do your homework, and accomplish other activities that might be more effectively done with access to a larger screen (M. Anderson, 2017).

Maura Seale points out that many internal documents that professional library associations produce assume that the biggest issue facing students today is too much information and too many information technologies. This assumption can lead to designing services for the haves while ignoring the have-nots, who are

> exceptions to this new and seemingly wonderful world of constant connectivity, abundant information, and material comfort. They obscure the very real issues around information access for those in poverty and even deny that poverty truly exists; can anyone claim to be poor if they have 500 TV channels, a home computer, a mobile device, a Wii, an xBox, a Playstation? (Seale, 2013, p. 158)

While it is useful to consider what makes information unique as a commodity because of its characteristic of being intangible, it still depends upon other goods and services in order to be communicated. Even as information seems to be increasingly free, access is increasingly a barrier for many. Information is intangible, but it still depends upon tangible objects for its expression. So, in some ways not much has changed since that nonpinpointable moment before the critical mass of information moved online.

This issue might not be one that librarians bring to the classroom in the form of a lesson; rather, it's something to keep in mind in understanding where students are coming from. It's important to design services and instruction for users with any level of access. The rest of this chapter considers economic factors that students should understand in order to cross the learning threshold and make ethical choices about information use.

Textbooks as Information Commodities

Students are most likely to feel the sting of information's commodification when it comes to textbook purchases. Prices have risen over 1,000 percent since 1977 (Popken, 2015), much faster than the overall consumer price index and at an unreasonable rate even compared to indexes known for bubbles, such as medical care and new home prices (Badkar, 2014). Because textbooks are such a major investment each term, students are very concerned with buyback and exchanges. One bookstore manager whom Amy talked to said that students used the campus store's buyback program like a pawn shop, selling back books needed for a yearlong sequence at the end of each term and then buying them again at a loss, because they needed the cash.

Of course, buybacks and exchanges don't solve the basic problem that the economic model of the textbook market is deeply flawed. Selection decisions are made by faculty who may not be aware of pricing, while the cost burden is placed on students, who don't have any choice in which course materials they will use (Senak, 2014). Major publishers needlessly issue new editions every few years in order to undercut the used book resale market. Access codes, at an average cost of $100 each, are becoming the new way for publishers to lock in a pay-to-play model where each student has to purchase their own log-on, which can't be shared, put on library course reserves, or resold (Senak, Donoghue, O'Connor Grant, & Steen, 2016).

Because the high price of course materials demonstrably interferes with students' ability to attain their educational goals (Florida Virtual Campus, 2016), there is an important case to be made for lowering or removing their cost. The open education movement argues that, especially when it comes to materials that support an undergraduate general education curriculum (highly enrolled courses that depend upon widely available information), this information ought to be freely available to students. This is accomplished through the use of openly licensed course materials as a solution to the problem because they can be accessed online for free or in print at low cost. Emerging research suggests that this approach not only saves money for students but also improves course outcomes, with significant positive impact on historically underserved populations such as Pell-eligible, nonwhite, and part-time students (Colvard, Watson, & Park, 2018).

Open educational resources can be confusing, though, because the model seems to shift costs from the student to the institution. The burden of additional labor placed upon faculty can appear insurmountable. While many authors share materials under an open license out of a desire to give back, and others receive onetime payments in the form of grants and stipends, authors are forgoing the possibility of ongoing royalty checks from publishers. Creating and maintaining open educational resources also relies on time and support from professionals in roles beyond faculty, such as librarians, instructional designers, IT, accessibility services, and distance learning.

The apparent cost to the institution may be most readily seen at the bookstore. Where there are very strong textbook affordability initiatives, the bookstore will necessarily take a hit to its bottom line. Most campus stores make a contribution back to the general fund out of revenue. It is clearly not ideal to have student financial aid money, some of which must be repaid with interest, flow from the government, through the students, to the bookstore, and from there to the general fund—with a significant offshoot of that stream being diverted to publisher profits—but it is also true that lost revenue must be offset in some way. While research suggests that institutions may be able to increase revenue through use of open educational resources to recover institutional costs, it is too soon to say whether these cost-neutral programs will be sustainable in light of systematic underfunding of higher education (Hilton, Fischer, Wiley, & Williams, 2016; Wiley, Williams, & Hilton, 2016).

As the open educational resources librarian for Oregon's 17 community colleges, Amy spent several years trying to figure out how to approach this problem before finally asking whether it is an economic problem at all, or rather an instructional design problem. Writing for Open Oregon Educational Resources, she says, "Is the purpose here to close the loop through [return on investment], or in the words of my former Portland State University colleague Bob Schroeder, is this 'bigger than the loop'?" (Open Oregon Educational Resources, 2017). Later in this chapter we consider other situations in which information commodities might not rightly belong to the information economy.

The cost of textbooks is an authentic problem with a direct impact on students, which makes it a good entry point for information literacy instruction. Librarians have an opportunity to frame the problem in terms of information commodities and propose open practices as a solution. When students learn about open educational resources, they generally want to use them in order to save money. However, from a threshold concepts perspective, telling students that we made their textbooks free by using open educational resources solves their affordability problem but potentially introduces new misunderstandings (Lin Hanick & Hofer, 2017). In the current moment of transition, in which students are beginning to take on activist roles around textbook affordability issues, students are learning deeply about the economics of the textbook market. A fuller understanding of information commodities acknowledges the value and labor represented by open educational resources as an information good.

Open licenses also provide an entry point into students understanding themselves as information creators through discussion of sharing with open licenses versus under traditional copyright. In an academic context, open pedagogy (also called open educational resources–enabled pedagogy) provides immediate opportunities for faculty to teach students about their copyright ownership and options for sharing as students leverage the affordances of open licenses to contribute to the course materials (Wiley, 2017).

As an information producer, you want your information to be used ethically. Open practices offer librarians the chance to support students as content creators in authentic settings, through teaching information literacy concepts such as copyright and open licensing, attributing open content, or developing a professional online identity. These lessons can be enriched through a deeper understanding of how the information commodities threshold concept fits into each of these topics.

Hidden Aspects of Information Commodities

As in the earlier example with newspapers, when the goods, value, or labor associated with information is not apparent to the user, misunderstandings about appropriate and ethical use crop up. Identifying places where the three characteristics in Marx's model of commodities are hidden illustrates why this threshold concept can be troublesome. Learning more about the economic systems that produce, reproduce, and disseminate information allows researchers to better understand the issues specific to information commodities.

When the *information good* itself—that is, the product as such—is obscured, the result is websites such as BuzzFeed and Cracked. The actual commodity in these examples is not the slideshow of animal pictures but the millions of views or clicks that the slideshow generates for advertisers. Similarly, while Facebook and Gmail provide services as a social network and a free email service, their real product is the information that users reveal about themselves. Online activist Eli Pariser (2011) writes that "while Gmail and Facebook may be helpful, free tools, they are also extremely effective and voracious extraction engines into which we pour the most intimate details of our lives." Both companies, in fact, can be better understood as advertising agencies.

Users are tracked, engaged, and sold, often without realizing a transaction has taken place at all. The consulting firm Cambridge Analytica declared bankruptcy following the 2018 scandal in which it was revealed that the company collected personal information about millions of Facebook users without permission, under the auspices of conducting academic research. April Glaser, writing for *Slate*, notes that the government has been slow to regulate this type of information exchange: "we still have no hint that meaningful regulations—that truly curb how companies are allowed to hand over user data to third parties and sell ads targeted at our precise interests, skin color, economic class, level of education, and even bigotries—are coming" (2018b). The momentary diversion of an online personality quiz could lead to an immortal data set about you and everyone else in your network, monetized all over again every election cycle. Unpacking the real product of an information commodity can be revelatory and lead to behavior changes to protect privacy—or advocacy for stronger policies. There is even a case to be made that if people own their data, they should be paid for its use. This idea is not especially new (e.g., De Bruin & Thiele, 2014), though unsurprisingly none of the major companies that have built a business model around selling user data have shown interest in this approach.

The *labor* of information commodities is another aspect that may not be visible to users. Comedian and YouTuber Gaby Dunn writes about her fans' expectation that online content will be available for free, and also without support from brand sponsors. Dunn describes uncomfortable interactions when online celebrities run into fans while waiting tables at their day jobs, because their online videos don't pay a living wage (2015).

In other cases, the labor might be related to dissemination, as Adrian Chen (2014) reveals in his *WIRED* article "The Laborers Who Keep Dick Pics and Beheadings Out of Your Facebook Feed." In a process that most social media users assume is automated, content moderators, many of them recent college graduates, most located in the Philippines, sift through reported posts to determine whether or not they violate community standards. The ranks of these employees are growing in the wake of the 2016 election meddling, with Facebook adding 4,000 additional content moderators in 2017 alone (Glaser, 2018a). Rob, a content moderator working for YouTube, spent his days screening for hate speech, sexual solicitation, and gore. About the last category, Rob says,

> If someone was uploading animal abuse, a lot of the time it was the person who did it. He was proud of that . . . And seeing it from the eyes of someone who was proud to do the f—d-up thing, rather than news reporting on the f—d-up thing—it just hurts you so much harder, for some reason. It just gives you a much darker view of humanity. (Chen, 2014)

Burnout is common, as are reports of paranoia, depression, and substance abuse. Chen writes, "Given that content moderators might very well comprise as much as half the total workforce for social media sites, it's worth pondering just what the long-term psychological toll of this work can be." The toll is difficult to measure, however, as long as companies continue to hide the labor done by content moderators. Microsoft, Google, and Facebook declined to speak to Chen for his article, and many other companies ask their content moderators to sign nondisclosure agreements. Social media companies clearly realize that users would be repelled by this side of the business.

In the context of academic libraries, the *value* of information commodities is often obscured. This is in contrast to the Information Has Value frame of the *Framework*; the concept's inclusion in a major professional document suggests that this concept is, or will soon be, widely taught. However, although librarians exert great effort to justify the value proposition of the library, they simultaneously undermine the perception of its value by hiding the cost of information at the point where the user encounters the information commodity. To give a few examples of this, consider that patrons are encouraged to access scholarly articles for free, attend free library programming, and get free research help from a librarian. This is despite the fact that public colleges and universities are paid for by tax dollars, and all types of academic libraries are supported by tuition dollars—the community has already paid for access. At some libraries the message seems to be, "Come to the library for free stuff!" Rather, the message should be, "You are already paying for access to a wealth of resources with your tuition and fees so use it while you still can!"

Positioning the library as a free resource leads to misunderstandings about the value of the holdings (this is the misunderstanding that the *Framework* primarily seeks to address). Free information sources and information services are still commodities and are not free to produce, acquire, or provide to patrons. Zoe Fisher writes that she leads a class discussion on information privilege using the case of Aaron Swartz, who downloaded articles from JSTOR in bulk:

> Swartz downloaded articles from JSTOR not because he wanted to read them, but because he wanted to bring them out from behind the paywall. I asked students to consider: Why would that matter? What were Swartz's motivations? Was his potential punishment just? What are the implications of "access or lack of access to information sources," as indicated in the knowledge practices of the Information Has Value frame? (Fisher, 2017, p. 355)

Other examples of users missing the value of library resources are more subtle. Outrage over reduced library hours fails to take into account the cost of paying staff and keeping the building open. Using textbook reserves collections as a free alternative to rising textbook costs complicates space considerations, seems to condone copyright violations as students photocopy far more of a text than can be justified by fair use, and creates the illusion of access without actually solving the problem of predatory pricing models. Even the perennial problem of librarians nagging faculty to contribute scholarly works to the institutional repository can be understood through the lens of rising database fees made unaffordable through budget cuts.

Further, marketing library resources and services as free can complicate advocacy for increased institutional investment in the library: How do you argue for the value of services and resources that are most recognizable for being, apparently, free? Librarians already may find it difficult to establish that the library is a unique collection curated for the needs of the student body, aligned with the institution's strategic goals. It can feel discouraging to have to repeatedly convince administrators that the library returns value to the institution and is not just a resource sink.

Information, viewed as a commodity, is a good, with value, created through labor. Uncovering these characteristics with students helps increase understanding about how reliable and reputable information is produced and shared, along with why it can be surprisingly expensive.

No Escape?

The point of the information commodities threshold concept is that students need to learn about the economics of information in order to become information literate. However, a new understanding of information as a commodity can potentially feel overwhelming. Once students see information as a commodity, all information sources may seem to operate under an ulterior motive. Reputable news sources like the *Wall Street Journal* and the *New York Times* are supported by advertising dollars and seek to increase views in the same way as sensational, clickbait sites like InfoWars and Addicting Info. The library's efforts at outreach can be seen as an attempt to improve circulation or gate count numbers to justify an increase in funding. Encouragement to "vote with your wallet" through careful selection of goods and participation in various boycotts makes it seem as if our most important role in society is as a consumer. When do we get to relate to information as citizens instead?

Personal exchanges of information are a good place to start in considering whether it is possible to be outside of the information economy. Telling your mom "I love you," for example, is not a commodity per Marx's definition. However, while that information may really be free, commodities crowd all around it. Was the information conveyed by text, which needed a phone and data plan? Was the statement made in an interview, on a TV show, or in a written work for hire? Has a greeting-card company coopted the national holiday of Mother's Day in order to monetize this exact sentiment? Other examples of information that might not seem to be a commodity are public safety information, such as an evacuation order before a hurricane makes landfall, or lifesaving medical knowledge, such as drug formulations and tests for highly infectious diseases, or civic documents like the study guide for U.S. citizenship tests. Yet, it's not too difficult to posit examples of this information, too, finding a place in the information economy.

There is always an economic context: even information that is apparently not owned by anyone at the moment of its creation can't escape from the information economy. And the thing that seems creepy, invasive, and genuinely new is the amount and character of the information that can now be monetized. When librarians urge students to protect their data, it's not just the photos they've uploaded to social networks that future employers shouldn't see, and weak email passwords that tip off bad actors to their bank passwords. It's also data about information consumption: websites visited, engagement with content, search terms used. There has always been an economic rationale for the invasion of privacy, but there now exists the technical means to enable an uncomfortable degree of tracking, monitoring, and control (Buckland, 2017). With this in mind, it's illustrative to look at Brand's famous quote in context:

> On the one hand information wants to be expensive, because it's so valuable. The right information in the right place just changes your life. On the other hand, information wants to be free, because the cost of getting it out is getting lower and lower all the time. So you have these two fighting against each other. (Brand, 1985, p. 49)

Brand highlights the relationship between the value of information and its slipperiness. When it is nearly impossible to lock down a commodity, people might not recognize its status as property, whether deliberately or inadvertently. If it doesn't belong to anyone, then it belongs to everyone—that is, it is in the commons. It seems to be free. By extension, there is tension between those who want to put more information into the commons—hackers, the open access movement, and the like—and those who want more protections—such as corporations that have invested in IT and groups concerned with data privacy. The freer information is, including information about information use, the more available it is to be scooped up for profit or exploitation. When information wants to be free, lack of privacy is inherent in the setup.

Yet, there is also ambiguity in Brand's use of the word "free," neatly summarized in the definition of free software: "To understand the concept, you should think of 'free' as in 'free speech,' not as in 'free beer.' " This distinction is sometimes indicated by the terms *libre* and *gratis*, respectively (Free Software Foundation, 1996). If information wants to be free, it might want to be gratis, as in publicly available, and it might want to be libre, as in intellectual freedom. Sarah Polkinghorne makes a useful distinction between intellectual freedom and open access. Intellectual freedom is a basic human right recognized by the United Nations. There are no rights associated with access, but rather permissions. The two ideas are closely related, and people who value one usually also value the other, yet they are not exactly the same thing (Future Librarians for Intellectual Freedom, 2016). Fighting to keep *Harry Potter* in the school library means that the library should have the right to purchase a copy of J. K. Rowling's copyrighted work, not that the library should be sent a free copy to put on the shelf.

Similarly, an information society must ask whether privacy is associated with rights, permissions, or something in between. Are we entitled to privacy or are we granted it? Do we opt in or opt out? These questions are under ongoing negotiation as new technologies and new norms arise.

Information Rights and Permissions

Saying that information is free doesn't necessarily mean that it's outside the information economy, because things that are free (gratis) can still be commodities that are owned privately or publicly. Still, it can be useful to consider when information is not private property. Some information is free in the sense that the public collectively owns it—that is, it's in the commons. Academic research is often paid for with taxpayer funds, so the resulting data, articles, and other intellectual properties can be understood as public goods. Creative works with a certain shelf life are in the public domain in order to encourage innovation. Fair use makes scholarly discourse and education possible by recognizing that we build on the achievements of others. These types of information are still not outside of the economy as a whole (i.e., they are still commodities according to Marx's definition), but they are removed from the need to be bought and sold because they are already available to the public.

Moving more information into the commons can seem to be an ethical stance because it removes economic barriers to access by broadly increasing permissions for use. Creative Commons, for example, is a nonprofit that is best known for developing open licenses that enable copyright holders to communicate reuse permissions to downstream users at the same time as they share their work. This is the most frequently used license type for open educational resources. The organization's vision statement is a wonderful expression of optimism: "Our vision is nothing less than realizing the full potential of the Internet—universal access to research and education, full participation in culture—to drive a new era of development, growth, and productivity" (Creative Commons, n.d.). At the same time, this statement seems to be the fullest logical extension of "information wants to be free," in that it doesn't address questions of personal privacy. Even more importantly, the Creative Commons vision also doesn't consider a worldview that doesn't see the commons as inherently good. In just the same way that Brand did, it elides the difference between open access information (gratis) and intellectual freedom (libre).

There has been resistance, however, to information being treated as automatically belonging in the Western commons by Indigenous groups. A colonialist worldview assumes that Indigenous culture, knowledge, land, and artifacts belong in the commons, free for the taking, and available for the general public to claim ownership over. As a result, individuals and communities today find themselves on the wrong side of legal access to, and control over, their own documents of cultural heritage (J. Anderson & Christen, 2013). This perspective fails to recognize both the right to sovereignty and the right to privacy of Indigenous nations.

Looked at in this way, the commons can be yet another site of oppression: "the concept of public domain is not accepted by many indigenous peoples for their knowledge" (Tulalip Tribes of Washington, 2003, p. 1). New licensing options attempt to return control of traditional information to the communities where they belong in order to let non-Indigenous users better understand appropriate use (Local Contexts, n.d.). Yet, the very attempt to establish tribes' right to their own heritage in Eurocentric terms can itself be seen as another violation. For example, writing of the Native American Graves Protection and Repatriation Act (NAGPRA), Elizabeth Joffrion and Lexie Tom write,

> When tribal and nontribal institutions work together to address Indigenous knowledge, culturally sensitive items, or sacred sites, it is important to recognize that these relationships exist within a cultural divide grounded in differing worldviews. From the Native perspective, NAGPRA was created in the context of a Western system of thought, and the modern cultural heritage institutions impacted by NAGPRA were created within and for the benefit of a dominant Western world. Due to a long history of oppressive and assimilative laws and policies that supported settler colonial society, the Western social order will always be linked to forced changes to ancient cultures with the intent of re-creating a society more recognizable to Western norms. (2016, pp. 7–8)

When knowledge is created in Switzerland, for example, it is subject to the copyright laws of that sovereign country. International users of that knowledge are expected to respect the intellectual property constraints of Switzerland. North American archivists would not presume to create a set of protocols to govern the use of Swiss documents. Why is this not also the case for Indigenous knowledge? While Swiss documents may need special protocols or oversight for use, the Swiss don't need to make a special case to determine the rights and permissions associated with their own intellectual property.

These conflicting views on rights and permissions play out in the library context, in particular around the *Protocols for Native American Archival Materials* (First Archivist Circle, 2006). Written by a group that included Native American representatives, the *Protocols* set out to establish improved relations between collecting institutions and tribes by offering guidelines for both archives/libraries and Native American communities to follow. Yet, in 2008, the Society of American Archivists declined to endorse this document; in 2012, a new group convened to revise the *Protocols* (Society of American Archivists, 2012) and there the matter stands (though many institutions are adopting the recommendations on their own nonetheless; Joffrion & Fernández, 2015).

What was the problem with the *Protocols*? Simply put, Native American requests for control over access to traditional knowledge are seen by some archivists as incompatible with major principles and values of the profession, such as open access to information, freedom of scholarly inquiry, and opposition to censorship (Mathiesen, 2012). By not endorsing the *Protocols*, though, archivists seem to suggest that intellectual freedom applies only to the users of information, and not to its creators, to establish terms of use that are valid in their contexts.

Taking a step back, it may be helpful to consider more broadly the ways that personal identity can come into conflict with institutional academia. For example, Māori academic librarian Nicola Andrews writes that, on the one hand, being Indigenous in academia can feel retraumatizing and recolonizing, as when universities fail to consider the provenance of the land where they are sited, permit sports teams to use offensive mascots and chants, or name buildings for colonizers or slaveholders (Andrews, 2018). On the other hand, and underlining the point that Indigenous groups represent a multitude of voices and opinions, Andrews also proposes that it may be healing for some to choose to share their knowledge "for the collective good" (p. 190). A diversity of opinions among Native Americans has emerged during the long process of considering the *Protocols*, reflecting in part the many ways that individuals choose to approach the sometimes conflicting values of personal and academic identities.

Andrews provides a valuable entry point for talking to marginalized students about the difficult-to-quantify emotional costs associated with their education and the ways by which they can reject, challenge, or improve an imperfect enterprise. As mentioned in Chapter 1, acknowledging and examining power structures using the threshold concept model need not be an endorsement of those structures. We can help students understand that if all information were free, as in free beer, it would all be in the commons or the public domain; and that if information were free, as in freedom of speech, its creators would all have the basic human right to define the terms of its ownership. Understanding this distinction prepares students of all backgrounds to be ethical users and creators of information in academic and other settings, and establish an identity as citizens rather than only as consumers. A full understanding of how information commodities function is also a way into identifying the information rights and human rights that defy commodification.

What about This Book?

At this point you may have flipped to the front matter of this book to check that it is under traditional copyright. Why isn't it openly licensed? What are the terms of our contract with ABC-CLIO? Are we getting paid to write this book?

We do hold the copyright to the work, though ABC-CLIO holds the right to publish, license, and sell our work. You won't see chapters of this book in an institutional repository because we don't have the right to put an open license on the content. (And if you ever see an action figure for one of the threshold concepts described in this book, it's because ABC-CLIO has the merchandising rights.)

We are getting paid: 10 percent on the first 1,000 copies and 12 percent after that (is it hard to sell more than 1,000 copies of a book about information literacy?). We don't know how much money we'll make, but it will feel fair to get financial compensation for all the hard work that went into this project. Also, Lori and Silvia are both in positions where having a book publication will enable them to make a good case in their tenure review or full professor evaluations, and these promotions come with increased compensation and job security.

We signed this contract just as Amy was transitioning into her current position as an open educational resources librarian and while she was on the very steep side of the learning curve about copyright and permissions. ABC-CLIO approached us about writing a book, and while we did shop the idea around to a couple of other possible publishers before we signed, none were interested. Having committed to the idea of a book, we went with the people who agreed that it would be published, and we didn't negotiate at all—either for rights or for payment.

All this being said, we don't think that ABC-CLIO is a villain in this scenario. They are providing valuable labor and services, particularly when considered in light of the relatively niche market for information literacy books as compared to the textbook market previously discussed in this chapter. We signed a standard publishing agreement. In fact, Silvia compared our contract with a couple of colleagues' contracts, and our terms were more favorable than theirs. We're participating in the current information economy, which, for all its flaws, is not inherently a problem. We can, however, be thoughtful about the limitations of these models.

We're including this section because we think that you, the reader, were probably wondering due to the content of this chapter. But transparency about the nuts and bolts of how information is sold and compensated can be illuminating for students too, especially in the context of encouraging students to share their own content. Their intellectual property may lead to monetary value, depending on the choices that they make. Take it from us: it's better to be informed than to take a blind "Terms of Service; Didn't Read" approach.

Applying the Threshold Concepts Criteria

Crossing this threshold is transformative because the act of using information is exposed as an economic and political choice that requires care and consideration. For example, Silvia remembers helping a student who came to an end-of-semester pop-up citation workshop. As she checked his bibliography, Silvia noticed that several of the student's citations for a paper in support of the Black Lives Matter movement came from Breitbart News. When asked about the use of the citations, the student said that he "wanted to use Eric Garner's last words," which were quoted in the Breitbart articles. Silvia pulled up the Breitbart site and went through the front page as well as the comments section with the student. She and the student talked about who owned the site, what it meant to use Breitbart as a source in this context, and what it meant to support the site with his viewership and citation. Then, she and the student found articles from Reuters and the *New York Times* that covered the same event. The student had not known that clicking through links in a search could function as a method of financial support.

While this student was not instantaneously transformed into an expert, he did make an irreversible shift: he understood that he plays an active role in the information economy, whether he wants to or not. Students who can identify economic influences on information sources can no longer see their information consumption as neutral. Likewise, students who understand the value of information can no longer consider any information to be unequivocally free. These understandings can be applied to intellectual property produced by students themselves as well.

The information commodities threshold concept integrates academic experiences into other familiar transactional situations, for example, with tangible commodities. By extension, it reveals the purpose guiding academic practices such as attribution, authentication for databases, and publication expectations for faculty. This concept connects the novice researcher to the network of scholars, agencies, institutions, and corporations producing and perpetuating the information they seek and use. Given the philosophical motives for open access publishing, institutional repositories, and other efforts to reduce the digital divide, this threshold concept may also introduce questions about the point at which information is not only a commodity but also a human right, as well as leading to critical questions about the concepts of private property and the commons from non-Western points of view.

This concept is borrowed from the field of economics, but it applies to information science because it prompts questions about the economic influences that affect information flow and its interaction with society. As mediators, facilitators, and creators, librarians both negotiate and disrupt the flow of information via economic systems. Librarians have a unique view on purchasing information in physical form and paying for access to digital content, which has led to strongly held professional principles relating to privacy, open access, and intellectual freedom.

The information commodities threshold concept is troublesome because so much information is readily available without an obvious cost. Information meets Marx's definition of a commodity (it is a good or service, has value, and is produced by human labor), but students can wind up with an incorrect sense of the value and function of information products and services because their characteristics as a commodity are often not apparent. Information is intangible, which makes it seem as if no one owns it and it belongs in the commons, even when it is private property or not appropriately understood as property at all. Understanding the information commodities threshold concept enables a student to identify the economic forces at play in their information landscape.

Teaching Information Commodities

Basic

Information Commodities and Ownership

At its most fundamental, the information commodities threshold concept asks students to value information as a good or service produced by labor. Students should understand the way that information interacts with economic systems; specifically, students should be able to identify the owner of an information source and the way that different owners can change the terms under which information can be accessed. The owner of a deli, for example, gets to decide how their counter will function. Will customers take a number and wait to be called? Do customers pay for their sandwich before it is made? Are substitutions allowed? Is avocado extra? Variations in ownership complicate student access to information, but it also explains the problem. A publisher's embargo on the most recent issue of a journal would explain why the full-text article is unavailable, and the acquisition of EasyBib's parent company by Chegg, an online textbook service, would explain why users now see more advertisements. This concept is also a way for students to understand the value of their own intellectual property and dictate the terms under which it can be shared or altered (e.g., through an understanding of copyright and open licenses).

Information Commodities and Citation

Even students who already have experience working with citation may struggle to see it as a useful part of a thoughtful research process. Students at this level may ask for help inserting the required number and type of sources into a paper they have already written. They may also ask a librarian to locate sources they quoted in their paper, having neglected to record bibliographic information at the time of use. These issues arise when citation is treated as an afterthought. The information commodities threshold concept can shift the focus away from procedural requirements for a comma versus a period, and instead highlight the way that citation represents participation in larger scholarly conversations that depend on other people's work.

Information Commodities and Plagiarism

Introducing students to plagiarism through information commodities can be a way to talk about gray areas related to intellectual property. As with comedy, music is rife with examples of reference and homage. When does sampling cross the line into stealing? How much credit should the creator of a remix get? How similar can two pop songs be before one can be said to be stealing from the other? Students should be able to apply the same reasoning to their information use to distinguish between legitimate use of information commodities and academic dishonesty.

Access to Commodified Information

While this may not always hold true, the most economically valuable information is usually the most difficult information to access. Compare, for instance, the difficulty of locating a market research report about the global frozen yogurt market for less than $2,000, against the ease with which an out-of-copyright classic like Jack London's *The Call of the Wild* can be found in a library, as a free PDF, or in a used bookstore. Students at this level should recognize that economic factors are likely to be prioritized over findability and usability when attempting to access information. This kind of commodification accounts for the variety of applications they must install and accounts they must create in order to read ebooks downloaded from the library. It also explains why physical books can be requested through interlibrary loan, but most electronic materials can only be accessed from the home campus.

Selling Free Information

When information is free to access (if not to produce), companies can monetize that information by creating proprietary wrappers around it. Students can use the information commodities threshold concept to understand why multiple access options exist for the same publicly available information and then select the option that best meets their immediate needs. If Census data and information about U.S. demographics are available through American FactFinder and Social Explorer, students should opt for the former if they want to work with tables and the latter if they want to interact with the data dynamically or graphically. Likewise, students should be able to use information directly from the open textbook platform OpenStax rather than through a proprietary publisher's platform that offers ancillary homework materials for a cost.

Information Commodification and Privacy

Just as hiding the cost of information can lead to misunderstandings about the value of libraries, information sources that hide their product can also prove to be troublesome. Information commodities provide an opportunity to talk about the relationship between privacy, the implications of commercial interests on net neutrality for web content, and the commodification of personal data. Students should develop a set of personal best practices for privacy on the basis of a nuanced understanding of commodified information; the successful student should feel empowered rather than paranoid when interacting with information sources.

Advanced

Producing Information Commodities in Higher Education

More advanced study of information commodities will focus on the economic systems that drive scholarly publication. As producers, students have decisions to make about how their intellectual property will be disseminated. Is it better to publish in a prestigious high-cost journal with a restrictive copyright agreement? Or is it more important to find a broader audience by publishing in an open access venue? Advanced students also need to understand the labor structure associated with producing information commodities. Not for nothing, after all, are academic job seekers referred to as being "on the market." Information commodities can be a way to clarify the publish-or-perish model of tenure, contingent faculty positions, travel support, labor union contracts, research leave, and predatory publishing.

Libraries and Information Commodities

Advanced explorations of information commodities should take into account the extent to which access in academic libraries continues to be restricted by socioeconomic conditions. The collection development policy at a community college will have very different priorities than that at a flagship research institution, designated as a Federal Depository Library. Reciprocal borrowing agreements and interlibrary loan cannot completely mitigate the difference in access between, say, Columbia University Libraries and Snow College in rural Ephraim, Utah. These differences impact the ease with which faculty and advanced students can pursue their research; can a scholar visit the Rare Book & Manuscript Library on campus to work with incunabula, or must she apply for funding and time to travel to another institution? Rather than talking about free library materials, librarians can present a more honest picture of the privileged access granted to students, which they will likely lose once they graduate. Some companies extend this connection even further in the hopes of gaining the loyalty of students. Westlaw, Bloomberg, and Lexis-Nexis all offer a range of perks to law school students, including discounted or free access to their databases, free printing, scholarships, or free lunches to the next generation of their paying customers.

Responsibilities Associated with Information Commodities

Experts have a responsibility to decide whether to protect information commodities at both the consumer and the creator level. On the one hand, an advanced understanding may lead to decisions about using and releasing work with open licenses or into the public domain, or other types of activism, in order to advance alternative economic models. On the other hand, experts may find ethical problems where current understandings of information commodities are not upheld, especially in a context in which the products of academic publishing are often portrayed as an open and available public good. For example, a footnote in a recent best-selling work of nonfiction written by two reputable scientists explains that most of the 600 scientific papers on which the book relied would be freely available online. The authors advise readers to explore Google Scholar, scientific journal websites, and the scientists' websites and, finally, recommend emailing researchers directly (Hare & Woods, 2013). Such suggestions paper over legal battles for fair use, library struggles to keep up with rising database costs, and the pressure academics face to produce high level work at a rate commensurate with their march toward tenure.

Takeaways

- The information commodities threshold concept is troublesome because so much information is readily available without an obvious cost. Still, information is sold, bought, and requires labor to produce.
- Positioning the library as a free source of information leads to misunderstandings about the value of information; we should, instead, be clear about the complexities of the information economy.
- Acknowledging and identifying the relationship between information and the economic systems that produce, reproduce, and disseminate information allows researchers to better negotiate the complicated territory of information value, proper attribution, and intellectual property.

For Further Consideration

- Given the philosophical motives for open access publishing, institutional repositories, and other efforts to reduce the digital divide, when do you think information shifts from being a commodity to a human right?
- Does your current elevator pitch for the library mention free books or free access to computers, databases, or research help? If so, how can you revise the way you talk about the library to better highlight its value?
- What are the copyright terms for your scholarship? Are they aligned with your professional and personal values?

References

American Library Association. (2000). *Information literacy competency standards for higher education*. Retrieved from http://www.ala.org/acrl/standards/informationliteracycompetency

Anderson, J., & Christen, K. (2013). "Chuck a copyright on it": Dilemmas of digital return and the possibilities for traditional knowledge licenses and labels. *Museum Anthropology Review, 7*(1–2), 105–126. Retrieved from http://scholarworks.dlib.indiana.edu/journals/index.php/mar/article/viewFile/2169/4251

Anderson, M. (2017, March 22). Digital divide persists even as lower-income Americans make gains in tech adoption. Retrieved from Pew Research Center website: http://www.pewresearch.org/fact-tank/2017/03/22/digital-divide-persists-even-as-lower-income-americans-make-gains-in-tech-adoption/

Andrews, N. (2018). Reflections on resistance, decolonization, and the historical trauma of libraries and academia. In K. P. Nicholson & M. Seale (Eds.), *The politics of theory and the practice of critical librarianship* (pp. 181–192). Sacramento, CA: Library Juice Press. Retrieved from https://osf.io/preprints/lissa/mva35/

Association of College & Research Libraries. (2014). *Framework for information literacy for higher education*. Retrieved from http://www.ala.org/acrl/standards/ilframework

Badkar, M. (2014, April 25). College textbook inflation is out of control. Retrieved from Business Insider website: http://www.businessinsider.com/textbook-price-inflation-2014-4

Brand, S. (1985, May). Hackers' conference 1984: Keep designing. *Whole Earth Review, 46*, 44–55.

Buckland, M. (2017). *Information and society*. Cambridge, MA: MIT Press.

Chen, A. (2014, October 23). The laborers who keep dick pics and beheadings out of your Facebook feed. *WIRED*. Retrieved from https://www.wired.com/2014/10/content-moderation/

Colvard, N., Watson, C. E., & Park, H. (2018). The impact of open educational resources on various student success metrics. *International Journal of Teaching and Learning in Higher Education, 30*(2), 262–276. Retrieved from http://www.isetl.org/ijtlhe/pdf/IJTLHE3386.pdf

Creative Commons. (n.d.). Mission and vision. Retrieved from https://creativecommons.org/about/mission-and-vision/

De Bruin, D., & Thiele, B. (2014, February 12). If you want my data, reward me. *Data Center Journal*. Retrieved from http://www.datacenterjournal.com/data-reward/

Dunn, G. (2015, December 14). Get rich or die vlogging: The sad economics of internet fame. Retrieved from Splinter website: https://splinternews.com/get-rich-or-die-vlogging-the-sad-economics-of-internet-1793853578

First Archivist Circle. (2006). *Protocols for Native American archival materials*. Retrieved from http://www2.nau.edu/libnap-p/

Fisher, Z. (2017). Facing the frames: Using the Framework as a guide for a credit-bearing information literacy course. *College & Research Libraries News, 78* (7), 354–358. Retrieved from http://crln.acrl.org/index.php/crlnews/article/view/16696/18175

Florida Virtual Campus. (2016). *2016 student textbook and course materials survey*. Retrieved from https://florida.theorangegrove.org/og/items/3a65c507-2510-42d7-814c-ffdefd394b6c/1/

Free Software Foundation. (1996). The free software definition. Retrieved from GNU Operating System website: http://www.gnu.org/philosophy/freesw.html

Future Librarians for Intellectual Freedom. (2016). Information was never free. In *CJSR-FM Podcast*. Retrieved from https://soundcloud.com/cjsrfm/flif-information-was-never-free

Glaser, A. (2018a, January 18). Want a terrible job? Facebook and Google may be hiring. *Slate*. Retrieved from https://slate.com/technology/2018/01/facebook-and-google-are-building-an-army-of-content-moderators-for-2018.html

Glaser, A. (2018b, May 7). The Cambridge Analytica scandal is over and nothing has changed. *Slate*. Retrieved from https://slate.com/technology/2018/05/the-cambridge-analytica-scandal-is-over-and-nothing-has-changed.html

Hare, B., & Woods, V. (2013). *The genius of dogs*. New York, NY: Plume.

Hilton, J. L., III, Fischer, L., Wiley, D., & Williams, L. (2016). Maintaining momentum toward graduation: OER and the course throughput rate. *International Review of Research in Open and Distributed Learning, 17*(6), 18–27. doi:10.19173/irrodl.v17i6.2686

Joffrion, E., & Fernández, N. (2015). Collaborations between tribal and nontribal organizations: Suggested best practices for sharing expertise, cultural resources, and knowledge. *American Archivist, 78*(1), 192–237. Retrieved from http://americanarchivist.org/doi/pdf/10.17723/0360-9081.78.1.192

Joffrion, E., & Tom, L. (2016). Broken promises: A case study in reconciliation. *Archival Issues: Journal of the Midwest Archives Conference, 37*(2), 7–22. Retrieved from https://cedar.wwu.edu/cgi/viewcontent.cgi?referer=https://scholar.google.com/&httpsredir=1&article=1050&context=library_facpubs

Lin Hanick, S., & Hofer, A. (2017). Opening the Framework: Connecting open education practices and information literacy. Retrieved from Open Oregon Educational Resources website: http://openoregon.org/opening-the-framework/

Local Contexts. (n.d.). *Traditional Knowledge (TK) labels*. Retrieved from http://localcontexts.org/tk-labels/

Marx, K. (1967). *Capital*. New York, NY: International Publishers.

Mathiesen, K. (2012). A defense of Native Americans' rights over their traditional cultural expressions. *American Archivist, 75*(2), 456–481.

Retrieved from http://americanarchivist.org/doi/pdf/10.17723/aarc.75.2.0073888331414314

Open Oregon Educational Resources. (2017, February 17). But is it sustainable? Retrieved from http://openoregon.org/but-is-it-sustainable/

Pariser, E. (2011). *The filter bubble: How the new personalized web is changing the way we think and the way we read.* New York, NY: Penguin.

Pew Research Center. (2018, April 27). One-in-five Americans own a smartphone, but do not have traditional broadband service. Retrieved from http://www.pewinternet.org/2018/04/30/declining-majority-of-online-adults-say-the-internet-has-been-good-for-society/pi_2018-04-30_internet-good-bad_0-02/

Popken, B. (2015, August 6). College textbook prices have risen 1,041 percent since 1977. NBC News. Retrieved from http://www.nbcnews.com/feature/freshman-year/college-textbook-prices-have-risen-812-percent-1978-n399926

Seale, M. (2013). Marketing information literacy. *Communications in Information Literacy, 7*(2), 154–160. Retrieved from https://pdxscholar.library.pdx.edu/cgi/viewcontent.cgi?article=1094&context=comminfolit

Seeber, K. P. (2016). The failed pedagogy of punishment: Moving discussions of plagiarism beyond detection and discipline. In N. Pagowsky & K. McElroy (Eds.), *Critical library pedagogy handbook* (pp. 131–138). Chicago, IL: ACRL Press.

Senak, E. (2014). *Fixing the broken textbook market: How students respond to high textbook costs and demand alternatives.* Retrieved from http://uspirg.org/sites/pirg/files/reports/NATIONAL%20Fixing%20Broken%20Textbooks%20Report1.pdf

Senak, E., Donoghue, R., O'Connor Grant, K., & Steen, K. (2016). *Access denied: The new face of the textbook monopoly.* Retrieved from http://www.studentpirgs.org/sites/student/files/reports/Access%20Denied%20-%20Final%20Report.pdf

Society of American Archivists. (2012). *Final report: Native American protocols forum working group.* Retrieved from https://www2.archivists.org/sites/all/files/0112-V-I-NativeAmProtocolsForum.pdf

Townsend, L., Brunetti, K., & Hofer, A. R. (2011). Threshold concepts and information literacy. *portal: Libraries and the Academy, 11*(3), 853–869. Retrieved from http://archives.pdx.edu/ds/psu/7417

Trevino, S., & Maron, M. (Host). (2010, May 27). *Willie Barcena/Steve Trevino/Carlos responds* [Audio podcast]. Retrieved from http://www.wtfpod.com/podcast/episodes/episode_76_willie_barcena_steve_trevino_carlos_responds

Tulalip Tribes of Washington. (2003, July 9). *Statement by the Tulalip Tribes of Washington on folklore, indigenous knowledge, and the public domain.* Retrieved from http://www.wipo.int/export/sites/www/tk/en/igc/ngo/tulaliptribes.pdf

Wikipedia. (2018, May 9). Commons. Retrieved from https://en.wikipedia.org/wiki/Commons

Wiley, D. (2017, May 2). *OER-enabled pedagogy*. Retrieved from https://opencontent.org/blog/archives/5009

Wiley, D., Williams, L., & Hilton, J. L., III. (2016). The Tidewater Z-Degree and the INTRO model for sustaining OER adoption. *Education Policy Analysis Archives, 23*(41), 1–15. doi:10.14507/epaa.v23.1828

Wong, A., & Maron, M. (Host). (2016, May 5). *Ali Wong* [Audio podcast]. Retrieved from http://www.wtfpod.com/podcast/52wyay702hls7pd1o8gs9q04tkjo4a?rq=ali%20wong

CHAPTER SIX

Organizing Systems

In seventh grade, Lori's social studies teacher required all of his students to visit the local university library. This wasn't a field trip—he just expected his students to find a way to get there on their own. University of California, Riverside might have been a smaller university campus, but its library seemed vast compared to the Chemawa Middle School library (this was before California started cutting their public school libraries and librarians). Lori wandered around the seemingly endless stacks, scared of the college students and library staff alike, and tried to find anything she could actually read and understand for her research project. It was quite possible to get lost in such a big library. But the signposts from the junior high school library could be found there as well: the card catalog, the current periodicals, the reference section. And there were new destinations, like the long rows of microfilm or the mysterious special collections.

Those of us of a certain age grew up with libraries, whether or not we used them regularly. Before the turn of the century, libraries represented one of the few places whose purpose was to store and disseminate all kinds of information. One of the things Lori notices today is that she still carries a mental model of information in her head that is based on the physicality and arrangement of those libraries. Formats are sorted into different sections because they have different shapes and are used more or less often. Reference books are in one area because of function. Regular books are sorted by subject and in a different, larger area because they often make up the bulk of the collection. Current magazines and newspapers are sometimes pulled out for easy access. The card catalog, with its three access points, was a physical index where you could get a sense of the scope and size of an entire library's collection, as well as experience the tactile pleasure of flipping through the cards.

We've all encountered faculty who, somewhat bewilderingly to us, just want the students to visit the library, to browse the stacks, to get a physical book off the shelf, as if entering the building will somehow teach students about information. The library as an organizing system and model for the information world helps explain this assignment, and it also helps explain some common practices of teaching librarians. We do things like bring in hard copies of various formats in an attempt to help students understand how those formats work. We are the folks likely to check the stacks for the print book when we do our own research. And back when we did bibliographic instruction, teaching students how to use the library really did give them a basic overview of the most common information formats and the organizing systems typically used to store and access them. Physical libraries were the primary organizing systems for information, and they made us feel the same way that a map makes us feel about the physical world—like we know where we stand and where we might go, and can find a route there.

This admittedly nostalgic view of libraries is offered here to make the point that the library as a space outlines a basic geography of information. Information geographies pop up everywhere. For example, a single issue of a magazine forms a geography. Some information is presented up front, including the table of contents, editorial message, or brief news items. Further into the publication, readers expect at least one big feature as well as minor features such as interviews and regular columns. It is accepted that all of this content will be interlaced with advertisements aimed at the demographic expected to be reading the magazine. These elements are placed to maximize ad revenue because that's how the magazine supports itself, though selling ads is not the primary purpose of the magazine. We see the content laid out adjacent or near other content, and it forms a recognizable geography of information placed just so: mountains of in-depth content, little brooks of amusing anecdotes or news, valleys of product reviews, and so on. Larger information geographies might include a website like Amazon.com or the search engines that roam the web or an archival digital collection. All of these information geographies are designed or arranged to make sense of collections of information.

We have noticed that our students often do not share the library's reference points, perhaps because their experience of information is multiple streams of apparently free content pouring in through a variety of devices. Information comes to them, and when they do seek it, that seeking is done through a single search box. The format threshold concept that we discussed in Chapter 4 arose from an understanding that many students don't have a conception that the information things they encounter share common structures and purposes. They similarly seem to have little idea of how the systems that organize, store, and deliver that information work. We propose that students can use these systems more effectively, critically, and responsibly if they know more about them.

This chapter will explore the organizing systems threshold concept by examining the traditional components of information organization (collections, description, and classification), looking at the rise of algorithms and search engines, and pausing to consider how organizing systems are used to search for and share information. Organizing systems offer a technical framework for information literacy, a structure built and maintained by people attempting to provide access to the world's information.

Organizing Systems Defined

Search is a mainstay in the instruction librarian wheelhouse, so we—Amy, Silvia, and Lori, along with our coauthor Korey—tried to figure out how to define a threshold concept related to search. As public services librarians, we knew there were probably technical threshold concepts that wouldn't necessarily spring to our minds right away, and we thought this might be hampering our ability to figure out a search threshold concept. We could get into the details of specific concepts like controlled vocabulary, keywords, Boolean operators, and limits, but we struggled to find something troublesome, unifying, and transformative to connect these kinds of concepts—though we know students often struggle to get useful and high-quality information out of both library and nonlibrary information systems.

Our first attempt at a search threshold concept was Good Searches Use Database Structure (Hofer, Townsend, & Brunetti, 2012, p. 402). We were trying to get at the idea that students should have some notion of how information systems are constructed in order to find information in them. The Association of College & Research Libraries' (ACRL) *Framework for Information Literacy for Higher Education* proposes Search Is Strategic Exploration (Association of College & Research Libraries, 2014). The concept that emerged from the Delphi study described in Chapter 2 was Information Structures (Townsend, Hofer, Lin Hanick, & Brunetti, 2016, p. 35). While this phrase is helpfully distinct from "information systems"—a term which is primarily associated with information technology—it again was a bit unsatisfying, though the content of the threshold concept was coming into view. While we agree with all of the aforementioned concepts, they felt unsatisfying because they didn't quite convey a complete picture of the technical and social structures around the organization and dissemination of information through information systems.

In researching this chapter, we came across Robert Glushko's (2016) groundbreaking book *The Discipline of Organizing* and it finally clicked into place: organizing systems.

Glushko's definition of an organizing system is as follows:

> An intentionally arranged collection of resources and the interactions they support. (2016, p. 502)

Where a resource is

> [a]nything of value that can support goal-oriented activity. This definition means that a resource can be a physical thing, a non-physical thing, information about physical things, or anything you want to organize. (Glushko, 2016, p. 505)

Glushko's definition of a resource aligns with Michael Buckland's concept of *information as thing*: objects that "are referred to as 'information' because they are regarded as being informative" (Buckland, 2017, p. 351). It also aligns with the concept of documents, which are the information things that move through these systems, often as distinct formats. People organize, preserve, and make documents accessible in organizing systems. Documents are a broader category than formats because they are not always created with intention or by people, but they serve as a kind of evidence. However, organizing systems are always created by people, with intention, even when that intention is relayed (or mislaid) via an algorithm.

Information things and the systems they swim in have gotten complicated. People manage documents and formats on a daily basis and engage with information systems so intricate that most of us really don't know how those systems work. We use these information things to communicate and act, whether that's in our personal or working lives, whether those things are meant to be fleeting or preserved for some time. Few of us could live our lives without managing, manipulating, creating, finding, and generally making regular use of all manner of documentary evidence.

We therefore propose the following definition for the threshold concept organizing systems:

> Organizing systems describe, categorize, preserve, and provide access to documents and information about documents. Though often mediated by computers, organizing systems are designed by humans and thus reflect and reproduce human understandings and biases.

Our students regularly encounter systems that make finding an increasingly large number and confusing variety of documents very easy, while obscuring the nature and function of both the documents themselves and the organizing systems that receive, store, and deliver those documents. It may seem that these systems have all the virtues of a card catalog while also being efficiently scoped to handle massive amounts of information. Taking a critical look at organizing systems reveals that they are still very human, and thus plagued by the faults shared by all human systems. Still, they often function in predictable ways that librarians can teach our students to understand. Comparing organizing systems such as web search engines to the systems used by libraries can help students trace out meaningful paths through a complex geography of information.

Classification

Humans classify. We organize the things in our environment, both abstractly and physically. We classify to make sense of things in order to survive (Brown, 1991, p. 133). But humans are also imperfect. We sort ourselves into families, tribes, and interest groups with antipathies and narrow perspectives: we hate, we love, and we are often unreasonable and irrational. And we classify accordingly. Librarians need a way to teach students to make effective use of classification systems while also acknowledging the imperfections inherent to these systems.

It might be helpful for students to think about our classifying impulse as arising from the need to stay alive in the natural world. All classifications begin locally and are most accurate when they stay local, oral, and practical. For instance, we know that mushrooms are delicious, but some mushrooms can kill us. We figure out a way to describe and classify mushrooms so that we can distinguish the poisonous mushrooms from the safe mushrooms. These classifications aren't quite as useful to the folks living one mountain over, where climate and ecology vary and produce different varieties of mushrooms. We pass these understandings along to our family and community—through words and eventually in recorded knowledge. As Buckland states, "Description is always and necessarily based in culture, because descriptions are based on the concepts, definitions, and understandings that have developed in a community" (2017, p. 91). Think, for example, about the possibility of a modern kitchen as a classification system—some drawers are reserved for sharp things used by ADULTS ONLY!, while the fondue pot is up high because it only gets used once a year. Used locally, classification systems adapt to changing circumstances and don't need to be understood by anyone we don't have regular conversations with.

However, when people gather in larger groups, divide up the labor, and begin exchanging goods and services, we start recording our classifications, which inevitably leads to problems. When we try to construct an abstract classification system for all knowledge, like the Library of Congress Subject Headings? We get that so wrong. When we leave the classifying to the wisdom of the crowds and the network? No better.

As experts in classification, librarians know that naming is culturally rooted and that language shifts. Librarians have always gotten it wrong, but it's not just us—classification systems will always be wrong to some extent, depending on the perspective of the user. The moment that classifications are fixed (in any form), they are almost immediately out of date and inaccurate (Cho, 2016).

Sanford Berman's efforts to update the Library of Congress Subject Headings are a visible and somewhat successful attempt to change what he described as "intellect-constricting rubbish that litters the LC list"—referencing such terms as "yellow peril," "mammies," and "sexual perversion" in his 1971 tract, *Prejudices and Antipathies* (Berman, 1993, p. 19). Berman encouraged librarians to find out how groups reference themselves in creating classifications. From the vantage point of the early 21st century, this advice seems obvious: it is unquestionably the most accurate and ethical way to reference a thing or group. Yet, it may not be the most efficient way to deliver information to library patrons, who are a diverse group of mixed communities, because there will never be one correct name for each information thing. Further, use of a community's preferred term may confuse other users who are searching for information on the same topic but use a different term.

An episode of *This American Life* about alternative street maps used by Chinese immigrants in New York City's Chinatown provides a vivid example of very individualized terms for information things. According to Mona, a cab company dispatcher, every street in the neighborhood is known by multiple names for the benefit of the various communities that live there. Orchard Street, for instance, is known by its English name, a Cantonese transliteration, a Mandarin transliteration, a Cantonese translation for orchard, a Mandarin translation for orchard, and then an additional handful of nicknames in all three languages. For these Chinese immigrants, many of the English names are unpronounceable, and the standard map is, as a result, unusable (Reiss, 2017). Clearly, one word or term will not always be the best word or term for everyone, even if it is technically correct. Yet, preferred terms are exactly what organizing systems demand. So why bother?

The reason that we need classification, for all its imperfections, is that in an information society we are represented by our documents: our social media presence, email style and signature, financial records, health records, and identification documents, such as driver's licenses and passports. As we move through the world, we generate a trail of documentary evidence that has to be managed (Buckland, 2017). And those documents are increasingly digital, subject to search, and available via networks variously corporate, governmental, and public. Therefore, the choices we make in naming, describing, and classifying information both enable us to navigate daily life and make us vulnerable to surveillance and control.

Addressing the fundamental problems of naming and classification with our students exposes them to one of the core concepts of organizing systems. Describing information things, whether their containers or their content, is important and useful. But it also highlights how all organizing systems must cope with the problems of language: terms that switch meaning depending on context, or that come to sound ill advised or offensive over time, or that mean the same thing with different spellings. The ongoing problem of classification in organizing systems does not change the value offered by controlled vocabularies in the retrieval of relevant information. So, even though we will never get it perfect, we agree with Berman that "simple honesty and our own professional commitment to elemental decency require that we try" (1991, p. 16). Classification systems hold a mirror up to common human understandings, needs, and mistakes.

Collections

When we classify, we are sorting ideas and documents into groups. Those groups are collections, which Glushko defines as

> a group of resources that have been selected for some purpose. (2016, p. 483)

The type of collection that people interact with most when using digital information is lists of search results. Lists are collections, and search results are collections of resources gathered by a search engine on the basis of our search terms. In a library catalog, that list is generated through a process of matching search terms against indexes of controlled vocabularies. Discovery systems and search engines create a list using an algorithm. Either way, the dynamically generated collections created through search are a useful way of filtering through a mass of irrelevant information.

Given the amount of information available, we need filters, but it's also important to keep in mind that filters can hide useful information by excluding it from the collection. Say, for example, you were looking for essays written by imprisoned British suffragettes during the early 20th century; you know that arrests dwindled by the start of World War I, so you limit your search of historical newspapers to the years between 1899 and 1914. In doing so, however, you may exclude results for essays published years after they were written, republications of essays first written for smaller audiences, or essays written retrospectively on the basis of notes from the time. Users should build their search strategy to account for the cracks in a filter through which useful information may slip.

Taking a step back, encouraging students to question what content is being searched (or not) complicates the idea that a single search tool can serve up all the information to meet a need. In other words, the parameters of the collection being searched are already filtering the collection that will be available in the list of search results. If students assume that their collection of search results is complete after searching only one collection, they miss out on understanding the choices and assumptions built into the system they're using. In E. L. Konigsburg's children's novel, *The View from Saturday*, a pivotal question in an Academic Bowl competition is won when the contestant correctly identifies Humpty Dumpty as appearing in *Through the Looking-Glass*, and not *Alice's Adventures in Wonderland*, as is popularly believed. A character explains, "How can you know what is missing if you've never met it? You must know of something's existence before you can notice its absence" (Konigsburg, 1998, p. 157). The same thinking can be applied to how users engage with collections. Until you know what can be found in a collection, you won't know what can't be found. Expertise in this area equips users with the ability to easily identify the boundaries of a collection. More practically, library databases can be used to illustrate the limitations of even expansive and expensive collections. After all, a SWOT analysis can't be found in *Project MUSE*, searching for engineering standards in Academic Search Complete will be unproductive, and Web of Science returns few results for something easily read and cited for a Public Speaking class.

Further, librarians are very aware that the reasons that information is collected and indexed in different locations has more to do with economic, disciplinary, and social conventions than with any qualities inherent to the content of the information. The expert understands that specific collections exist and how to find them, and also that those collections can be searched with precision once you understand how they are scoped and arranged. This is entirely different from searching across collections with a single search box: single search solutions offer less control than separate searches of collections because they hide the seams created by stitching together disparate collections (Sherratt, 2015). Students might have more patience and perseverance for searching multiple sources once they understand why the tools that promise to search most things (Google, library discovery platforms) won't answer all inquiries.

Collections, whether carefully curated or dynamically generated through search, are created for a purpose. That purpose may be to make accessible documents of a certain type, such as scholarly journal articles; to preserve information items of a particular type, such as archival photos; or to satisfy a basic information need, such as the search results returned by a search engine with an answer to the question "When does Daylight Savings Time begin?" Organizing systems within cultural heritage institutions and libraries can be broadly characterized as "collections of collections" (Glushko, 2016, p. 49).

The web disrupts the notion of "collections of collections," however, because it is not purposefully organized as it is being built (it is constantly being constructed and deconstructed and reconstructed). Rather, collections are organized for the user by individual websites and as information is retrieved using search engines. As we discuss in the next section, these web collection creators are algorithmic proxies for human decision making.

Algorithms Are Not Neutral

In the early days of the web and browsers, a number of start-ups attempted to make online information accessible through organizing systems. Some of these tried to get the job done with hierarchical directories and other strategies that relied on describing and categorizing the information on the web. The sheer amount of content, though, quickly overtook the capacity of human elbow grease to catalog the web. These days, the organizing systems that most of us interact with on a daily basis are search engines, usually Google, that rely on algorithms instead. Algorithms have become so central to so many aspects of life at this point that it's essential for students to be exposed to this concept.

Unlike a library catalog, algorithms don't match keywords against carefully organized indexes of controlled vocabularies prepared by people, but they rather use programmed metrics to identify relevant information that is indexed by machines on the basis of characteristics that they can recognize. According to Christopher Steiner, in *Automate This*, algorithms are "decision trees" based on a series of "binary choices" (2012, p. 6). This makes algorithms sound relatively simple—but, in fact, algorithms have developed into complex networks that can be fed hundreds of variables in order to produce a set of results. Google, the 500-pound gorilla of search, uses an algorithm that was initially designed around a principle derived from academic citation-analysis practices, which treats citations as recommendations (Noble, 2018). Generally, the more prestigious (in this case, popular) the recommender, the more weight the recommendation is given by the algorithm. The exact makeup of the algorithm is proprietary information, but we know that it usually works, so it seems like magic.

Opening the hood on Google's search algorithm can show students that the search engine as organizing system doesn't actually give us access to all of the information in the network; in fact, it's impossible to know exactly what we are searching. Google uses information about the individual user, especially if the user happens to be logged into his or her Google account—including search history, geographic location, political leanings, specific demographic information, shopping preferences, emails, and more. This customization can cause previous browsing or searching habits to influence and limit future search results, creating an echo chamber of biased information tailored to individual predispositions. Eli Pariser's influential book, *The Filter Bubble*, contends that this personalization can cause people to "become trapped in a you loop," which aims to generate "compulsive" clicking (2011, pp. 125, 127). In a world where search engines filter an overwhelming torrent of information into something usable, systems that attempt to make search perfect for individuals may in fact limit their perspective to what they already know or believe. And to be completely clear, the aim of this personalization is to capture desired consumer behavior—eyes or clicks on ads—since, as we discussed in Chapter 5, Google's search engine is a product that supports its advertising business.

Students are probably used to thinking of algorithms, if they think of algorithms at all, as neutral computing processes that help make the world run more efficiently. In fact, online search algorithms not only lead to filter bubbles but also replicate societal biases and paradigms of the dominant culture, even while they simultaneously seem to strip their results of human intention. Safiya Noble's research has made a major contribution toward documenting the ways that Google reproduces racist and sexist biases in its search results. Noble did a simple search for the term "black girls," thinking of her young niece, and retrieved pornography (2018, p. 32). More searches yielded similar stereotypes of women and people of color held by the dominant culture. She notes that in a feedback loop that has the potential to erode journalistic ethics, "algorithmically driven analytics . . . place pressure on journalists to modify their content" in order to generate more clicks and more advertising dollars (2018, p. 154).

Lori and her friend Sarah ran into this issue when they were doing research for a book chapter about their experiences as Native women academic librarians. Their Google search for "Native American women" did not bring up pornography, but well over half of the image results portrayed

Native women in traditional rather than modern clothing, a significant minority were sexualized (sexy squaw Halloween costumes, anyone?), and over a third were historic images. A dominant stereotype of Native people, even in the era of Dakota Access Pipeline protests and large urban Native populations, is that they live in the past. When the mass media admits that modern Native people exist, they are portrayed in traditional clothing or regalia, such as that worn for ceremonies or powwows. Most Native people, whether urban or rez, are more likely to wear blue jeans or business clothing on a typical day, just like everyone else. This brings up the question: Who are these Google results for?

So far we've seen that algorithms create personal filter bubbles and filter search results into collections with built-in toxic biases. If we stop right here, this is already most of the way to a compelling information literacy instruction session. Students can consider the commercial and ideological interests powering their daily interactions with algorithms, whether it's a search engine or other opt-in services such as Google Maps indicating the fastest route from Point A to Point B on the basis of current traffic conditions, Spotify finding a new song on the basis of past music preferences, and Lyft matching them with a nearby driver. Yet, algorithms pervade modern life, including the criminal justice, social services, and insurance systems, in ways that have implications far beyond individual information use, and create opportunities for even larger classroom discussions about social justice.

Take, for instance, the case of algorithms used by the criminal justice system to predict outcomes such as whether a criminal will reoffend or show up for a trial. ProPublica investigated one such algorithm produced by the company Northpointe, which claims to make a risk assessment as to whether a defendant will reoffend (Angwin, Larson, Mattu, & Kirchner, 2016). Using the scores produced by one county, ProPublica found that the algorithm was more likely to identify black defendants as high risk to commit future crimes and white defendants as low risk. The algorithm doesn't use race as a metric, yet somehow, through consideration of a variety of factors from employment status to whether parents have criminal records, it's still racist. And because algorithms seem neutral, these results are treated as objective information by the people who use the system. Despite the intention of the algorithm designer that the score not be used to decide sentencing, and the intention by the courts that it be used only to lighten sentences and keep people out of jail or prison, judges still rely on Northpointe scores when making sentencing decisions.

In her book *Automating Inequality*, Virginia Eubanks further explores the implementation of algorithms in a variety of systems that make life-altering determinations about people living in poverty. For example, the Allegheny Family Screening Tool tries to predict which children are at greater risk of abuse, using records compiled from various governmental databases such as welfare, public schools, and Medicaid. Eubanks found the algorithm flawed, inaccurate, and "guaranteed to produce thousands of false negatives and positives annually"—mistakes that could result in children staying in abusive homes or being forced out of loving but low-income homes (2018, p. 146). One of the women profiled in the book talks about how her grocery purchases are monitored electronically by a social worker and warns, "You should pay attention to what happens to us. You're next" (2018, p. 9). Librarians should encourage students to think carefully about who might be next, and why; in which social contexts are people made vulnerable by the collection and processing of personal information?

We've seen that even when deployed to aid decision making in extremely sensitive and important situations, algorithms often get it wrong. Yet, people still tend to imbue them with an almost supernatural authority. As Ian Bogost (2015) says, "The next time you hear someone talking about algorithms, replace the term with 'God' and ask yourself if the meaning changes." When students are introduced to these ideas, it might seem as if the solution is to purge your life of algorithms. Experts, on the other hand, know that just as we need classification systems, we also need algorithms in order to make sense of the vast quantity of information all around us. It's not that search is broken; it was never perfect in the first place, because organizing systems are made by humans.

Using Organizing Systems

So far we've taken a deep dive into classification, collections, and algorithms. These are concepts that we want students to have a critical understanding of when they approach an organizing system. When they are acquainted with the elements that make up organizing systems, they are better prepared to be more effective users of those systems. For example, Twitter was originally designed as a system to communicate limited text messages in a public forum. Certain parameters were established for the information (initially 140 characters, lately 280 characters and images/videos, subject description with hashtags, user names beginning with @), and then people were invited to contribute information. Twitter designed and maintains the search algorithm, as well as a list of Trends documenting popular topics. Users not only contribute content through tweets but can also create a personalized collection of content by following other Twitter users, and they can create stories made up of multiple tweets using Twitter

Moments. Use of the system varies by users, but an understanding of its structure is important to retrieving useful and enjoyable information from it. A less savvy user might accidentally tweet something that was intended as a direct message, mix up hashtags with handles, or mistake a retweet for original content and credit the wrong source.

Our group of coauthors' understanding of search has benefited from Virginia Tucker's doctoral research on threshold concepts, which identified four threshold concepts for search: "information environment," "information structures," "information vocabularies," and "concept fusion" (2012, p. 5). Tucker compared professional searchers with novice searchers who were trying to develop professional-level skills. Her work highlights the understandings that expert searchers use—that is, the learning thresholds that they have crossed. For our purposes, working with students who are probably not going to go on to become professional searchers, the organizing systems threshold concept as proposed in this chapter is a good place to begin (and the beauty of the threshold concept approach is that both conceptualizations can be right).

In approaching the organizing systems threshold concept, there are two aspects to using organizing systems: creating or contributing to them and retrieving information from them. In the fairly recent past, the creation and maintenance of these systems was left to librarians and information companies like EBSCO and ProQuest. Now, however, these systems are increasingly being built by tech companies or individual developers and populated with information by ordinary people. And our students regularly contribute information to organizing systems, through social media platforms like Instagram, Twitter, and Facebook, or to the private organizing systems on their phones or personal computers, or in advanced data-intensive research where they may need to include appropriate metadata for reuse and sharing. Given the power of current digital organizing systems, our students are increasingly content creators who make contributions, both small and large, directly to the organizing systems that store and disseminate that content. This is where understanding the structure of the systems and how to describe and structure the content they add to the system is useful. Librarians can work with students to help them contribute content to library information systems, like institutional repositories. Librarians can also help students create websites that search engines can find and participate effectively on various social media platforms.

Retrieving information from these systems has become both easier, as user interfaces are designed with novice searchers in mind, and more difficult, as the emphasis on a single search box reduces control. However, librarians can still teach students how search works, whether it's in systems that use a controlled vocabulary and match against search terms or systems that use algorithms to create collections that are returned to users on the basis of search terms. We can work with students to develop strong keywords, vary their search terms, and use language effectively when searching. We can continue to teach Boolean logic and subject searching on the basis of controlled vocabularies. We can show students how limiters work to filter content and how different systems allow varying levels of control using those limiters. We can especially work to help our students see the increasing complexity of the geography of information, using the concept of organizing systems. We can expose them to useful collections, help them understand why collections are organized in particular ways, make sense of the scope of different kinds of collections, and help them learn how to find new collections.

We quoted Stewart Brand in Chapter 5, "Information Commodities," as saying that information wants to be free, but Tucker points to what Brand said just before this, about the value of information: "the right information in the right place just changes your life" (Brand, 1985, p. 49). We believe that our students will be just as likely to *place* that information as they will be to discover it—and that's why we have chosen the organizing systems emphasis.

Applying the Threshold Concepts Criteria

At first glance, the threshold concept organizing systems may not seem troublesome. College-age students, in particular, seem to move deftly through the digital world. Librarians don't often encounter undergraduates who struggle to accomplish regular computing tasks such as word processing and using browsers to move around the web. Yet, our students still struggle to move beyond Googling—and what we mean by Googling is finding and selecting information on the web by relying almost wholly on the judgment of an algorithm to find relevant information, employing few (if any) filters or limits, being relatively careless when selecting search terms, and using just one general tool. And yet, Googling is comfortable, so it may be troublesome for the novice to leave the comfort zone of their preferred search strategy; while the ultimate result may be more efficient, good search requires learning new concepts and skills and is not always intuitive. Additionally, students often lack a mental model that makes sense of the information environment, which can make information retrieval seem haphazard and arbitrary—thus the need for a single dependable tool rather than exploring nonobvious collections and tools. Searching within complex information structures requires effort, patience, and persistence—affective qualities that indicate a troublesome concept.

Understanding organizing systems is a transformative shift because it reveals a complex and imperfect underlying geography of information and the information things that populate it. This threshold concept also reveals the very human nature of organizing systems, even when filtered through technology and seemingly divorced from human decisions. It shifts the perspective from a single search box where words are tossed pell-mell to a multiplicity of unique collections with multiple means of access. Retrieving information from specialized organizing systems is more complex but often offers more control; once mastered, advanced users may be resentful of a one-size-fits-all discovery layer. For example, PubMed is well known for its MeSH (Medical Subject Headings), which grant searchers a great deal of granular control through the use of an extensive, specialized, controlled vocabulary and search building functions. Using PubMed as an expert requires an investment of time, but the ability to retrieve precise and relevant results is the reward. Additionally, the experts' perspective on using organizing systems includes an understanding of how their own contributions can be better structured for inclusion in and distribution by these systems. This concept extends from personal information management through effective use of folders and tags as organizing tools, to networked uses such as tagging photos on Instagram and sharing collections in citation management software, to using metadata standards (existing and developing) for the gathering of research data into repositories. Adding appropriate metadata to data makes it possible to share information more effectively but requires care and thought so that information doesn't get lost.

This threshold concept is irreversible because once the complexity of the information landscape is revealed, the geography is filled in with hills and valleys, beautifully ordered farms and wilderness areas, and crisscrossed with access roads, both paved and rocky. It's impossible to go back to seeing it as a flat, featureless plain with one point of access. Organizing systems can be found in almost every task one undertakes in a modern information society, and once the novice recognizes them, they remain in sight. The skills required to use organizing systems may fade or require updating. However, the core understandings around the use of language in classification and description, common information structures, and algorithmic decision making remain, as does the ability to recognize organizing systems in your life.

The organizing systems threshold concept integrates previously unrelated concepts such as where and how to find authoritative information, the ethical implications associated with the systems you choose to use, and what your rights are when you contribute to a system. Common lessons on brainstorming keywords, Boolean operator activities, and exploration of subject databases newly relate to understanding organizing systems as a whole. This threshold concept also integrates ideas about format, because formats make up the majority of information things that organizing systems house and distribute.

Organizing systems are the most direct connection that librarians can make to our disciplinary field of information science and form the technical foundations of information literacy. This concept is bounded by information science because librarians are trained in, concerned with, and often produce information structures, as well as organize and make accessible collections of information, both physical and digital.

Teaching Organizing Systems

Basic

Defining Information and Knowledge

Librarians deal with information and knowledge as they impact our daily lives. When librarians talk about knowledge, we are usually referring to collections of recorded information as well as the information that lives in our minds. We (Amy, Silvia, and Lori) do not spend a lot of time worrying about the epistemological questions that concern the nature of truth as it relates to knowledge. For us, there is what humans believe to be true, and the distinction between that and truth is for philosophers. Librarians should make it clear to our students that our definition of information is practical, not philosophical or mathematical. In Chapter 4, we recommended teaching students about information as thing to help them understand formats. Information as thing is an equally important concept with respect to organizing systems, because organizing systems contain physical information things—aka documents—whether those things are on paper or in bits and bytes. Organizing systems organize information things, or things that inform, many of which are instances of specific formats and most of which can be used as evidence. Those foundational understandings can give students a place to start building their own mental model of a geography of information.

Marking and Parking

Organizing systems work because humans (or their algorithmic proxies) make decisions about how to describe information things. As Glushko says, "We organize both physical and digital things and we organize the information about physical and digital things" (2016, p. 26). Sometimes those information things come to us with embedded metadata or bibliographic information that tells us how they want to be described or that contains basic facts about their structure—such as number of pages, date of publication, subject descriptors, and authorship. Introducing the idea of a surrogate is useful here when thinking about digital organizing systems. Librarians can engage students with activities around describing and classifying interesting objects and explore how language from person to person varies and how everybody represents meaning a bit differently. This is productive when we start asking students to think about keywords and search terms. We can also address how we use descriptions to help classify information for discovery. This brings in common classification systems used in libraries and reveals both the benefits and the perils of attempting to categorize knowledge in abstract ways. We can also look at how the culturally embedded and constantly shifting nature of language complicates this work and how we are fighting an ongoing, but worthwhile, battle in trying to accurately and helpfully describe the things and people in our world.

Basic Structure of Common Digital Organizing Systems

Students often understand little about how digital organizing systems are structured and the mechanisms used to retrieve information from them. Search engines, because of their proprietary algorithms, are especially likely to seem to work by magic. However, learning the basic structure of the web and how search engines work is helpful in understanding the kinds of information that web searching is likely to return and why. Additionally, learning how common library systems, like the catalog, archival digital collections, and commonly used databases like Web of Science or those offered by EBSCOhost, differ from search engines can help students understand the value of using different systems for different tasks. It can also reinforce the idea that one system is not sufficient for all information needs and that there is a benefit to carefully crafted digital collections that serve a specialized audience.

Navigation Tools

Understanding how organizing systems are structured and the underlying classification and naming helps students construct a geography of information. In this geography, finding and selection techniques are akin to navigation tools. Here we can teach students the skills of searching: how to develop keywords and search terms, how Boolean searching works, tricks like truncation and wildcards, how to take advantage of controlled vocabularies, and advanced limiters like file format or domain name. We can also introduce the idea that searching is only a starting point and that other techniques such as citation chaining and informed browsing can be more productive at different points in the research process.

People Organize Information

This theme permeates the organizing systems threshold concept, and yet it cannot be overemphasized. Information does not organize itself, nor do computers organize it by themselves. All information is organized according to decisions that humans make, whether directly about a given piece of information, as in assigning a subject heading, or through design decisions made while constructing an organizing system, or through building search algorithms. This impacts both how we retrieve information from organizing systems, as in choosing search terms, and how we organize and describe information for inclusion within organizing systems. We can encourage students to treat organizing systems with the same skepticism they would when evaluating a specific piece of information. Sometimes organizing systems can fade into the background, like a wall painted a neutral color, but focusing on the human side can help students foreground the systems, even if momentarily, and maintain a critical stance.

Advanced

Structuring Information and Data for Inclusion within Organizing Systems

Initial forays into this area are often taken in students' personal lives, through titling and tagging content for social media. The importance of these skills has increased with the rise of data-intensive research, institutional repositories, and personal information management systems. The ability to structure data and other information for inclusion in organizing systems is especially important as students develop into information creators, particularly in an academic context. For example, metadata creation in the context of data sets is dependent on the disciplinary context and technical considerations, in addition to granting agency and data repository requirements. The growing data curation movement in academic research and librarianship has created a wealth of educational and curricular resources from organizations such as IASSIST (International Association for Social Science Information Services and Technology), DataONE, ICPSR (Inter-university Consortium for Political and Social Research), and the

Digital Curation Centre, as well as libraries with well-established data programs, such as Purdue University Libraries, MIT Libraries, the University of Minnesota Libraries, and Lori's institution, the University of New Mexico University Libraries. Whether creating keywords and other basic metadata for their dissertation's inclusion in the institutional repository, designing and developing complex technical metadata in the context of a large research project, or simply creating an efficient and productive personal information management system, information creation requires that we consider how it will eventually be distributed in organizing systems.

Advanced Search Techniques for Specialized Systems

As students advance academically and professionally, we can teach them to take advantage of specialized collections. First, we can expose them to unique collections and databases: for example, archival collections like the New Mexico Digital Collections for humanists, databases of academic society publications like ASCE (American Society of Civil Engineers) for engineers, publicly available repositories like PubMed for health sciences, professionally oriented databases like IBISWorld for marketing, and data repositories like ICPSR for social scientists. Second, we can show them how to best use these collections, which typically involves taking advantage of the unique organizing systems that have been developed around organizing specific formats for discovery and dissemination. These systems are often less intuitive than the single search boxes offered by the new library discovery systems and web search engines. But they are often more powerful and allow the searcher more control through advanced filtering, limiters, and specialized controlled vocabularies that we can teach users to take advantage of.

Takeaways

- While it is now easy to find huge amounts of many types of information very quickly, the nature and function of that information, as well as the organizing systems that receive, store, and deliver information, are not so easy to understand.
- Search engines often return accurate and useful results, but they also replicate societal biases and paradigms constructed by the dominant culture.
- When individuals use organizing systems, they are just as likely to contribute information as they are to find it. When such systems span the corporate, governmental, and public spheres, the choices we make in naming, describing, and classifying information affect both our immediate lived experiences and society in general.

For Further Consideration

- Organizing systems create geographies of information that we navigate using our ability to search for and choose information. Think about the geographies of information you navigate daily, from a newspaper to a restaurant menu to an online store. Which navigation skills seem universal? What seems unique to that particular geography?
- Algorithms, though designed by humans with human intentions, seem more neutral than humans. How can librarians help users correct this misunderstanding?
- Language varies from person to person, which means that naming, classification, and meaning all vary as well. Still, most organizing systems demand a controlled vocabulary. How do you navigate this tension in your work as a librarian?

References

Angwin, J., Larson, J., Mattu, S., & Kirchner, L. (2016, May 23). Machine bias. Retrieved from ProPublica website: https://www.propublica.org/article/machine-bias-risk-assessments-in-criminal-sentencing

Association of College & Research Libraries. (2014). *Framework for information literacy for higher education*. Retrieved from http://www.ala.org/acrl/standards/ilframework

Berman, S. (1993). *Prejudices and antipathies*. Jefferson, NC: McFarland & Co. Retrieved from http://www.sanfordberman.org/prejant.htm

Bogost, I. (2015, January 15). The cathedral of computation. *The Atlantic*. Retrieved from https://www.theatlantic.com/technology/archive/2015/01/the-cathedral-of-computation/384300/

Brand, S. (1985). Hackers' conference 1984: Keep designing. *Whole Earth Review*, *46*, 44–55.

Brown, D. E. (1991). *Human universals*. New York, NY: McGraw-Hill.

Buckland, M. (2017). *Information and society*. Cambridge, MA: MIT Press.

Cho, J. S. (2016). *Producing discursive change: From "illegal aliens" to "unauthorized immigration" in library catalogs*. Retrieved from https://academicworks.cuny.edu/gc_etds/1559

Eubanks, V. (2018). *Automating inequality : How high-tech tools profile, police, and punish the poor*. New York, NY: St. Martin's Press.

Glushko, R. J. (2016). *The discipline of organizing: Core concepts edition*. Sebastopol, CA: O'Reilly Media.

Hofer, A. R., Townsend, L., & Brunetti, K. (2012). Troublesome concepts and information literacy: Investigating threshold concepts for IL instruction. *portal: Libraries and the Academy, 12*(4), 387–405. Retrieved from https://pdxscholar.library.pdx.edu/ulib_fac/60/

Konigsburg, E. L. (1998). *The view from Saturday*. New York, NY: Atheneum Books for Young Readers.

Noble, S. U. (2018). *Algorithms of oppression: How search engines reinforce racism*. New York, NY: New York University Press.

Pariser, E. (2011). *The filter bubble: What the internet is hiding from you*. New York, NY: Penguin Press.

Reiss, A. (2017, August 4). 622: Who you gonna call, Act two: A road by any other name. *This American Life*. Retrieved from https://www.thisamericanlife.org/622/who-you-gonna-call

Sherratt, T. (2015, February 3). Seams and edges: Dreams of aggregation, access & discovery in a broken world. *ALIA Online*. Retrieved from http://discontents.com.au/seams-and-edges-dreams-of-aggregation-access-discovery-in-a-broken-world/

Steiner, C. (2012). *Automate this: How algorithms came to rule our world*. New York, NY: Portfolio/Penguin.

Townsend, L., Hofer, A., Lin Hanick, S., & Brunetti, K. (2016). Identifying threshold concepts for information literacy: A Delphi study. *Communications in Information Literacy, 10*(1), 23–49. Retrieved from https://doi.org/10.15760/comminfolit.2016.10.1.13

Tucker, V. M. (2012). *Acquiring search expertise: Learning experiences and threshold concepts* (Doctoral dissertation). Queensland University of Technology, Brisbane, Australia. Retrieved from https://eprints.qut.edu.au/63652/

CHAPTER SEVEN

Research Process

Imagine you've just returned home after a successful trip to IKEA. Your living room is now crowded with a pile of flat boxes. You open the first box to find a set of paper directions where a funny little character leads you through the process of building your bookcase or chair or dresser. Included is a set of tools: maybe an Allen wrench, some small wooden plugs, and a few screws. In a couple of hours, depending on your aptitude for this sort of thing, you've either got a useful piece of furniture or an angry cat and spouse (or perhaps both).

Now imagine you are a master carpenter. You've spent years building the skills and knowledge necessary to design and construct beautiful, useful, custom pieces of furniture. You've assembled a large and carefully chosen collection of tools. When you begin a project, there are no directions or pre-engineered materials. You may hold a picture in your mind of a final product; you may sketch it down in detail. If it's an original piece, you know that you will likely make some mistakes along the way, try some new technique or material that doesn't work quite as expected, and have to try again. The design and build process, while generally predictable, will vary from project to project. Each step of the process will require multiple decisions, careful judgment, and finely honed skills. Parts of the process may stall or have to be redone. But, having gone through this process many times, you know that you will persist. And though it may not look exactly like your original design, you will eventually produce a functional, custom piece of furniture.

At the University of New Mexico, the University Libraries Instruction Working Group brainstormed the idea of "IKEA research" to describe the kind of research process that lower-division undergraduates are expected to master. Original research, asking novel questions to discover new knowledge, is typically the province of advanced graduate students and research faculty. IKEA research isn't useless, but it's a very different process. The space between the two is where students stretch toward new understandings and cross through the liminal space to become researchers. Given that librarians know the difference between IKEA research and original research, where does information literacy instruction fit into that process? Is it possible to help students assemble an IKEA shelf while also helping them move toward the stance and skill set of a master carpenter?

This chapter will explore the research process threshold concept by defining the research process, reviewing Carol Collier Kuhlthau's seminal writing on the affective side of search, dipping into the literature on creativity and curiosity as they connect to the research process, and exploring how the concept of ignorance can help our students make sense of research and become experts themselves. We've found that the research process is a topic that lends itself to lots and lots of metaphors (as in "IKEA research") and also that doing research on the research process can become all too real.

Research Process Defined

Browsing academic library websites shows how librarians tend to define the research process and communicate it to students. It's usually presented as a series of linear steps, often acknowledged as iterative. It sometimes overlaps with the writing process for lower-division undergraduates. Table 7.1 offers a few examples (Elmer E. Rasmuson Library, 2016; Engle, 2012; Georgia Tech Library, 2016).

Librarians often teach students these versions of the research process during instruction sessions and reference interactions. However, we also provide services for those who have already passed through the research process threshold and are producing original research. Therefore, subject librarians are usually familiar with the kinds of questions asked by researchers in a given field and the types of evidence acceptable within that field. We know what original scholarly research is and how it differs from other forms of research such as that undertaken in journalism or lower-division undergraduate writing classes. Our research process lists are typically designed with that undergraduate in mind. But while they might help a student complete a class assignment, they also offer a limited view of research—just the IKEA view. They seem to say that research mostly takes place in the library, that inquiry only happens during the topic development step, and that you'll feel much better once you actually start searching for sources.

Table 7.1 Linear Research Process Models

• Define your topic • Write a thesis or problem statement • Make an outline • Develop a Search Strategy • Evaluate your sources • Take careful notes • Writing and revising the paper • Document your sources	• Identify and develop your topic • Find background information • Use catalogs to find books and media • Use indexes to find periodical articles • Find internet resources • Evaluate what you find • Cite what you find using a standard format	• Develop a topic • Locate information • Evaluate and analyze information • Write, organize, and communicate information • Cite sources

The examples in Table 7.1 are not chosen to show that librarians don't understand how real research works but rather to emphasize that it's difficult to give accurate, concrete advice in the liminal space. Research process lists tend to stay at the IKEA level when they don't differentiate between the relatively easy and the really difficult steps. Developing a unique line of inquiry is far more challenging than compiling citations, but such lists put these two tasks on pretty much equal footing. Because they are structured linearly, as lists, the iterative nature of research is often not represented in an obvious way. Nor do they take into account the way that inquiry is essential to all the steps of the research process, long after it has been checked off on the list. As you evaluate and analyze information, for instance, you may also be adjusting, narrowing, or correcting your field of inquiry. In short, these lists represent IKEA research, rather than research as a master carpenter understands the term, which means that the IKEA researcher might not see what the differences are.

In an information literacy context, a definition of the research process needs to include what both novices and experts do. It must be broad enough to encompass investigations into new knowledge in the academic disciplines, as well as the pursuit of information that is necessary in our personal and working lives. Scholars approach their research in a more structured way than people do when researching ordinary things, with established criteria relating to the quality and purpose of their work. Most of our students will not become scholars, but they will gain transferable skills by learning how academic research is done.

We advocate for an approach to the research process that encompasses both scholarly and nonscholarly research, and therefore use the following definition:

> The research process is characterized by the formulation of an inquiry based on existing ignorance, the pursuit of information to answer, explore, and/or re-formulate the inquiry, the creation of new understandings in answering the inquiry using an appropriate method, and the communication of those new understandings to interested members of the community.

By defining the research process in this way, we bring into view the community where that research is situated. Community norms and disciplinary understandings shape not only *which* questions can be asked but also *how* the questions can be asked and answered; research is never conducted in a vacuum. The primary concern of the research process is not a search for information or even the finding of an answer or the solution to a problem, but the formulation of a meaningful inquiry.

Uncertainty and Other Uncomfortable Feelings

No discussion of the research process would be complete without considering Kuhlthau's groundbreaking research on the information search process. Initially working with a small group of high-performing high school students, Kuhlthau observed that the beginning of the research process was marked by feelings of uncertainty and frustration. In subsequent studies with different groups of library users and professionals, she developed a broadly applicable model of the research process that correlates commonly experienced feelings with each stage in the model. Summarizing her key insight, Kuhlthau writes,

> This research has revealed that people experience the process of information seeking holistically as an interplay of thoughts, feelings and actions . . . One of the more surprising findings was "the dip" . . . after a search had been initiated during the exploration stage. However, this experience is also one of the most recognizable to both librarians and library users when the model is presented to them. Users tend to think that they are the only ones to experience "the dip" before they become aware that it is a common occurrence in the [information search process]. (Kuhlthau, 1999)

Kuhlthau proposes different ways that librarians can intervene at various stages in the research process, taking into account the likely underlying feelings the student may be experiencing. Many of her recommendations have gained traction in reference and instruction settings, such as collaborative brainstorming activities, assigning research journals, tailoring assistance to the stage of the process on the basis of information elicited in a reference interview, and even simply acknowledging and normalizing how the student may be feeling (Kuhlthau, 1994). Kuhlthau's work is widely influential, included in library school syllabi, and has led to general acceptance of the idea that librarians should consider the whole person, including their emotions, when providing research assistance. Yet, it's relatively rare to see a model shared with students that includes affect, even though Kuhlthau definitely advises doing this (1994). Why does this knowledge about the affective side of research, then, sometimes stay in the background, as in the examples in Table 7.1?

We can't answer this question for all librarians, but we do have an idea: we think that librarians may hesitate to share what we know about affect at the beginning of the research process with students precisely because it is so uncomfortable. Kuhlthau finds that once the students in her study arrive at the stage of the process where they can begin collecting sources, they feel confident and curious. But before that, they move through uncomfortable emotions such as confusion and doubt. Similarly, Alison Head and Michael Eisenberg of Project Information Literacy find that college students struggle with fear of failure as they begin their research, likening the task of choosing a research topic to gambling:

> The beginning of research is when the first bets were placed. Choosing a topic is fraught with risk for many students. As one student acknowledged in interviews: either a topic worked well or it failed when it was too late to change it. (2010, p. 32)

Understandably, students want to rush past what's horrible and get straight to the part where they are self-assuredly looking for evidence. Searching is the relatively straightforward process of gathering information; it is where students start to feel better about their project, and it is also where librarians might feel most confident in helping students. Yet, as Holliday and Rogers (2013) assert, "learning about" is the primary goal, not "finding sources" (p. 265). The affective qualities associated with the research process are not reserved for novices alone; in the next section, we explore how creativity and curiosity manifest for expert researchers as well.

Becoming Expert Researchers

The difficulty of the transition from novice to expert through the research process threshold concept can be explored through a closer examination of a population that many academic librarians are quite familiar with: graduate students. Researcher Barbara Lovitts has examined the traits of graduate students whose dissertations succeed in making "an original and significant contribution to knowledge" (2008, p. 297). Her research highlights the differences between excellent course-takers (information consumers) and excellent independent researchers (information creators), and finds that one of the key differences is what she calls creative intelligence. Faculty describe creative students as "idea generators" or "idea factories" and admit that students who are mediocre course-takers may often make highly successful researchers and vice versa (p. 304). Despite the importance of creative intelligence in defining the transition to expert researcher, though, faculty members seem to regard this trait as inborn; they do not teach or otherwise enhance the ability through direct intervention. Unsurprisingly, faculty can struggle to guide students through this liminal space and can in fact find it difficult to explain their own approach to research, for they have reached the other side of the threshold.

In fact, highly successful research faculty aren't able to articulate exactly how they use creativity in their research, yet they do recognize its importance (Cravens, Ulibarri, Cornelius, Royalty, & Nabergoj, 2014). These faculty describe the beginning of the research process, the one Kuhlthau found most anxiety provoking in her study, as the most exciting and motivating part—even when they are stuck, because that is when they reexamine assumptions and rethink their framing. Faculty openly discussed the possibility and inevitability of failure, a notion terrifying to both undergraduate and graduate students, as a "normal part of the process of producing original research" (p. 237). Though these beginnings are an uncertain space, just as for the novices, instead of describing their primary experience as frustrating and discouraging, expert researchers found it exciting. (If you are reading this and thinking "I can't relate! I hate failing," consider whether being a professional researcher is your primary assignment.) These expert researchers understood the linchpin of the research process as the formulation and articulation of an inquiry. But how can creativity be better understood in this context?

Creativity is often viewed as a magical trait, possessed in great measure by geniuses. Psychologists have sought to understand creativity through an exploration of the great minds of Leonardo da Vinci, Jane Austen, Albert Einstein, Prince, and so on. However, in academic and scholarly work, creativity is associated with an original approach to solving new problems, which is why faculty bring up creativity again and again when speaking of research. Political scientist Li Bennich-Björkman, for example, pushes back against the idea of creativity as a "sign of genius and an ability reserved for the very few." Rather, she writes that an original scholarly contribution should, "apart from being novel, also be valuable, appropriate or relevant to the problem which it is supposed to address" (1997, p. 23). Psychologists James Kaufman and Ronald Beghetto propose that creativity is experienced by everyone and is a skill that can be developed, not a mystical ability (2009). Original research, and therefore creativity, must be used to ask questions that create new knowledge within the existing discourse of the discipline and, therefore, is something that can and should be taught.

However, creativity remains a trait that is freighted with value, particularly in the academic realm. Scholars associate originality with authenticity and integrity, while judging "unoriginal work as a sign of moral failure" (Guetzkow, Lamont, & Mallard, 2004, p. 191). Is it surprising, then, that students entering the academic context, simultaneously facing dire warnings against plagiarism and repeated urging from well-meaning instructors to come up with their own take, feel like they are gambling against the house when starting a research project?

While asking good questions involves creativity, curiosity is a trait that is at the heart of inquiry. Yet, students hesitate to indulge their natural curiosity in an academic context, though the possession of intellectual curiosity is a trait of the expert and is seen among academics as an essential part of becoming a researcher. Hannel Rempel and Anne-Marie Deitering (2017), in exploring the concept of curiosity in the research process, were intrigued by the lack of originality in undergraduate papers. These student papers were "lifeless" and described a research process "almost completely devoid of curiosity" (n.p.). They realized that students were playing it safe and that the negative affect described in Kuhlthau's work was manifesting as an avoidance of curiosity or any investment in topics they cared about. The research process wasn't used by these novices to pose new and interesting questions but to confirm existing beliefs or explore commonplace topics (e.g., medical marijuana, global warming) in the hope of avoiding failure. The joy and passion of curiosity can be sidelined by fear, in favor of a (weak) guarantee of academic success. In contrast, expert researchers know that failure is inevitable and use the uncertain beginnings of the research process as a place to explore and prepare for the work ahead. Can we help our students make that connection, not only admitting that the research process begins in anxiety but also understanding that this energy can be recast as excitement, perhaps employing some techniques to lower the stakes, to help them move through the challenges ahead?

Ignorance in the Research Process

Let's talk about ignorance. A common assumption is that the research process is important because the pursuit of knowledge is fundamentally noble. By extension, one might paint ignorance as an evil to be banished, perhaps even a boogeyman to run away from, certainly something to be ashamed of. Ignorance, especially in the post-truth era, can seem like an enemy that librarians must teach students to do battle with. However, in developing the research process threshold concept, we found ignorance to be a friend and working partner. We think that the concept of ignorance can help reduce student anxiety and negative affect by clarifying the goals of research.

In his book *Ignorance: How It Drives Science*, Stuart Firestein (2012) argues that scientists are driven by seeking new questions rather than finding answers. Part of the satisfaction in pursuing ignorance is in proving the past wrong, whether the past is your own previous understanding or the understandings of your discipline. Rather than seeing ignorance as something to be avoided at all costs, in this view scientists actively pursue the discovery of new ignorance. The University of Arizona's medical school has operationalized this approach in their Curriculum on Medical Ignorance. Among the curriculum goals, they seek to

> [i]mprove skills to recognize and deal productively with ignorance, uncertainty, and the unknown: questioning critically and creatively focusing on raising, listening to, analyzing, prioritizing, and answering questions from different points of view . . . Reinforce positive attitudes and values of curiosity, optimism, humility, self-confidence, and skepticism. (University of Arizona Health Sciences Center, 2017)

In recasting ignorance as not just acceptable, but as a sought-after and productive state, this curriculum transforms ignorance from something to fear into a positive mind-set for asking good questions about what isn't already known. This approach can be helpful in pursuing inquiry in any discipline (not just the sciences), because a primary purpose of research is to uncover new ignorance, not to confirm old ideas.

Identifying and articulating useful research questions in an academic setting is difficult intellectual work requiring an existing foundation of knowledge. Applying information to a problem—or using it as evidence in an argument or for inspiration in a creative endeavor—requires that the researcher understand what qualifies as disciplinary evidence. Engaging in the information creation process is an extension of the analytical and creative thinking processes. All of these are paid for in blood, sweat, and tears.

The novice researcher will often collect information on a topic, summarize, and recommunicate it, without understanding how to ask and answer an original question. The expert recognizes that the process of inquiry, research, and creation is iterative, requiring researchers to move through uncertainty repeatedly as they make mistakes, correct earlier misapprehensions, and progress toward new understandings and further inquiry. Understanding the relationship between inquiry and ignorance crucially helps shift the meaning of research from gathering information about what is already known to asking questions about the unknown. Educational theorist John Dewey encapsulated this: "As the saying goes, a question well put is half answered. Problem and solution stand out completely at the same time. Up to that point, our grasp of the problem has been more or less vague and tentative" (as cited in Kuhlthau, 2004, p. 16). And the initial struggle of the novice highlights the centrality of inquiry formulation to the research process and reveals it as *the* problem for students.

Inquiry Is Not an Individual Pursuit

Inquiry formulation does not, however, happen in isolation. Novice researchers seek to join an ongoing conversation in which new knowledge is negotiated and mediated by the norms of a practitioner community. The expert has moved through most of the understandings available on a particular topic—what humanists might call the corpus—and is therefore also an expert in his or her own ignorance and the collective ignorance of the discipline. The expert's questions are informed by those understandings, and their inquiry creates new knowledge and ignorance, both personal and collective. The beginner is struggling to move through established understandings, barely knows enough to sketch the boundaries of their current state of ignorance, and may not connect that struggle, that personal inquiry and contention with ignorance, to the struggle that the expert experiences. They are not in a position to be creative in the same way as the expert because they have not learned enough about the context of their discipline. However, when an inquiry is formed, new connections are made, and this iterative process, from the creation of an inquiry, to seeking out existing knowledge, to the selection of relevant information, to the development and testing of an informed inquiry, and the subsequent analysis and synthesis of the results, is the same one that experts engage with in the creation of new knowledge.

The metaphor of scholarship as a conversation is useful because it emphasizes that these processes take place in the context of a community that includes experts, novices, and apprentices. Developing expertise is a process, and learners can be assisted by those more expert in the field as well as those with allied expertise (e.g., librarians) who can assist in developing skills and understanding. Generally speaking, communities uphold standards and exert influence on the content produced within those guidelines. Medical student residencies and student-teacher internship requirements enable communities of practice to ensure that novices receive advice and guidance in practice and conceptual knowledge acquisition, and ensure that standards are upheld in a rigorous way. As we discussed in Chapter 3, "Authority," however, communities at times have difficulty negotiating new standards or shared understandings and can silence dissenters (e.g., consider the fate of Galileo).

While understanding scholarship as a conversation democratizes research and opens the door to previously underrepresented content creators, it would be disingenuous not to also acknowledge the barriers to entry to scholarly conversations. Just as Wikipedians have their own rules and culture for contribution, scholars have expectations about credentials, impact, style, and other criteria for inclusion. Raising questions about this issue can be part of the process of knowledge creation, as in literary criticism where research into voices excluded from the traditional canon has opened new disciplines of study. A crucial part of the research process, then, is access to scholarly conversations.

Kuhlthau usefully points out that "the expert is rarely at the true beginning, as is the novice who holds only a few constructs on the topic" (2004, p. 93). The work a researcher does to both construct meaning from information and reincorporate that meaning into the process of inquiry is an act of creation, as is communicating those results in an appropriate format to the larger community. Moving from consuming information to creating it, in this community context, distinguishes the novice from the expert. Barbara Fister writes of wanting for her students:

> A chance to investigate a question that genuinely matters to them, to say something in their own voice, something that isn't formulaic, that hasn't been said before so it can be cited ... permission to turn the conversation in a new direction or to apply the tools of inquiry to their own lives and communities. (2017, p. x)

As we described previously, creativity is one of the markers of the expert researcher. However, novices also need to figure out how to be creative in a specific context (a threshold that readers of this book can likely relate to).

A Single Step versus the Whole Entire Process

To bring together the ideas we've considered so far, we argue that inquiry defines the entire research process rather than representing a single step of that process. Information literacy has traditionally been defined as starting with an information need, which students are often asked to define through a process of topic development (Association of College & Research Libraries, 2006). The student, as characterized by Andrew Abbott, "might think that the answer to any possible question or puzzle is out there somewhere in the library or online, and the 'research' means finding that answer" (2014, p. 1). The real work of the research process, though, is in making sense of that information and exploring meaningful research questions that lead to new understandings. In a review of Kuhlthau's book, *Seeking Meaning*, Marcia Bates observes,

> As long as the old model prevails, formulating the topic of a paper will be seen to involve plucking a topic like an apple off a tree—a single task that precedes the real business of gathering information and writing the paper. (1994, p. 474)

Topic development, therefore, is a tricky phrase because it attempts to simplify and contain an inherently messy undertaking and may in fact obscure the entire purpose of the research process.

Making research more palatable for students by limiting inquiry to the topic development step of the model, when inquiry actually is essential to the entire research process, does students a disservice. We had great difficulty in thinking of another situation where a whole process is boiled down and made to represent just one step of that process—probably because doing this doesn't make very much sense. We came up with three different metaphors to help clarify our meaning here. Before we start, it may be helpful to know that while writing this book, this group of coauthors also adopted two puppies and a kitten. Dog people, here we go.*

First, the way that some research models outline topic development is like giving a puppy a bath. Rosie *hates* baths. Correction: Rosie hates the *idea* of baths. Once she is being lathered, rinsed, and dried, it's not so bad.

---

*Cat people, here's a metaphor for you: When Silvia visited Portland and met Wendell, she bought him one green mouse toy and one gray mouse toy, which are called Silvia and Conor, respectively. Three months later, Silvia had lost an ear and her stuffing was coming out, while Conor was like new. The novice (human) doesn't see the difference between the toys (lines of inquiry). The expert (Wendell) has a clear favorite for reasons that are not apparent to the outsider.

At the first sign of running water, however, she takes off running. The challenge of bathing Rosie is in chasing her all over the house, catching her, and getting her into the bathtub without also getting fear-pee all over the floors. It would not be very helpful to Lori if all of the available advice about how best to bathe a dog treated this prebath battle as an easy first step to take before you move on to choosing the type of shampoo that is best suited for a particular breed, using a rubber brush like a Zoom Groom to get into the undercoat, and making sure to keep water temperatures tepid. Likewise, when librarians teach the research process with a simple step-by-step model, equal weight is given to topic development, searching, evaluating, and using sources. Searching, evaluating, and using sources are important skills, but they are meaningless until you've tracked down a line of inquiry worth pursuing. Coming up with a topic and getting Rosie into the bathtub are uniquely difficult parts of a process, but they are rarely acknowledged as such.

Second, picking a topic is a lot like going for a ride in a car. Puppies, or novices, may find their first car rides to be terrifying. They are getting into a fast-moving machine, entering into the wild unknown. Will they live in the car forever? Is this a journey to their doom? Older dogs, or experts, know that car rides are a means to an end. Sure, there is a bit of uncertainty and discomfort, but the dominant emotion is excitement, not fear. For every vet visit, there are countless rides to hike in the mountains, visit great smelling friends, and bark at the ocean. You may not know where you're going, but it'll probably be interesting. There may even be a chance to put your head outside the window or chase an unfamiliar leaf. In developing an inquiry, uncertainty is a given. Novices may see this uncertainty as frustrating or confusing; an expert will treat uncertainty as possibility and opportunity.

Third, developing an inquiry is like giving a puppy a basket of balls. For Norbert's first birthday, he received a dozen balls in a basket, one ball for each month of his first year of life. There were balls in a rainbow of colors, squeaky balls, spiky balls, and hollow balls with treats hidden inside. For all of his delight, Norbert also had to deal with new challenges. This was not the linear game of fetch to which he was accustomed, where one standard tennis ball is thrown and retrieved. He scampered after one ball, only to be distracted by another. He tried to bring back two balls at once but dropped the ball in his mouth when trying to pick up the second ball. Initially, a research topic may feel like a tidy basket of balls, where the basket is the inquiry holding in a range of possible research directions. As you develop your inquiry, however, the basket tips over, and suddenly you find yourself chasing ideas in every direction. Maybe one idea feels great, so you settle in and try to get the biscuit hidden inside. Then, you see a fuzzy ball out of the corner of your eye, and you're off again.

Silvia once met with an engineering student from a Technical Writing class who unknowingly put a bow on our dog metaphors. His initial topic was one specific car: the Honda Civic Type R. That's it. In his library instruction session, he learned how to find articles from trade publications and scholarly journals. He found a few articles about the Civic Type R and spent the rest of the time looking at his phone. In a follow-up session, Silvia focused her instruction on refining research topics. "Can you answer your research question in one sentence?" she asked. "If you can, you also need to ask, 'so what?' " At this point, the student realized that his topic was much too narrow. He knew how to give a dog a bath, but the dog was *not* in the bathtub. He grew concerned about having to start over and considered switching his topic to solar panels. He knew he could find, choose, and use information, but without a solid inquiry, he was lost. As a novice, he was willing to give up on a topic he cared about to avoid the challenge of trying to make it work. As an expert, Silvia convinced him to get back in the car because research is always more fun if you choose a topic that excites you. "Tell me why you like cars, and I bet you'll have a topic," Silvia said. "I feel like I'm in a ball pit," he replied, "there's too much to say and I can't get up." (Silvia had not told him about the basket of balls—this was his own description!) After an intense reference interview and a one-on-one consultation-slash-pep-talk, Silvia worked with the student to craft a new topic: How has the use of front-wheel drive, the V6 engine, and hybrid technology in nonluxury cars allowed nonprofessionals to maximize performance in racing conditions? Even with a topic in hand, however, it is worth remembering that this student's process of inquiry was far from over. Away from the library, he would need to read articles that revealed new areas of ignorance, develop ideas about the best evidence to include, and work to communicate everything he learned.

Nonlinearity

Other writers, too, often turn to extended metaphors in trying to describe what it feels like to engage in the kind of inquiry that creates new knowledge. It was not hard to find several interesting examples. Teaching assistant and PhD student Maja Maksimović writes, "I feel that my research is calling me, evokes me and rejects me. We are in a relationship, conflict, misunderstanding and friendship" (2015, p. 2). Doctoral student Sarah Elliott described her struggle to shift her worldview to that of professional researcher as a tug-of-war (Elliott, Glynn, & Morris, 2016). A doctoral student interviewed by Gina Wisker and Gillian Robinson described their creative academic process as "something between a wandering minstrel I suppose and the person who paints the white lines down the middle of the road" (Wisker & Robinson, 2014, p. 57).

Metaphors are a productive tool for describing the research process. Marybeth Meszaros and Allison Lewis warn that when applying conceptual metaphor theory to academic librarianship, "conventional metaphors can squelch unconventional, critical thinking" (2015, p. 56). Yet, *unconventional* metaphors can, at least on a temporary basis, enable new understandings. Extended metaphors can, in fact, turn into models for finding new understandings of a topic or problem. Models are considered by some to be a type of metaphor, as in the following definition from *The Blackwell Guide to the Philosophy of Science*:

> A model is an interpretative description of a phenomenon that facilitates access to that phenomenon . . . Facilitating access usually involves focusing on specific aspects of a phenomenon, sometimes deliberately disregarding others. As a result, models tend to be partial descriptions only . . . Models and metaphors exploit the strategy of understanding something in terms of something else that is better understood and more familiar; they exploit the analogy relationship suggested by a metaphor or explored in a model. (Bailer-Jones, 2002, pp. 108–109, 118)

We began this chapter by asking whether it is possible to help students do well on typical undergraduate research assignments (IKEA research) while also helping them understand how these assignments relate to what professional researchers do (master carpenters). We propose that the answer may in part lie in the models, or metaphors, that we present to students. Many models, as we have seen, focus on the stepwise aspect of research; we propose that students would also benefit from models that focus on the nonlinearity of research—that is, the ways that inquiry is essential throughout the process.

For example, North Carolina State University Libraries created a short video that directly addresses why students get stuck when their mental model of the research process is "a one-way street" (i.e., linear). The video offers an alternative model of research as a cycle, assisted by animation, in order to show that "picking your topic is intertwined with finding and reading sources and writing and editing your paper. Picking your topic IS research" (NCSU Libraries, 2013). By embracing the nonlinear research process, the video validates the feelings students will later experience; when students arrive at the twisty, overlapping steps of the process, they'll know that they're doing everything right.

In another example, Sarah Polkinghorne shares a visualization with students that divides search into "Internal: you create" and "External: you learn, adapt to, contribute to, critique" (2016, p. 82). The model is designed for the purpose of prompting discussion about search practices without a predefined beginning-middle-end structure. Instead, the searcher is in the middle of the model. On one side are the parts of the process that the searcher has direct control over: your topic, words you might use in a search. On the other side are the parts of the process that the searcher doesn't control but can make use of, challenge, learn from, and perhaps add to: information sources and organizing systems. Polkinghorne writes that students respond to her model with greater awareness of the complexity of search; perhaps the model enables novices to articulate aspects that did not seem worthy of comment in relation to a linear model (Polkinghorne, 2016).

Rempel and Deitering write about curiosity as something that is "sparked"; this choice of words emphasizes that curiosity is nonlinear, relying rather on sudden and discontinuous leaps of thought. They realized that librarian intervention needs to come before topic selection—maybe this is "step zero" in the typical research process list. How can librarians help students make the connection not only that the research process begins in anxiety and fear but also that this energy can be harnessed and redirected to help them move through the challenges ahead? They suggest a number of techniques that can reduce anxiety by scaffolding exploration through low-stakes activities. For example, they encourage students to take a self-assessment on the basis of recent research into different types of curiosities, which is paired with reflective activities about how this insight might be applied in an academic setting. They use Oregon State University's news feed of press releases about faculty research to help students understand the context and purpose of scholarly formats. They also recommend working closely with disciplinary faculty when possible to redesign assignments in a way that will break the habit of relying on familiar topics (Rempel & Deitering, 2017).

Applying the Threshold Concepts Criteria

Crossing this threshold is transformative because it reveals the purpose of research conducted in the library, the lab, and beyond; research is positioned as one means by which new knowledge may be created, and it connects the novice in the classroom to a broad web of thinkers and creators who transcend space and time. The stages of the research process in a linear model—defining an information need, searching for information, and using information—are placed in perspective. Research is no longer simply the retrieval and compilation of discrete facts about a topic but is shown to solve problems, answer questions, and generate new lines of inquiry through the discovery of new ignorance.

The research process concept is irreversible because once you understand the purpose of research as the development of new inquiry rather than confirming prior understandings, you will not mistake reportage for research and will recognize the difference in your own work and the work of others. It is not possible to return to the idea of a lone genius with a lightbulb over his or her head or to treat one's own work as produced in a vacuum. Here is a true story about how challenging this aspect of the research process can be. Silvia did not fully cross the threshold on the research process until nearly four years into her first job as a librarian and several classes into her MA in English. In preparing an annotated bibliography for a paper examining references to Shakespeare's tragedies in George Eliot's novels, she was excited to discover several books and many articles already written about the topic. In her mind, coming up with a topic that so many scholars had already addressed meant that she was onto something good. When her annotated bibliography was returned, her professor circled these sources and asked, "How is your paper different?" "It's not," Silvia thought, "but why does that matter? This is just a paper for class." It took several more drafts, many office visits, and much frustration before Silvia managed to articulate how her paper would do more than report on, and replicate, previous works on the topic. Now on the other side, Silvia cannot separate the concept of research from novel inquiry.

This concept is integrative because it brings together the skills necessary for developing an inquiry about a topic and combines them with those required for finding and communicating information. Scholarly conventions, like citation and referencing institutional affiliations, which beginners may have observed, are now understood to be part of an entire culture that produces knowledge rather than isolated lessons about format or authority. It integrates the undergraduate topic development process with the kind of inquiry that expert researchers do. And it situates research within a community, because research is part of a scholarly conversation.

This threshold concept is troublesome because it might seem like asking questions should be easy and that ignorance is an evil to be banished. Good questions may be perceived as springing forth whole from the creative mind rather than as the culmination of research applied to existing ignorance. It may not be obvious or comfortable to consider knowledge being negotiated rather than fixed. One particularly troublesome area might be background research in service of developing an inquiry. For the novice, the copious reading associated with background research may feel like a waste of time; it's all the more frustrating if the reading doesn't even wind up counting toward the number of sources your instructor required for the assignment.

Experts, however, tend to use background research as a way to figure out which lines of inquiry to follow. One way we frame this is to compare background research to planning a travel itinerary. Say you are going on a weeklong vacation to Hawaii and you'd like to eat everything the islands have to offer. It may be tempting to start making reservations, but another way to go about things is to consider what you don't know about Hawaiian cuisine. As you read, you may find out that poke and sashimi are different, though both feature fresh fish served raw. Or, you'll discover that Hawaiians are the second-largest consumers of spam, after Guam, and that you should definitely try it in sushi (or skip it altogether). You'll learn that colonialism and immigration have influenced a number of dishes and look for the way loco moco blends multiple influences. Maybe you've never had breadfruit, winged beans, or mountain apples, and this will be your chance. Once you know about what you want to eat, *then* you can start researching specific restaurants. After all, how can you find the best malasada if you didn't even know this amazing combination of fried dough and custard existed?

While the research process is a priority throughout academia, information science emphasizes an examination of the process by which new knowledge is created, discovered, and disseminated, more than the intellectual results of such research. Librarians have a unique perspective because we are familiar with varied paths of inquiry that span across disciplines and are well positioned to offer insight on how to structure a question, where to ask it, and how to adjust on the basis of new information. More often than not, librarians meet students at their point of need; most one-shot library instruction sessions, after all, are scheduled just as, or just after, students start the research process. Librarians can validate the feelings of discomfort that students experience in the first stages of building an inquiry and perhaps intervene when curiosity is sacrificed in pursuit of a safe research topic.

Teaching the Research Process

Basic

Research/Science as the Pursuit of Ignorance

Scholars are driven by what they don't know, more than the much smaller number of things that they do know. The goal of research isn't to find, understand, memorize, and recommunicate a body of knowledge, but to learn enough to identify the next horizon of ignorance. The goal is to pose better, more informed questions, some of which might be answerable or partially answerable using disciplinary methodologies. Research is perhaps best approached as an exploration of personal and societal ignorance rather than as a problem to solve or an answer to be found. If the research process is one grounded in the production of new ignorance, it moves the novice away from basic misconceptions. For example, that research is: out of reach for them personally, about finding existing facts to answer relatively simplistic questions, the reporting of information discovered through basic search processes like a search engine query, or easy (as in "this should be easy; why am I struggling/stupid?"). Librarians can bring in experts to discuss what they don't know and communicate the excitement that research represents to the expert. Librarians can also support the exploration of novice ignorance by creating spaces that encourage students to admit when they don't know something and celebrate the generation of new questions as a result.

Question Formulation (IKEA Research)

Generating good questions can seem to be a talent, like creativity, that some possess and some don't. However, the art of questioning is one that can be taught. Using the Question Formulation Techniques developed by the Right Question Institute (2018; detailed further in Chapter 9) and the pedagogical approaches used in programs such as the University of Arizona Curriculum on Medical Ignorance, librarians can center the process of constructing and improving questions in learning. With straightforward and concrete guidance, students can improve their ability to ask pertinent and meaningful questions, which can also help reduce the anxiety that is intrinsic to the exploratory stages of the research process. Librarians can teach students how to ask questions and use curiosity to lead them down new paths despite a natural fear of failure. Yes, there are no stupid questions, but students can also learn to ask smarter questions. And sometimes the most ignorant beginner's questions can overturn an entire field of knowledge. After all, Maya Lin was a 21-year-old undergraduate student at Yale when she submitted her controversial and moving design for the Vietnam Veterans Memorial. After studying monuments and memorials from the past, Lin noted that most "carried larger, more general messages about a leader's victory or accomplishments rather than the lives lost" and wondered, "what then would bring back the memory of a person?" (Lin, 2000). A complete novice with no professional design experience, Lin proposed a design that was initially criticized for being unpatriotic, bleak, and unremarkable. Today, the Vietnam Veterans Memorial is one of the most visited memorials in Washington, DC, and widely acknowledged as a major milestone in 20th-century art.

Research Process Model and Experience

What is the reality of how doing research feels? How do experts cope with the ambiguity and fear? Negative affect around the research process includes feelings of uncertainty, struggles with the fear of failure, and feelings of stupidity when faced with difficult understandings or complexities beyond the scope of initial investigations. Novices and experts alike may share feelings of isolation, which creates a funny paradox where we always feel alone when doing research, even though the act of research is undertaken to increase knowledge and knowledge is generated in the context of a community. Understanding the affective side of research can help a student move past the initial and expected negative feelings around topic selection and preresearch into the more comfortable phases of focus formulation and information collection (Kuhlthau, 2004). The expert has learned to cope with these negative feelings and transform early uncertainty into excitement. The expert experiences early phases of research as exciting, creative, and energy generating, even while acknowledging ambivalence and the possibility of failure. Repeated exposure to the research process cycle, through a variety of projects where creativity and ignorance are centered, can help acclimate the novice to the difficulties while emphasizing the positives.

Scholars Are People Having Conversations

Conducting research often feels lonely. However, new knowledge is always negotiated and created in the context of a community, as represented by individuals, scholarly disciplines, and professions, which can be compared to a conversation. Why are these conversations difficult to approach, let alone engage in? Some modes of conversation have high barriers to access—for example, in many disciplines publication and dissemination of new ideas occur almost entirely in extremely expensive journals. Other parts of the scholarly conversation would be almost impossible to commodify—for example, colleagues discussing a project while taking a walk around campus—yet this mode of conversation may be difficult to access for the novice for entirely different social reasons. Still, these conversations become more approachable when students understand that *people* are responsible for the production of new knowledge, rather than artifacts like dusty books in the library and journal article pdfs found through database searches. This understanding also uncovers the connections between pieces of scholarly or professional literature as exchanges between researchers and innovators who are engaged in inquiry around interconnected topics. The metaphor of the conversation is limited but potentially transformative, once students grasp that all research is communication between people who are pursuing new ways of understanding, creating, and acting in the world.

Bibliographies as Conversation

Influential conversations take place in many environments. In the music world, for instance, Beyoncé, Usher, and Madonna all list Michael Jackson as a source of inspiration. Likewise, Michael Jackson named Diana Ross, James Brown, Frankie Lymon, Fred Astaire, and many others as his influences. A superfan even made an infographic illustrating this web of influence that functions much like a citation map generated by Web of Science (Sheldon, 2013). Read as an ongoing conversation, the bibliography of a scholarly paper becomes a point of access for the novice researcher.

Advanced

Knowledge Is Created/Negotiated in a Community

Original research is generated by individuals and groups of people. New knowledge, however, is built in the context of existing knowledge and must contend with the structures, norms, and expectations of a disciplinary community. At the upper undergraduate or graduate level, this understanding helps ground the literature review as an exploration of our current state of disciplinary ignorance. This understanding also expands the earlier framing of scholarship as a conversation to scholarship as a network of conversations shared within a community of inquiry.

Question Formulation in the Pursuit of Original Research

At this level, meaningful and skilled questions lead to the generation of original research. New knowledge is created by effective problem framing, the application of disciplinary methodologies, and prioritizing the discovery of new ignorance. Advancing students are learning how to develop questions that can be answered and the techniques to discover answers. The goal of generating, recognizing, and prioritizing interesting questions shifts from the efficient and critical consumption of knowledge to the creative generation of new knowledge or the improvement of existing approaches and processes in a profession. Here, students engage directly with the discipline. As they confront the realities of working as a practitioner in the field, they will also seek out more dynamic forms of apprenticeship; they are no longer getting through one class on a subject but preparing for a career in the discipline. Most students at this level are already accustomed to producing excellent work. The shift, however, comes when their work moves from competent to competitive. It is no longer enough to write a good paper; the research product must withstand the peer review process and include original insights that contribute to the disciplinary conversation.

Disciplinary Methodologies

Disciplinary structures (theoretical foundations and core understandings) facilitate and shape the creation of new knowledge. These foundational assumptions and understandings can both help and hinder the discovery of new knowledge. Disciplinary methodologies dictate the structure of research questions and the kind of evidence considered valid. Advanced students learn the specifics of these disciplinary and professional approaches from experts in their field of study.

Literature Review as Scholarly Conversation

In the academic context, a basic step toward this concept is the realization that citation has a function beyond the negative purpose of avoiding plagiarism. At a more advanced level, writing a literature review demonstrates awareness of the existing strands of scholarly discourse already happening around a topic. In some cases, close study of existing scholarly conversations will lead to a new inquiry as a literature review reveals gaps in the conversation. In fact, this conversation—that is, the scholarly literature—makes the most sense when it is approached with a research question in mind. While not a format that lends itself to reading for pleasure, academic papers become compelling when approached with a question, and that question must in turn be informed by the scholarly conversation.

Takeaways

- The research process is centered on novel inquiry, rather than identifying answers to questions.
- Frustration, doubt, and insecurity should be normalized for the novice researcher so that they may find a way into the excitement, creativity, and curiosity with which expert researchers approach the process.

- Although the research process can feel isolating, it is, in fact, centered within disciplinary communities, communities of inquiry, and communities of practice.

For Further Consideration

- Can you remember the feeling of being an undergraduate and realizing that you could not ask an original question? Do you remember the first time you asked an original question?
- Though it is seldom acknowledged, much of the research process is defined by affect. What do you do, as an instructor, to mitigate anxiety when working with students on the research process? What can you do to encourage students to practice curiosity and take risks rather than pick safe topics?
- What are the limits of knowledge in library and information science? Where should librarians seek new ignorance?

References

Abbott, A. (2014). *Digital paper: A manual for research and writing with library and internet materials*. Chicago, IL: The University of Chicago Press.

Association of College & Research Libraries. (2006). *Presidential committee on information literacy: Final report*. Retrieved from http://www.ala.org/acrl/publications/whitepapers/presidential

Bailer-Jones, D. M. (2002). Models, metaphors and analogies. In P. K. Machamer & M. Silberstein (Eds.), *The Blackwell guide to the philosophy of science* (pp. 108–127). Malden, MA: Blackwell. Retrieved from http://www.zolaist.org/wiki/images/a/ad/Models,_Metaphors,_and_Analogies.pdf

Bates, M. J. (1994). Seeking meaning: A process approach to library and information services by Carol Collier Kuhlthau. *Library Quarterly: Information, Community, Policy, 64*(4), 473–475.

Bennich-Björkman, L. (1997). *Organising innovative research: The inner life of university departments*. Oxford, England: Elsevier Science, Ltd.

Cravens, A. E., Ulibarri, N., Cornelius, M., Royalty, A., & Nabergoj, A. S. (2014). Reflecting, iterating, and tolerating ambiguity: Highlighting the creative process of scientific and scholarly research for doctoral education. *International Journal of Doctoral Studies, 9*, 229–247. Retrieved from http://ijds.org/Volume9/IJDSv9p229-247Cravens0637.pdf

Elliott, S., Glynn, A., & Morris, J. (2016). From practitioner to researcher: A threshold concept—A personal reflection on my own "tug of war." *International Journal of Practice-Based Learning in Health and Social Care, 4*(1), 78–87. doi:10.18552/ijpblhsc.v4i1.203 78

Elmer E. Rasmuson Library. (2016, August 25). Library research process. Retrieved from the University of Alaska Fairbanks website: http://library.uaf.edu/ls101-reading-library-research-process

Engle, M. (2012, September 18). The seven steps of the research process. Retrieved from Cornell University Library website: https://olinuris.library.cornell.edu/content/seven-steps-research-process

Firestein, S. (2012). *Ignorance: How it drives science*. Oxford, England: Oxford University Press.

Fister, B. (2017). Foreword. In A. Deitering, R. Schroeder, & R. Stoddart (Eds.), *The self as subject: Autoethnographic research into identity, culture, and academic librarianship* (pp. vii–xii). Chicago, IL: Association of College & Research Libraries.

Georgia Tech Library. (2016, September 26). Research process: A step-by-step guide: Get started. Retrieved from http://libguides.gatech.edu/researchprocess

Guetzkow, J., Lamont, M., & Mallard, G. (2004). What is originality in the humanities and the social sciences? *American Sociological Review, 69*(2), 190–212. doi:10.1177/000312240406900203

Head, A. J., & Eisenberg, M. B. (2010). *Truth be told: How college students evaluate and use information in the digital age*. Retrieved from http://www.projectinfolit.org/uploads/2/7/5/4/27541717/pil_fall2010_survey_fullreport1.pdf

Holliday, W., & Rogers, J. (2013). Talking about information literacy: The mediating role of discourse in a college writing classroom. *portal: Libraries and the Academy, 13*(3), 257–271. doi:10.1353/pla.2013.0025

Kaufman, J. C., & Beghetto, R. A. (2009). Beyond big and little: The four C model of creativity. *Review of General Psychology, 13*(1), 1–12. doi:10.1037/a0013688

Kuhlthau, C. C. (1994). Students and the information search process: Zones of intervention for librarians. *Advances in Librarianship, 18*, 57–72. Retrieved from https://www.researchgate.net/profile/Carol_Kuhlthau/publication/235299125_Students_and_the_Information_Search_Process_Zones_of_Intervention_for_Librarians/links/55bce01f08aec0e5f44453fa/Students-and-the-Information-Search-Process-Zones-of-Intervention-for-Librarians.pdf

Kuhlthau, C. C. (1999). Accommodating the user's information search process: Challenges for information retrieval system designers. *Bulletin of the Association for Information Science and Technology, 25*(3), 12–16.

Kuhlthau, C. C. (2004). *Seeking meaning: A process approach to library and information services*. Westport, CT: Libraries Unlimited.

Lin, M. (2000, November 2). Making the memorial. *New York Review of Books*. Retrieved from http://www.nybooks.com/articles/2000/11/02/making-the-memorial/

Lovitts, B. E. (2008). The transition to independent research: Who makes it, who doesn't, and why. *Journal of Higher Education, 79*(3), 296–325. Retrieved from https://doi.org/10.1353/jhe.0.0006

Maksimović, M. (2015). *Research process as a liminal space—Blurring the boundaries between art and science*. Presentation at the 3rd Conference on arts-based research and arts research, Faculty of Fine Arts, University of Porto, Porto, Portugal. Retrieved from http://3c.nea.fba.up.pt/sites/3c.nea.fba.up.pt/files/FINAL_Research%20Process%20as%20a%20Liminal%20Space%20Maja%20Maksimovic.pdf

Meszaros, M., & Lewis, A. M. (2015). Librarianspeak: Metaphors that reflect (and shape) the ethos and practice of academic librarianship. In T. A. Swanson & H. Jagman (Eds.), *Not just where to click: Teaching students how to think about information* (pp. 53–85). Chicago, IL: Association of College & Research Libraries.

NCSU Libraries. (2013). Picking your topic IS research! Retrieved from https://www.lib.ncsu.edu/tutorials/picking_topic/

Polkinghorne, S. (2016). Critical consciousness and search: An introductory visualization. In N. Pagowsky & K. McElroy (Eds.), *Critical library pedagogy handbook* (pp. 81–86). Chicago, IL: American Library Association. Retrieved from https://doi.org/10.7939/R3FX7454P

Rempel, H. G., & Deitering, A. M. (2017). Sparking-curiosity—Librarians' role in encouraging exploration. *In the Library with the Lead Pipe*. Retrieved from http://www.inthelibrarywiththeleadpipe.org/2017/sparking-curiosity/

The Right Question Institute. (2018). Teach students to ask their own questions. Retrieved from http://rightquestion.org/education/

Sheldon, C. (2013, May). *Getting to the research roots: Musical metaphors for citation tracking*. Paper presented at LOEX, Nashville, TN.

University of Arizona Health Sciences Center. (2017). Curriculum on medical ignorance.Retrieved from Q-Cubed website: http://ignorance.medicine.arizona.edu/programs/curriculum-medical-ignorance

Wisker, G., & Robinson, G. (2014). Experiences of the creative doctorate: Minstrels and white lines. *Critical Studies in Teaching and Learning (CriSTaL)*, 2(2), 49–67. doi:10.14426/cristal.v2i2.36

PART III

Threshold Concepts for Information Literacy in Practice

CHAPTER EIGHT

Assessment and Threshold Concepts

Do threshold concepts belong to a discussion of assessment and accreditation when so much good work has already been done by the library profession in these areas? Our group of authors initially wondered whether we were suggesting that librarians add another screwdriver to an already overstuffed assessment toolbox. Threshold concepts work well with curriculum maps, inquiry-based curriculum, and rubrics. They are likewise compatible with statewide standards and regional accreditation language. That's well and good, but really, who needs another screwdriver?

We hope, though, that with this chapter we are offering something different. Threshold concepts give librarians a language to use with disciplinary faculty and accrediting bodies that is distinct from what we had before. The language in regional accreditation standards may have been based on the Association of College & Research Libraries (ACRL) *Information Literacy Competency Standards for Higher Education* (American Library Association, 2000), but that same accreditation language is also compatible with the ACRL *Framework for Information Literacy for Higher Education* (2014) and may even be better explained by using the *Framework* and threshold concepts.

Thinking about this from a different direction, we also considered the medical maxim, "First do no harm." Threshold concepts don't disrupt what we need to do on the level of accreditation, and they also can help us in the classroom. They do no harm to our current assessment practices, so we can leverage their use in developing pedagogical content.

Finally, let's return to our toolbox metaphor: it's not that we are offering someone with a screwdriver . . . another screwdriver. Rather, we are offering an electric drill to someone with a toolbox already stocked with a screwdriver, tape measure, hammer, pliers, a wrench, and a professional code. Each tool serves a different immediate purpose while contributing to a broader project goal. And that screwdriver is still useful.

The Value Proposition for Information Literacy

The current climate in higher education prioritizes assessment and data-driven decisions. In this era of tightening budgets and enrollment fluctuations, institutions must demonstrate their value. This pressure is amplified for each academic unit, and the library is no exception. Librarians such as Debra Gilchrist and Megan Oakleaf have done tremendous work to develop strategies that focus on student learning in a way that will keep libraries relevant in the 21st century (e.g., Gilchrist & Oakleaf, 2012; Oakleaf, 2010). As such, the assessment of student learning has been central to librarians' argument for the value of academic libraries.

To demonstrate value, librarians count contact hours, questions asked, materials circulated, volumes owned, services offered and used, and improved test scores as a proxy for learning outcomes met. The old *Standards* lent themselves fairly well to a checklist-style approach to assessment. Michaela D. Willi Hooper and Emily Scharf usefully point out, however, that "outcomes-based education and transformative learning appear to be at odds in several ways" (2016, p. 84). Most problematic, this approach makes certain assumptions about what is valuable—on the basis of what can be counted.

Outcomes assessment certainly has its detractors. In one useful critique, political philosophy scholar James F. Pontuso and feminist economist Saranna R. Thorton (2008) compare two quarterbacks who play in the same league. The first is naturally talented and seldom practices; the second is motivated and works hard. Both quarterbacks produce similar results in terms of yards gained passing or touchdown, but these numbers cannot be used to evaluate their coach's efficacy. Outcomes assessment does not, Pontuso and Thorton argue, "allow individual colleges to assess student learning—while simultaneously controlling for student aptitude, willingness and ability to do college level academic work, and other such variables" (p. 63). Their argument also calls into question the extent to which instructors can take credit for student outcomes, given variations in prior learning and natural inclination.

Likewise, writing for the social justice–oriented journal *Radical Teacher*, Michael Bennett and Jacqueline Brady (2014) urge faculty to acknowledge that "it is not the slight variation in internal pedagogical practices that create an achievement gap but the huge structural inequalities that are everywhere evident in the widely divergent resources available to students and faculty of different classes" (p. 148). In teaching to and measuring our teaching on the programmatic level with curriculum maps, rubrics, or other metrics, we imply that student success can be manipulated and adjusted like worker output in a factory, "obscuring the fact that better educational opportunities require fundamental social change" (p. 149). Traditional assessment methods flatten student learning narratives, failing to capture lived experiences.

Teaching with threshold concepts is a reminder to avoid thinking of students as raw materials upon whom *this* learning experience, followed by *that* learning experience, will result in a product: the *information literate lifelong learner*. Assessing threshold concept acquisition requires authentic assessment of meaningful content and is unlikely to demonstrate quantitative value the way that outcomes assessment does. Though the threshold concept approach to teaching and learning does not necessarily produce the type of data that administrators use to make a case for a bigger budget allocation, we hold that this is a feature, not a bug. Threshold concepts help us teach what cannot be counted.

Assessing Conceptual Learning

Assessment of conceptual learning is a complex, even daunting, area of inquiry. Assessing threshold concept acquisition can show us where learners struggle in a course. It can show us what helps them learn, and it can push us to improve our teaching. Student movement through learning thresholds is gradual, iterative, and challenging to quantify within the confines of a one-shot session, or even a semester-length course.

Threshold concepts will not simplify the relationship between information literacy instruction and assessment. By nature, students will need to revisit threshold concepts again and again before they are able to integrate formerly disparate facts with new disciplinary understandings. Even after students cross the threshold, they may need to revisit earlier material. Without sufficient time, students may gain superficial knowledge to pass a test but won't develop a nuanced understanding of the material. This has implications for assessing when a student has approached or crossed a threshold, and may seem to disqualify the threshold concept approach for one-shot library instruction altogether. Indeed, no student will cross a threshold in one hour, let alone master all of the concepts proposed in Part II of this book.

This particular issue with assessing conceptual learning has been discussed by some of the sharpest thinkers in information literacy instruction. For example, Barbara Fister writes persuasively that "librarians don't teach students how to be information literate . . . it has to be learned over several years, because it's complicated and needs lots of practice ... Having good guides helps, but this kind of learning only happens in the doing of it" (2015, p. 7). While we would love to fill our classrooms with one *aha!* moment after another, sudden, transformative awareness is unlikely to dawn on a student as she is participating in a group project or completing a homework assignment. This moment is more likely to be experienced quietly, gradually, outside of the midterm exam, the research paper, or the company of a librarian. If students do not cross a threshold in an hour or semester, then what is it that we measure in order to demonstrate the value of our instruction session?

Meredith Farkas writes that work produced by a student who understands a new concept can look identical to that produced by a student who is only "mimicking good papers s/he has seen before without ever actually internalizing any of the larger lessons ... How do you know when a student has made it over the hill of a threshold concept?" (Farkas, 2014). This question echoes one raised by Jan Meyer and Ray Land: "How might we get away from traditional assessment regimes in which a student can produce the 'right' answer while retaining fundamental misconceptions?" (Meyer & Land, 2005). An example for information literacy might be when a student knows that articles categorized as peer reviewed are scholarly but doesn't know how to differentiate between that article and one from a newspaper or magazine. How do we get away from testing memorized answers or mimicry and find out what learners truly understand?

Assessment of conceptual learning must move beyond rewarding students for producing recordable answers, in order to authentically reveal transformative learning. Activities and assignments should ask students to do more than mimic the formal products of the discipline, be it writing a research paper or a mathematical proof. Instead, assessments must prompt reflective, introspective, or imaginative responses to learning that will help instructors understand whether students can integrate and apply new disciplinary knowledge.

Take, for example, learning to drive a car. Your driving skill is typically evaluated using both a written test (to make sure you know important laws or penalties) and a practical test (to make sure you can apply what you've learned). Driving tests are good tests of new concepts, but they can still fail to demonstrate authentic learning; a student can pass both tests and still be not only inexpert, but even not a very good driver, with very significant consequences. You might pass your driving test at low speeds and using extreme caution, only to clip a car in your blind spot the next day, skid on black ice in your first winter, or forget to signal when the evaluator isn't sitting in the passenger seat. Or, using the same license, you could feel like an expert driver in rural Iowa but a novice in Central London. Driving tests work as a valid form of authentic assessment, capturing the start of the transition away from novice thinking, but they leave much learning unmeasured. The same argument might be made regarding professional gatekeeping tests, such as the fundamentals of engineering exam, the bar exam for lawyers, and the boards for doctors.

In considering how to assess learning for information literacy concepts, it is productive to consider how one might assess other big ideas like *equality* or *honesty*. To learn about equality, students can cover a range of interpretations from Thomas Hobbes to bell hooks or look to social and political examples like the ratification of the Fourteenth and Nineteenth Amendments, the Stonewall riots, and the passage of the Affordable Care Act. A unit on honesty might start with stories about George Washington and the cherry tree or Pinocchio and then transition into discussions about the classic game theory exercise, the prisoner's dilemma, or plagiarism by journalists like Jonah Lehrer and Stephen Glass. Students might be asked to demonstrate their understanding via reflective writing or role playing or by presenting arguments for two different perspectives. Assessment for these lessons might consider the sophistication of a student's thesis statement, the student's ability to define these ideas in their own words, or basic fact retention. Developing, expanding, and complicating these concepts in the classroom is useful and *is* teaching even if we are not able to *prove* that the student has embraced these ideas and will move through life as an egalitarian truth-teller. Likewise, it is possible to teach, and assess, information literacy threshold concepts like authority or information commodities, even if students do not cross the threshold.

Consider a spatial metaphor (Figure 8.1). A threshold, after all, is a doorway, and its Latin translation is *limen* (as in "liminal"). The liminal space is where transformation takes place, but it is also where learners might get stuck—where they don't fully grasp the threshold concept. At this point, they might wander around the liminal space, turn around and head back the way they came in, or pass through the threshold.

Meyer and Land refer to this as "variation theory" (2005). Showing progress is going to look different for everyone because our students start out with very different backgrounds and experiences. Indeed, Meyer and Land reject the idea of "one definitive and total conceptual understanding available" (2005, p. 383). Instead, activities and assignments should be designed to accommodate variation while also enabling librarians to assess how students are progressing in their understandings.

After all, students do not start a course in the same place, nor do they learn at the same pace. At its simplest, assessing threshold concept

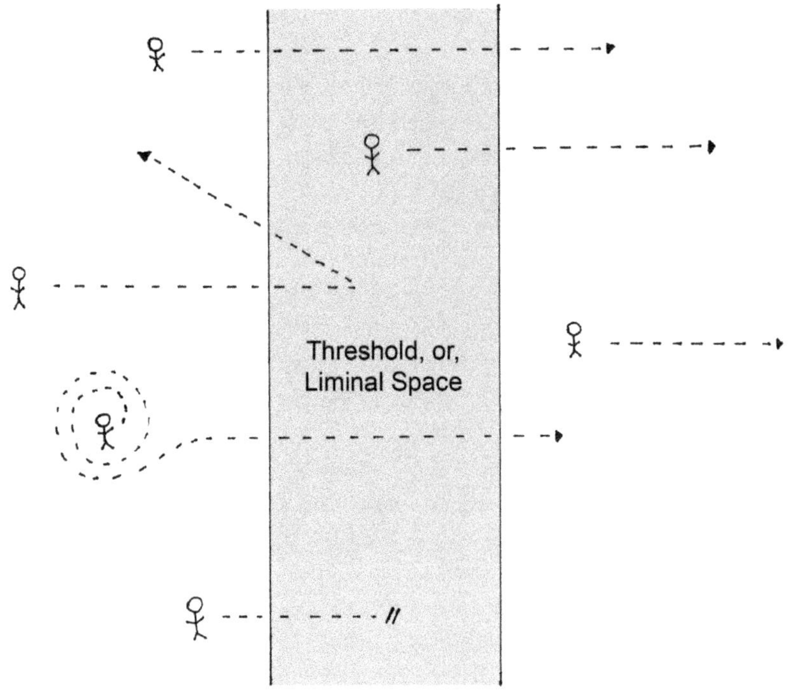

Figure 8.1 Meyer and Land's variation theory.

acquisition asks you to find out where your students are so you can correct a misconception or clarify with an additional example. When students are first introduced to a threshold concept, they bring different levels of existing knowledge. Some students may have gone through a peer-revision process in their English class and will be able compare it to the academic peer-review process. Others may have participated in an elementary school science fair and can make a connection between a hypothesis and a thesis statement. There are many ways that students can reach their undergraduate courses more and less prepared for what awaits them.

Our lived experiences are not uniform. Our learning experiences should not be uniform. To return to the picture of a threshold concept as a doorway in the distance, imagine the learners approaching it from all directions. One person might have their hand on the handle. When this student is introduced to a threshold concept for the first time, they may walk right through the door because they have had exposure to similar ideas, or were offered an example to which they could relate. The student's peers may take twice as long because they are several blocks away from the door or because they stopped to get a coffee. Still others may walk around in a circle for a bit or sit down in one place for three months. In order to assess student learning, and our own effectiveness as instructors, we need to find a way to externalize the internal ontological and cognitive shifts that indicate an approach to and crossing of a learning threshold.

Nonprotocol Activity and Assignment Design

Classroom activities and assignments externalize learning transformations, but at times the rules of the game can hide whether or not students understand the big, conceptual ideas (Meyer & Land, 2005). For higher education, the rules of the game include citation styles, sentence-level grammar issues, and unfamiliar vocabulary in academic writing. In a library context, the rules of the game might be the knowledge that you can check out books without spending money or being comfortable with asking a librarian for help.

Meyer and Land (2005) suggest that one way to assess conceptual understanding is to produce informally structured assignments that can help us see whether students are engaging with the concept, in order to bracket the rules of the game as a separate learning objective. What would this type of instructional design—with an emphasis on nonprotocol assignments and activities—look like?

In the language of educational theory, one answer is to use stimuli with unstructured protocol (Meyer & Land, 2010). In everyday terms, this means using assignments (stimuli) that do not explicitly prioritize the rules of the game (protocol). Peter Davies and Jean Mangan (2008) propose three types of learning activities to meet this goal: (1) reflective exercises that compare how students approach a problem with the way an expert would approach the problem, (2) problem-focused exercises that ask students to suggest explanations for a problem, and (3) threshold network exercises that give students a problem and a list of concepts that can be used to make sense of the problem.

For example, in the information literacy context, Davies and Mangan's learning activities might look like this: (1) having students record the steps they took to find sources on a topic and then, after seeing a librarian demonstrate expert search methods, writing a reflection comparing their own approach with the librarian's approach; (2) asking students to suggest explanations for why there are so many different places to search for information, be it in hundreds of different library databases, thousands of different newspapers, or millions of web results; and (3) discussing copyright law, economic models for open access publishing, and editorial and peer-review processes in order to help explain why textbooks are so expensive.

Activities along these lines that might be used in information literacy instruction are many. Because of the new approach in the *Framework*, librarians have published and presented extensively on assessment of conceptual learning, offering ready examples. Prompts for informal writing samples such as diary entries and blog posts, or oral and visual rather than written work, can all reveal the ways that students interact with the course content, but do not require perfect citations or the use of an academic tone. Oakleaf (2014) encourages librarians to write learning outcomes for threshold concepts and to use "active learning strategies . . . which are simultaneously active assessment strategies" (p. 512). Her examples include asking students to sketch the relationship between often and rarely cited articles; listing, discussing, and reporting areas of disagreement or consensus for websites on the same topic; and brainstorming about author characteristics that indicate credibility.

These activities are not necessarily an enormous change from current practice. The emphasis is simply changed to activities where students can successfully demonstrate learning without relying on protocol; each of these examples asks students to focus on articulating what they do or do not know rather than making sure their margins are the correct width or that everything is written in the third person.

Threshold Concepts and Bibliographic Instruction

Bibliographic instruction, on the other hand, is well suited to address the rules of the game, which students also need to learn in order to succeed. Many librarians consider the term "bibliographic instruction" to have been superseded by "information literacy," but we find that it is useful to think of the terms as referring to two separate areas of instruction. Bibliographic instruction can offer students an entry point into the rules of the game and perhaps bring a threshold into view.

Librarians can expect to encounter a wide variation in how students approach the rules of the game. Prior experience will shape habits of mind and practiced behaviors like being able to take productive notes during a lecture, attending office hours, or knowing email etiquette when writing to an instructor. Student populations are no longer the traditional well-off children of educated parents who once were the majority of the college bound. More than a third of 5- to 17-year-olds in the United States are first-generation students, and these students often begin college with less academic preparation (Choy, 2001). These students are also more likely to delay college entry, need remedial coursework, or drop out of college (Engle, 2007).

Offering students bibliographic instruction has the potential to impact not just retention, but also graduation rates (Cook, 2014). Spending an hour or a full semester focusing on specific skills (how to use databases, how to use reference works, how to put together citations, etc.) is constructive. It is a productive approach because learning the rules of the game allows you to not only join but also win the game.

For instance, a session for a Communication and Journalism class on the History of Mass Media may start by asking students for their proposed research topics. From there, a discussion of the assignment requirements may lead into an examination of the nature of primary versus secondary sources. Conceptual ideas are only briefly introduced, and the bulk of the hour is devoted to database demonstrations and individual experimentation. This class is successful: students pay attention and ask questions. The instruction session meets learners at their point of need, students are engaged by active learning techniques, and the library resources presented are the sort that are difficult to find on the open web. This session can be assessed using existing methods like pre- and posttests, surveys, and student work analysis.

How does this relate to a threshold concept approach to instruction? While it's not possible to cover a threshold concept in a one-shot session in the same way as in a semester-length class, that doesn't mean abandoning the complexity, ambiguity, and flexibility of conceptual teaching. In a bibliographic instruction setting, your conceptual approach might help guide the examples you choose or the way you explain something. But that doesn't mean that librarians should stop teaching the rules of the game.

Affective Learning and Threshold Concepts

Acknowledging the affective aspects of teaching with threshold concepts can create a safer, more inclusive learning space. Working with threshold concepts is uncomfortable and humbling. By recognizing these negative feelings, we can begin to mitigate them.

For new students, for example, there is much about the research process that can feel unfamiliar. To demystify the college library itself, an instruction session might connect the academic library to public and national libraries. In 2016, the White House produced a video to introduce Dr. Carla Hayden as the nominee for the next Librarian of Congress; this video does an excellent job of outlining the function, value, and future of not only the Library of Congress but also public libraries in Baltimore. Before watching the video, students are asked to write for one minute in response to the prompt "why do we need libraries?" After watching the video, students talk to each other about what they wrote down, and what they would add after watching the video. They are also asked to share one story about a recent or childhood visit to the library. On the basis of student responses, connections can be drawn between the academic library, public libraries, and the Library of Congress. Students may remember going to the library for storytime or tutoring, which can be related to library programs or reference assistance. Or, they may notice that the Library of Congress serves the U.S. Congress, which can lead to a discussion about the type of research done by members of Congress to prepare for a vote or when writing a bill and the type of research done by college students.

Anonymous tools like Poll Everywhere can help destigmatize the experience of not getting new concepts right away. One example of a productive poll question is, "What makes a source scholarly?" Sometimes, responses from a group of first-year students may show that most of them know that "peer-review" and "scholarly journals" are the expected answers. When these phrases come up over and over, it's time to start pushing on those answers to get at questions about authority and scholarly discourse. Follow-up questions might cover, "What do you look for when you check your classmate's writing?" "What percentage of journal articles do you think are rejected?" "Is a Yelp review written by a food expert scholarly?" "Is Pepsi's CEO an expert on soft drinks? Is she a good source of information if she tells you Pepsi makes the best soft drinks?" Discussion questions contextualize student responses and build on prior knowledge. No single student response is put on the line or used to represent the entire group, providing cover for those who feel uncomfortable struggling in public. We can go on to ask "Does the value of a source change depending on who is reading it?" "What's the difference between an opinion and an argument?" Anonymizing or aggregating student responses allows for variation while helping students feel heard.

When student responses are solicited, it is only after they have the opportunity to brainstorm, practice, or explore on their own. When working alone, students should also have a safety net for mitigating the affective qualities related to searching. For instance, before starting a search in a database, students can be encouraged to write down as many keywords and ideas relating to their topic as they can. Then, when one search doesn't work, they have alternative searches at the ready.

With the threshold concept approach, students and teachers are encouraged to acknowledge rather than conceal discomfort and frustration; confusion or even anger reflects not incompetence, but progress toward a threshold. Doubt is a part of the process, and uncertainty is allowed.

Programmatic Assessment

Threshold concepts have the potential to shift librarians' approach to programmatic assessment of information literacy by providing more robust language for conveying our content that still aligns with institutional, statewide, and regional standards. Assessment tools such as rubrics and curriculum maps clarify where threshold concepts fit with existing curricula. It is also possible to compare the language used to address information literacy by the six regional higher education accreditors in the United States to offer ideas about how to use threshold concepts on a wider stage (while not undertaken here, this analysis could be applied to accreditation standards in other countries as well).

Meyer and Land (2010) compare learners' movement through a threshold to progress around a racetrack with fence or ditch obstacles. Learners must overcome the highs of misplaced confidence and the lows of self-doubt in order to cross the finish line. Using threshold concepts " 'rattles the cage' of a linear approach to curriculum design that assumes standard and homogenised outcomes" (Land, Cousin, Meyer, & Davies, 2005, p. 60). Students will also need plenty of time to complete their laps around the track, which suggests that assessment is well suited to evaluation on a programmatic level. For example, how do English majors analyze irony in lower- versus upper-level courses? Can recent MLIS graduates illustrate the structure of a database?

As we have seen, however, the crossing of thresholds cannot be easily captured or measured within traditional assessment methods; forcing threshold concept assessment into current success metrics is unproductive. Threshold concepts *can* be effectively used to guide instructional design and to contextualize information-seeking skills. Assessment might capture progress in the liminal space or movement through a threshold. The threshold concept model offers a meaningful way to improve teaching practice, but we certainly would not recommend it as the only assessment structure in your instruction program. When used alongside other assessment methods, however, threshold concepts can be useful for improving library instruction on the programmatic or statewide level. Four examples follow.

Champlain College's Multiple Model Approach

Champlain College has long used an inquiry-based curriculum for its information literacy program, but also finds room to experiment with threshold concepts and the *Framework*. For example, Alan Carbery (2014a, 2014b) describes using the Scholarly Discourse threshold concept to recontextualize an annotated bibliography assignment by asking students to choose sources that contributed in different ways to the conversation (a first-person account, an expert opinion). These documents, like the annotated bibliography, gather relevant sources and highlight what is useful or contradictory in the source. By structuring the assignment around a threshold concept, Carbery turned a potentially frustrating assignment into a useful, transferable learning experience. Threshold concepts do not replace the demonstrably effective inquiry-based information literacy curriculum, but they are an additional means by which Carbery and his colleagues may improve student learning.

LaGuardia Community College's Rubric-Based Approach

Rubrics are a flexible programmatic assessment tool compatible with a threshold concept approach. Oakleaf (2008) recommends use of rubrics for information literacy assessment because, in addition to clearly conveying expectations to students, they offer the opportunity for librarians to express a shared vision for student learning. Threshold concepts can replace or be used alongside current dimensions to organize content without disrupting the measurable elements in dimension descriptions. Using threshold concepts in rubrics indicates departmental support for conceptual learning and can also remind individual instructors to prioritize conceptual learning when designing activities and assignments.

The Association of American Colleges & Universities (AAC&U) and Carleton College have created two widely used information literacy rubrics. Both rubrics contain an information evaluation dimension; AAC&U (2010) uses an "Evaluate information and its sources critically" dimension, and Carleton (Gould Library Reference and Instruction Department, 2012) uses "Evaluation of sources." In the "Capstone" scale level of AAC&U's rubric, the student "thoroughly (systematically and methodically) analyzes own and others' assumptions and carefully evaluates the relevance of contexts when presenting a position." Similarly, in the "Very Strong" scale level of Carleton's rubric, "sources employed demonstrate sophisticated independent thought." The Authority threshold concept could be incorporated into these dimensions and be evaluated using the existing descriptions. Its inclusion would not take anything away from the importance of information evaluation, nor would it require that student work be read differently.

Rubrics need not be rewritten to accommodate the threshold concept approach and can, in fact, serve as a way to evaluate conceptual learning on a programmatic level. At LaGuardia Community College, Silvia participated in updating the *Core Competencies and Abilities* (2014). The Inquiry and Problem Solving rubric (which replaced the one for Research and Information Literacy) offers many entry points for library instruction sessions and credit courses. When designing activities and assignments, librarians might look at the dimensions and translate "Define and contextualize the problem/question" into Research Process, or "Gather and analyze evidence to test hypothesis/solution" into Authority or Format. While teaching to information literacy threshold concepts by including certain big picture examples, and connecting assignments to experiences outside of the classroom, librarians can also put aside the threshold concept lens and focus on the dimension descriptions when scoring student work.

To make these connections more accessible to disciplinary faculty, Silvia and her colleagues created a list of library instruction modules to be used in hour-long sessions, as shown in Table 8.1 (Lin Hanick et al., 2015; reprinted with permission).

In subsequent semesters, Silvia and her colleagues extended the work they did with the aforementioned modules by mapping each of their First Year Seminar library instruction sessions to a frame from the *Framework*, the *Core Competencies* for her campus, the library resources to be taught, and an activity for the session, as shown in Table 8.2 (Lin Hanick et al., 2018; reprinted with permission).

Simultaneously inspired by threshold concepts, the ACRL *Framework*, and locally developed Core Competencies, the modules and the library instruction map for First Year Seminars gave disciplinary faculty a clear sense of the concepts and skills that could be taught or introduced in a library visit. Disciplinary faculty responded well to offerings that aligned with their teaching priorities, while Silvia and her colleagues enjoyed the more ambitious approach to library instruction.

University of New Mexico Curriculum Map

Curriculum mapping offers an opportunity to step back and understand at the highest levels what is being taught, when, and where. This approach was originally applied in K–12 settings (e.g., Kuhlthau, 1987) and has since been adopted in higher education for programs, for disciplines, and in libraries. College and university librarians have written extensively about the need to integrate information literacy into the curriculum, especially where librarians are limited to one-shot instruction, and curriculum maps can be an effective tool to meet these needs (Buchanan, Webb, Houk, & Tingelstad, 2015).

Table 8.1 Library Instruction Modules Used at LaGuardia Community College (CUNY)

Title	Choose This Module If . . .	Students Will . . .
A Source is a Source: Web Search Engines vs. Subscription Databases	• You want students to know the difference between Google and library databases • You want to introduce the concept of "academic" or "peer-reviewed" sources • You want to talk about how different disciplines produce scholarship	• Demonstrate ability to select appropriate search tools • Be able to filter results and understand how results are retrieved • Understand the importance of authority & credibility
Joining an Ongoing Conversation: Acquiring Background Knowledge and Terminology	• Your students are new to the discipline • Your students are still developing topics • You want students to explore their topics broadly	• Learn where to find background knowledge • Learn why citation is important • Understand using bibliographies to find information
Why Do We Cite?: MLA, APA, and the Bibliography	• Your students will be using outside information in their writing • You want students to know when to use a book versus a newspaper article versus a magazine • You want students to understand the value of citation	• Correctly identify information format based on citation • Understand the difference between source types • Be able to select appropriate search tool based on info format • Understand how a bibliography is organized

That's My Job: Career Research as Strategic Exploration	• You plan to use the "Career Planning" module in the FYS ePortfolio • You want students to use the Occupational Outlook Handbook and library databases • You want students to explore the structure of various professions	• Be able to identify/use appropriate search tools for career research • Learn how to develop career related vocabulary • Understand connection between seemingly disparate tools and careers • Learn where to find and how to use readymade subject guides
Don't Re-invent the Wheel: Using Bibliographies to Save Time	• You want students to be able to locate a book or article based on a citation • Your students will be using "academic" or "peer-reviewed" sources references • You want students to see the way scholarly information builds off of previous research	• Be able to locate bibliography and in-text references • Learn how to determine information format from a citation/reference • Learn how to do a title search to locate specific information
Research as Inquiry: Finding Credible, Authoritative Information	• Your students have a formal research assignment • Your students need help with topic development • You want students to search the library catalog and databases	• Understand the importance of identifying their research need • Learn to develop basic research question and thesis statement • Be able to develop basic research strategy

Table 8.2 Library Instruction Map for First Year Seminars at LaGuardia Community College (CUNY)

Course Name	Frame	Core Competency	Resources	Activity
BTF 101—Business and Technology	Searching as Strategic Exploration Information Has Value	Integrative Learning Inquiry & Problem Solving Integrative Learning Global Learning	*Business Insights* *Wall Street Journal* Business Source Complete	Profiling the Global Impact of a Company
ECF 090—Engineering and Computer Science	Research as Inquiry	Integrative Learning Global Learning	Career Research Guide Applied Science & Tech Source *New York Times*	Exploring Careers and Industry Problems
CJF 101—Criminal Justice	Authority	Integrative Learning Global Learning	Opposing or Global Viewpoints Criminal Justice Abstracts ProPublica website	Evaluating Reliability in Sources
HSF 101—Health Sciences	Research as Inquiry	Inquiry & Problem Solving Integrative Learning Global Learning I & PS, Integrative Learning	CINAHL Academic Search Complete	"Cultural Competency" for Your Field

LIF 101—LA, Social Science and Humanities	Information Has Value	Integrative Learning Integrative Learning	Gale Virtual Reference Library Database Subject Matrix	The Value of Libraries and Identifying Info Needs
LMF 101—Math and Science	Searching as Strategic Exploration	Inquiry & Problem Solving Integrative Learning Integrative Learning Global Learning	Access Science Credo, Gale Virtual Reference Science Magazine	Transhumanism and Disciplinary Research
NSF 100—Natural Sciences	Searching as Strategic Exploration	Inquiry & Problem Solving Integrative Learning Global Learning	Career Research Guide General Science OneSearch	Exploring Careers and Industry Problems
SYF 101—Psychology	Searching as Strategic Exploration Scholarship as a Conversation	Inquiry & Problem Solving Integrative Learning Global Learning	Credo, Gale Virtual Reference	Scholarly Conversations and Citation

Just as course redesign starts with reexamining learning objectives, curriculum mapping looks at all of the library's instructional offerings in order to ensure that they are appropriately distributed. This is a heavy lift but may bring to light places to find efficiencies or eliminate overlaps, and provides insight into how student learning might be assessed.

At the University of New Mexico (UNM), the University Libraries Instruction Working Group created a curriculum map to organize the library's teaching (Townsend, Hurley, Potter, Cooper, & Hessney-Moore, 2015). The curriculum map deliberately targets specific information literacy topics, not the crossing of thresholds; the table is designed to show what we teach in a class, not to suggest that students will master a threshold concept during the class or that they will be evaluated for doing so. Topics are organized by three basic categories: Searching/Finding, Choosing/Evaluating, and Using. The topics (the row headers in Table 8.3) can be taught with any of the overlapping threshold concepts for information literacy, but the topics themselves don't change.

The purpose of the curriculum map is twofold. First, it gives liaison librarians a tool to customize their curricula for the academic departments they work with. It has proven to be a useful communication aid in helping disciplinary faculty understand what librarians will teach and what disciplinary faculty need to know about it. Second, it provides a top-level view of what students learn and when. The map has also helped UNM librarians design the lower- and upper-division credit courses that they teach.

Table 8.3 (Townsend et al., 2015; reprinted with permission) shows UNM's curriculum map with information literacy topics organized by level. Table 8.4 (Townsend et al., 2015; reprinted with permission), which follows, reorganizes the same topics by threshold concept. Again, the goal is not to suggest that students will cross the threshold for a concept in an hour, but rather to see how information literacy topics at various student levels map to threshold concepts.

The UNM map is an example of a threshold concept approach allowing for greater flexibility in program design than librarians previously had with the *Standards* as a guiding document. The *Standards* provided specific premade learning objectives that could be customized for the local context. Using threshold concepts and the new *Framework* offered a way to reconsider where current learning objectives fit the curriculum and where learning objectives could be added in order to address big ideas in a more comprehensive way. Students aren't expected to get a degree in information literacy, but they can make progress with conceptual content over several courses or throughout their degree program rather than collecting discrete skills here and there throughout their undergraduate experience.

Table 8.3 Library Instruction Learning Objectives by Level at University of New Mexico

Level	Searching/Finding	Choosing/Evaluating	Using
Threshold Concepts	• Information structures • Format • Information commodities	• Authority • Format • Research process	• Research process • Information commodities • Scholarly discourse • Information structures
High School	• Specific databases, multidisciplinary resources available to NM residents or free online • Boolean, truncation, wildcard • Keywords	• Specific databases, multidisciplinary resources available to NM residents or free online • Boolean, truncation, wildcard • Keywords	• Research is a thing—it exists • Introduction to citation/plagiarism • Online etiquette & using social media wisely
Lower Division	• Platonic database and multidisciplinary databases • Boolean, truncation, wildcard • Keywords • Advanced Googling	• Scholarly vs. popular • Website evaluation • Information formats (basic) • Establishing credibility (authority)	• Topic development • Research as a process • Research solves problems and answers questions • Filling gaps in personal knowledge • Citation basics & plagiarism
Upper Division	• Disciplinary databases • Citation chaining (mostly backwards through references) • Data, primary sources, & primary research • Google Scholar	• Nature of scholarly sources & peer review • Primary sources & information formats in the discipline • Original/primary research • Filter bubble • Knowledge commons	• Asking meaningful questions (not yet original) • Understanding how questions get answered in a discipline • Structure of and recognizing gaps in disciplinary knowledge • IKEA research

(continued)

Table 8.3 *(continued)*

Level	Searching/Finding	Choosing/Evaluating	Using
			• Filling gaps in personal knowledge • Citation management • Copyright as students (fair use, creative commons, disciplinary stuff like image rights) • Ethics in information use (e.g. privacy, social media)
Graduate	• Citation chaining (backwards and forwards through references, Web of Science, Google Scholar) • Building knowledge about individual sources of expertise in discipline • Data, primary sources & primary research • Literature reviews • Journal metrics • Advanced Google Scholar	• Journals in which to publish • Advanced disciplinary techniques for evaluation (including statistical analysis, expertise in disciplinary methodology) • Literature reviews • Primary sources in the discipline • Original/primary research	• Asking original questions • Identifying gaps in disciplinary knowledge and how they can be filled • Data management & issues in data • Open access • Advanced citation management • Copyright (as an information creator & user) • Ethics in information creation (e.g. privacy for researchers)

Table 8.4 Library Instruction Topics by Threshold Concept at University of New Mexico

Threshold Concept	High School	Lower Division	Upper Division	Graduate
Authority	• Tool selection • Encourage skepticism! Who wrote the source, what organization, etc. • Basic web evaluation	• Establishing credibility (authority—it's fluid, contextual, cultural, subject to social, political influences) • Web evaluation • Scholarly vs. popular	• Nature of scholarly sources & peer review • Filter bubble • Literature reviews (basic & purpose)	• Building knowledge about individual sources of expertise in discipline • Filter bubble • Disciplinary models for establishing authority
Format	• Tool selection	• Information formats (basic) • Information cycles (social science, science, humanities): how they influence format and channels of dissemination • Web evaluation	• Nature of scholarly sources & peer review • Primary sources & information formats in the discipline • Disciplinary information cycles • Original/primary research (finding and designing) • Advanced web evaluation	• Original/primary research (finding, designing and conducting) • Using and finding primary sources and evidence in the discipline • Using disciplinary information cycles to create new knowledge

(continued)

Table 8.4 *(continued)*

Threshold Concept	High School	Lower Division	Upper Division	Graduate
Information Commodities	• Introduction to citation/plagiarism • Using social media wisely	• Citation basics & plagiarism • Copyright basics—existence of copyright law and the concept of fair use • Library's role in information cycle • Social media and the filter bubble	• Copyright as students (fair use, creative commons, disciplinary stuff like image rights) • Filter bubble • Knowledge commons	• Open access • Copyright as professionals, in the context of publishing, presenting, selling • Filter bubble • Choosing journals for publishing
Information Structures	• Specific databases, multidisciplinary resources available to NM residents or free online • Boolean, truncation, wildcard • Keywords	• "Platonic database" and multidisciplinary databases • Boolean, truncation, wildcard • Keywords • Advanced Googling	• Disciplinary databases • Google Scholar • Citation management	• Citation chaining (backwards and forwards through references, Web of Science, Google Scholar) • Advanced Google Scholar • Advanced citation/knowledge management • Data management & issues in data

Research Process	• Relevance of sources to issue • Research is a thing—evidence comes from research	• Research solves problems and answers questions • Filling gaps in personal knowledge • Information cycles (social science, science, humanities): how new knowledge is created & disseminated	• Asking meaningful questions (not yet original) • Understanding how questions get answered in a discipline • Disciplinary information cycles	• Asking original questions • Identifying gaps in disciplinary knowledge and how they can be filled • Using and finding primary sources and evidence in the discipline • Literature reviews (purpose and writing of)
Scholarly Discourse			• Citation chaining (mostly backwards through references) • Structure of and recognizing gaps in disciplinary knowledge • Literature reviews (basic & purpose) • IKEA research	• Citation chaining (backwards and forwards through references, Web of Science, Google Scholar) • Literature reviews (purpose and writing of) • Identifying gaps in disciplinary knowledge and how they can be filled • Choosing journals for publishing

New Mexico Statewide General Education Curriculum

In New Mexico, a conceptual learning approach to information literacy has extended beyond individual institutions. When the *Statewide General Education Curriculum* was revised in 2018, librarians used the *Framework* to advocate for the inclusion of information literacy for the first time. Information and digital literacy are now listed under the Communications content area for New Mexico's General Education Curriculum. The component skills for the outcome cover each of the five threshold concepts explored in this book, as shown in Table 8.5 (New Mexico Statewide General Education, 2018).

While the titles and outcomes may differ from those used in Part II of this book, it is clear from the short descriptions that they speak to the same conceptual ideas. As a member of the working group that wrote the information and digital literacy skills outcomes, Lori reports that using the language of threshold concepts was central to their effort; the threshold concept approach successfully framed the unique disciplinary content introduced via information literacy.

Table 8.5 Comparison of Component Skills from the New Mexico *Statewide General Education Curriculum* and Threshold Concepts for Information Literacy

Component Skill	Threshold Concepts for Information Literacy
Authority and Value of Information Recognize the interdependent nature of the authority and value of information, and use this knowledge ethically when selecting, using, and creating information.	Authority Information Commodities
Digital Literacy Understand, communicate, compute, create, and design in digital environments.	
Information Structures Select, use, produce, organize, and share information employing appropriate information formats, collections, systems, and applications.	Organizing Systems Format
Research as Inquiry Engage in an iterative process of inquiry that defines a problem or poses a question and, through research, generates a reasonable solution or answer.	Research Process

Threshold Concepts and Accreditation Standards

For many institutions, programmatic assessment is tied to accreditation standards. It is a tremendous victory for information literacy advocates that the library's contributions to student learning and the campus community are acknowledged and quantified in these documents. In many cases, the inclusion of the library represents years, if not decades, of advocacy. In order to better understand the relationship between accreditation standards and the threshold concept model, we took a closer look at the language in regional accreditation standards.

For the purposes of this conversation, Table 8.6 identifies mentions of information literacy or library instruction. It does not quote standards addressing collections, infrastructure, or requirements for the library as a physical space, nor does it consider national, professional, or other specialized accreditors. If you happen to be the kind of person who can't stand reading this type of language, just skip to the information for your own accrediting body.

Taken as a whole, the standards that relate to information literacy instruction exemplify what Grant Wiggins and Jay McTighe (2005) call "the nebulous problem": they are so vague that many different interpretations can be plausibly made. For this reason, all of the standards can be compatible with a threshold concept approach to information literacy instruction. This table demonstrates that where there is language in accreditation standards about information literacy or library instruction, the new *Framework*—with its conceptual approach—will respond flexibly to the challenge presented by those standards. Correlatively, for the accrediting agencies that say nothing about the library at all, there are usually statements about critical thinking or lifelong learning that the *Framework* is likely to map to.

The table is here to demonstrate that as a model and a teaching approach, threshold concepts do not run counter to the goals of our regional accreditation standards. Middle States, the New England Association, and Western Association of Schools and Colleges (WASC) all mention information literacy alongside their commitment to critical thinking or reasoning, ethics, and diversity—and threshold concepts can help us teach those things. The Northwest Commission and the Southern Association want to be sure that students receive regular instruction on how to obtain, evaluate, and use information resources. Threshold concepts can help us teach these things too. The accreditation standards speak to the work academic librarians do now and will continue to do, and threshold concepts don't interfere with that.

Table 8.6 Mentions of Information Literacy or Library Instruction in Regional Accreditation Standards

Accrediting Organization	Where Mentioned	Information Literacy–Related Language
Middle States Commission on Higher Education	Standard III, Criteria 5b	At institutions that offer undergraduate education, a general education program, free standing or integrated into academic disciplines, that . . . offers a curriculum designed so that students acquire and demonstrate essential skills including at least oral and written communication, scientific and quantitative reasoning, critical analysis and reasoning, technological competency, and information literacy. Consistent with mission, the general education program also includes the study of values, ethics, and diverse perspectives. (Middle States, 2015)
New England Association of Schools and Colleges Commission on Institutions of Higher Education	Standard 4.12	Expectations for student achievement, independent learning, information literacy, skills in inquiry, and critical judgment are appropriate to the subject matter and degree level and in keeping with generally accepted practice. (New England, 2016)
	Standard 4.15	Graduates successfully completing an undergraduate program demonstrate competence in written and oral communication in English; the ability for scientific and quantitative reasoning, for critical analysis and logical thinking; and the capability for continuing learning, including the skills of information literacy. They also demonstrate knowledge and understanding of scientific, historical, and social phenomena, and a knowledge and appreciation of the aesthetic and ethical dimensions of humankind. (New England, 2016)
Northwest Commission on Colleges and Universities	2.C.6	Faculty with teaching responsibilities, in partnership with library and information resources personnel, ensure that the use of library and information resources is integrated into the learning process. (Northwest Commission, 2018)
	2.E.3	Consistent with its mission and core themes, the institution provides appropriate instruction and support for students, faculty, staff, administrators, and others (as appropriate) to enhance their efficiency and effectiveness in obtaining, evaluating, and using library and information resources that support its programs and services, wherever offered and however delivered. (Northwest Commission, 2018)

North Central Association of Colleges and Schools Higher Learning Commission	2.E.2	Students are offered guidance in the ethical use of information resources. (Higher Learning Commission, 2014)
	3.D.5	The institution provides to students guidance in the effective use of research and information resources. (Higher Learning Commission, 2014)
Southern Association of Colleges and Schools Commission on Colleges	11.3	The institution provides . . . access to regular and timely instruction in the use of the library and other learning/information resources. (Southern Association, 2018)
Accrediting Commission for Community and Junior Colleges, Western Association of Schools and Colleges	2.B.1	Learning support services include, but are not limited to, library collections, tutoring, learning centers, computer laboratories, learning technology, and ongoing instruction for users of library and other learning support services. (Accrediting Commission, 2014)
	2.B.3	The institution evaluates library and other learning support services to assure their adequacy in meeting identified student needs. Evaluation of these services includes evidence that they contribute to the attainment of student learning outcomes. The institution uses the results of these evaluations as the basis for improvement. (Accrediting Commission, 2014)
Western Association of Schools and Colleges Senior College and University Commission	Standard 2.2a	Undergraduate programs engage students in an integrated course of study of sufficient breadth and depth to prepare them for work, citizenship, and lifelong learning. These programs ensure the development of core competencies including, but not limited to, written and oral communication, quantitative reasoning, information literacy, and critical thinking. In addition, undergraduate programs actively foster creativity, innovation, an appreciation for diversity, ethical and civic responsibility, civic engagement, and the ability to work with others. Baccalaureate programs also ensure breadth for all students in cultural and aesthetic, social and political, and scientific and technical knowledge expected of educated persons. Baccalaureate degrees include significant in-depth study in a given area of knowledge (typically described in terms of a program or major). (Western Association, 2013)

While threshold concepts require a different assessment approach on the activity or assignment level, this approach aligns with what accreditation standards expect of academic libraries. This is not to suggest that all of the work is done. Just as librarians have worked for years to introduce information literacy into assessment documents, so, too, must we champion conceptual teaching. How can these documents better position librarians as subject matter experts contributing to student learning? Do our accreditation documents reflect our commitment to conceptual teaching, or do they measure whether we have taught skills?

Threshold Concepts: Not Another Screwdriver

Threshold concepts extend and improve our existing teaching practices by connecting skills to the underlying big ideas; teaching conceptually helps make those hard-won skills transferable. In order to assess student progress through a threshold, activities and assignments should prioritize the student voice rather than the ability to follow the rules of the game. Still, the threshold concept model is most useful for disrupting our teaching habits and shaking up where we've settled into complacency; the threshold concept approach asks us to see anew the experience of our students, question our assumptions, and adjust our teaching and assessment accordingly. Used alongside our existing formal and informal assessment tools, threshold concepts help build a reflective and sustainable teaching practice.

Takeaways

- Assessing threshold concept acquisition is not simple; as instructors, we need to make external the internalized ontological and cognitive shifts that indicate an approach to and crossing of a learning threshold.
- Students will need to revisit threshold concepts again and again before they are able to integrate formerly disparate facts with new disciplinary understandings. This is not likely to happen in one hour or one semester.
- The threshold concept approach should be used as way for instructors to define their disciplinary content, but it does not undermine existing assessment methods; this approach can be used alongside the assessment methods that work for your local context.

For Further Consideration

- Successful assessment of threshold concept acquisition needs to consider the affective side of learning. How can you tell when a student is still in the liminal space? What can you do to minimize the student's discomfort or confusion in the liminal space?

- Consider an information literacy lesson that you have given in the past. How would you teach this lesson to emphasize mastery of academic protocol? How would you teach this lesson to minimize protocol requirements?
- How can the threshold concept approach work with your local assessment or accreditation priorities?

References

Accrediting Commission for Community and Junior Colleges, Western Association of Schools and Colleges. (2014). *Accreditation standards*. Retrieved from https://accjc.org/wp-content/uploads/Accreditation-Standards_-Adopted-June-2014.pdf

American Library Association. (2000). *Information literacy competency standards for higher education*. Retrieved from http://www.ala.org/acrl/standards/informationliteracycompetency

Association of American Colleges & Universities. (2010). Information literacy VALUE rubric. In T. L. Rhodes (Ed.), *Assessing outcomes and improving achievement: Tips and tools for using rubrics*. Washington, DC: Association of American Colleges & Universities. Retrieved from https://www.aacu.org/value/rubrics/information-literacy

Association of College & Research Libraries. (2014). *Framework for information literacy for higher education*. Retrieved from http://www.ala.org/acrl/standards/ilframework

Bennett, M., & Brady, J. (2014). A radical critique of the learning outcomes assessment movement. *Radical Teacher, 40*(5), 510–514. doi:10.5406/radicalteacher.94.0034

Buchanan, H., Webb, K. K., Houk, A. H., & Tingelstad, C. (2015). Curriculum mapping in academic libraries. *New Review of Academic Librarianship, 21*(1), 94–111. doi:10.1080/13614533.2014.1001413

Carbery, A. (2014a, March 4). Teaching to threshold concepts in information literacy [Web log post]. Retrieved from https://edlibbs.wordpress.com/2014/03/04/teaching-to-threshold-concepts-in-information-literacy/

Carbery, A. (2014b, July 2). Things and frames [Web log post]. Retrieved from https://edlibbs.wordpress.com/2014/07/02/things-frames/

Choy, S. P. (2001). *Students whose parents did not go to college: Postsecondary access, persistence, and attainment*. Washington, DC: National Center for Education Statistics. Retrieved from https://nces.ed.gov/pubs2001/2001072_Essay.pdf

Cook, J. M. (2014). A library credit course and student success rates: A longitudinal study. *College & Research Libraries, 75*(3), 272–283. doi:10.5860/crl12-424

Davies, P., & Mangan, J. (2008). Embedding threshold concepts: From theory to pedagogical principles to learning activities. In R. Land, J. H. F. Meyer, & J. Smith (Eds.), *Threshold concepts within the disciplines* (pp. 37–50). Rotterdam, the Netherlands: Sense Publishers.

Engle, J. (2007). Postsecondary access and success for first-generation college students. *American Academic, 3*, 25–48. Retrieved from http://citeseerx.ist.psu.edu/viewdoc/download?doi=10.1.1.296.7903&rep=rep1&type=pdf

Farkas, M. (2014). Getting into the gray areas with the draft Framework for Information Literacy for Higher Education [Web log post]. Retrieved from http://meredith.wolfwater.com/wordpress/2014/03/03/getting-into-the-gray-areas-with-the-draft-framework-for-information-literacy-for-higher-education/

Fister, B. (2015). *The liminal library: Making our libraries sites of transformative learning*. Paper presented at the Librarians' Information Literacy Annual Conference, Newcastle University, Newcastle upon Tyne. Retrieved from http://barbarafister.com/LiminalLibrary.pdf

Gilchrist, D., & Oakleaf, M. (2012, April). *An essential partner: The librarian's role in student learning assessment*. Urbana, IL: University of Illinois and Indiana University, National Institute for Learning Outcomes Assessment. Retrieved from http://www.learningoutcomeassessment.org/occasionalpaperfourteen.htm

Gould Library Reference and Instruction Department. (2012). *Information literacy in student writing rubric and codebook*. Northfield, MN: Carleton College. Retrieved from http://go.carleton.edu/ILSW

Kuhlthau, C. C. (1987). *Information skills for an information society: A review of research. An ERIC Information Analysis product*. Syracuse, NY: Information Resources Publications. Retrieved from https://files.eric.ed.gov/fulltext/ED297740.pdf

LaGuardia Community College. (2014). *Core competencies and abilities*. Retrieved from https://www.laguardia.edu/assessment/assignment-library/

Land, R., Cousin, G., Meyer, J. H. F., & Davies, P. (2005). Threshold concepts and troublesome knowledge (3): Implications for course design and evaluation. In C. Rust (Ed.), *Improving student learning diversity and inclusivity* (pp. 53–64). Oxford, England: Oxford Center for Staff and Learning Development. Retrieved from http://www.ee.ucl.ac.uk/~mflanaga/ISL04-pp53-64-Land-et-al.pdf

Lin Hanick, S., Keyes, C., Letnikova, G., McDermott, I., McHale, C., Ovadia, S., . . . Stern, C. (2018). *Library instruction map for First Year Seminars at LaGuardia Community College (CUNY)*. Unpublished internal document.

Lin Hanick, S., Keyes, C., Letnikova, G., McHale, C., Ovadia, S., Rojas, A., & Stern, C. (2015). *Library instruction modules used at LaGuardia Community College (CUNY)*. Unpublished internal document.

Meyer, J. H. F., & Land, R. (2005). Threshold concepts and troublesome knowledge (2): Epistemological considerations and a conceptual framework for teaching and learning. *Higher Education: The International Journal of Higher*

Education and Educational Planning, 49(3), 373–388. doi:10.1007/s10734-004-6779-5

Meyer, J. H. F., & Land, R. (2010). Threshold concepts and troublesome knowledge: The dynamics of assessment. In R. Land, J. H. F. Meyer, & C. Baillie (Eds.), *Threshold concepts and transformational learning* (pp. 61–79). Rotterdam, the Netherlands: Sense Publishers.

Middle States Commission on Higher Education. (2015). *Standards for accreditation and requirements of affiliation*. Retrieved from http://www.msche.org/publications/RevisedStandardsFINAL.pdf

New England Association of Schools and Colleges Commission on Institutions of Higher Education. (2016). *Standards for accreditation*. Retrieved from https://cihe.neasc.org/standards-policies/standards-accreditation/standards-effective-july-1-2016

New Mexico Statewide General Education. (2018). *Statewide general education steering committee final report*. Retrieved from https://provost.nmsu.edu/state-wide-gen-ed/

North Central Association of Colleges and Schools Higher Learning Commission. (2014). *The criteria for accreditation and core components*. Retrieved from https://www.hlcommission.org/Criteria-Eligibility-and-Candidacy/criteria-and-core-components.html

Northwest Commission on Colleges and Universities. (2018). *NWCCU standards*. Retrieved from http://www.nwccu.org/accreditation/standards-policies/standards/

Oakleaf, M. (2008). Dangers and opportunities: A conceptual map of information literacy assessment tools. *portal: Libraries and the Academy, 8*(3), 233–253. doi:10.1353/pla.0.0011

Oakleaf, M. (2010). *The value of academic libraries: A comprehensive research review and report*. Retrieved from http://www.ala.org/acrl/sites/ala.org.acrl/files/content/issues/value/val_report.pdf

Oakleaf, M. (2014). A roadmap for assessing student learning using the new Framework for Information Literacy for Higher Education. *Journal of Academic Librarianship, 40*(5), 510–514. doi:10.1016/j.acalib.2014.08.001

Pontuso, J. F., & Thorton, S. R. (2008). Is outcomes assessment hurting higher education? *Thought & Action*, 61–69. Retrieved from http://www.nea.org/assets/img/PubThoughtAndAction/TAA_08_08.pdf

Southern Association of Colleges and Schools Commission on Colleges. (2018). *The principles of accreditation: Foundations for quality enhancement*. Retrieved from http://www.sacscoc.org/pdf/2018PrinciplesOfAcreditation.pdf

Townsend, L., Hurley, D., Potter, R., Cooper, L., & Hessney-Moore, S. (2015). *Curriculum map for UNM Library*. Unpublished internal document.

Western Association of Schools and Colleges Senior College and University Commission. (2013). *Standard 2: Achieving educational objectives through core functions*. Retrieved from https://www.wscuc.org/resources/handbook-accreditation-2013/part-ii-core-commitments-and-standards-accreditation/wasc-standards-accreditation-2013/standard-2-achieving-educational-objectives-through-core-functions

Wiggins, G. P., & McTighe, J. (2005). *Understanding by design*. Alexandria, VA: Association for Supervision and Curriculum Development.

Willi Hooper, M. D., & Scharf, E. (2017). Connecting and reflecting: Transformative learning in academic libraries. *Journal of Transformative Education, 15*(1), 79–94. doi:10.1177/1541344616670033

CHAPTER NINE

Designing Activities for Conceptual Teaching

Educational researcher Glynis Cousin writes that, in general, research into threshold concepts tackles three questions:

> a. What do academics consider to be fundamental to a grasp of their subject?
> b. What do students find difficult to grasp?
> c. What curriculum design interventions can support mastery of these difficulties? (Cousin, 2009, p. 206)

This chapter looks at the third question.

Too often, assessments create just a snapshot of student learning. The photograph may be vivid, but it captures only one moment in the learning process; the scope of view is necessarily limited by the edge of the frame. Likewise, many assignments ask only for part of the story: the correct answer, the name of a database, the phrase "scholarly source." Out of context, these answers may represent real mastery or just surface-level understanding—there is no way to tell the difference.

Assignments that ask students to interrogate the edges of the frame, to delve into why a source was created, the cost of information, the way we classify information, the way we use information, and who holds authority, shift the focus from mimicking the right rules to grappling with conceptual understandings. By striving to follow students as they learn, we can acknowledge variation in student experience and discover when and how learning is happening.

These assignments will resemble those we already give. We don't have to reject research papers or fact-based quizzes, but we can supplement our courses with other assignments that tell us where students are. These assignments can be informal, fun, or just aim to give learners a chance to tell us how they're doing.

When it comes to teaching with threshold concepts, there is no substitute for time on task. Students do not cross thresholds without enough time. A credit course is likely the best way to get beyond the doorway of the threshold, but a one-hour library instruction session can be used to introduce students to a new concept, helping a threshold come into view. The activities in this chapter are designed to be used in class to introduce a threshold concept and/or practice the rules of the game, while the assignments are designed to assess a student's progress through a learning threshold (though some activities and assignments may do both).

When delving into examples of assignments and activities, remember that threshold concepts address content, not pedagogy. This theory guides what we teach, not how we teach. The following examples reveal Amy, Lori, and Silvia's preferences for active learning, problem-based learning, and constructivist paradigms, but our pedagogical habits should not be mistaken for components of the threshold concept approach.

Activities

Why Buy the (Library) Cow

Threshold Concepts: Format, Information Commodities, Organizing Systems

Activity time: 10 minutes

Prep time: 5–10 minutes

Students are asked to search one set of keywords in Google and then replicate the search in a library database. Together, the class identifies the types of sources in their search results and talks about which sources might be useful. This activity is a quick way to demonstrate the difference between the open web and library resources.

The class starts by searching together on Google for a topic related to their assignment. For instance, if the research project should address the intersection of technology and identity, the whole class can search for "social media AND advertising" on Google. In small groups or as a class, students are asked:

- What do these results have in common?
- Are these results useful?
- Which result would you use for your paper?

Next, the class searches for the same terms in a library database and answers the same questions listed previously. This activity is an opportunity to talk about how the open web and library databases can both be useful for understanding a topic while highlighting the added value of resources found through the library. Students should also be prompted to consider what each set of results prioritizes in terms of currency, geographic focus, advertising (or lack thereof), and filtering options.

Are You in a Filter Bubble?

Threshold Concepts: Authority, Information Commodities
Activity time: 15 minutes
Prep time: 5–10 minutes

After a brief lecture on filter bubbles, the class is divided into four groups and assigned a question. Each group has five minutes for discussion and two minutes to report out to the class.

- When does information customization help you? When does it hurt you?
- How do page ranks affect search results? Is this a good way to organize searches?
- In addition to relevance, what other factors should you consider when you look for information?
- Do you mind if Google tracks your information? How do you stop your information from being tracked?

I Am an Expert—Ask Me Anything

Threshold Concepts: Research Process
Activity Time: 10–15 minutes
Prep time: 5 minutes

To prepare for this activity, inspired by Dan Rothstein and Luz Santana's (2014) Question Formulation Technique, you should pick an image, a video, or an artifact that represents an area where you possess unexpected expertise. Consider a topic that will be unfamiliar to most students; the goal is for the class to start the activity at the same place, information-wise. Lori has used short recordings from a live stream of bears in the wild, and Silvia has used an engraving from William Hogarth's satirical series *A Rake's Progress* (explore, 2018; Shesgreen, 1973).

Share your image, video, or artifact with the class, and ask students to write down as many questions as possible. For this first step, students should not worry about the quality of the questions—they are aiming for quantity. Next, have students form pairs and sort their questions into closed- and open-ended questions. Pairs should choose the three best questions from their list and rank them accordingly. Chat with students while they work through this process, giving feedback on the questions.

Returning to the larger group, ask students to share their best questions, talking through closed- and open-ended questions, clarifying as needed. *Answer* their questions (you are an expert!), and discuss those that you were not able to answer. Do you need more information? What are the limits to your expertise? What information do you need in order to answer their question?

After you've answered a good number of questions, direct students to return to their pairs and write new questions on the basis of what they now know. Encourage students to share their second set of questions with the class, highlighting how their questions have changed after they knew more about the topic. End by connecting this activity to the research process. This activity suggests that asking good questions is a skill that can be taught and improved in order to overcome the typical feelings of dread, anxiety, and fear and tap the potential for exploration, wonder, and productivity.

Beyond the CRAAP Test

Threshold Concepts: Authority, Research Process
Activity Time: 30–40 minutes
Prep time: 5–10 minutes

The CRAAP test is a popular way to teach source evaluation; using a funny acronym, students look for a source's Currency, Relevance, Authority, Accuracy, and Purpose (Meriam Library, 2017). While the CRAAP test is a good place to start, the proliferation of heavily biased news networks or fake news sites can make web sources increasingly difficult to evaluate. This activity introduces nuance into source evaluation by asking students to look more closely at context and to consider authority as a moving target.

In small groups, students are given election endorsements from news sources that all pass the CRAAP test—that is, each endorsement comes from a news source with a reputation for being truthful. For an assignment ahead of the 2016 presidential election, we used

- Hillary Clinton's endorsement from the *New York Times*
- Hillary Clinton's endorsement from *Vogue*
- Donald Trump's endorsement from the *Las Vegas Review Journal*
- Gary Johnson's endorsement from the *Chicago Tribune*

Students are asked to discuss, first in small groups and then as a class:

- What evidence is cited?
- What arguments are made?
- How does an endorsement from *Vogue* (a luxury fashion magazine) differ from that of the *New York Times*?
- If you read the *Las Vegas Review Journal*'s endorsement of Trump, it passes the CRAAP test. Still, what do you make of the fact that it is Trump's *only* endorsement from a major paper?

Web Evaluation: Don't Take Their Word for It

Threshold Concepts: Authority, Format
Activity time: 30 minutes
Prep time: 20–30 minutes

This activity is designed for students who are researching topics on the open web. After a brief lecture on searching the web and website evaluation, students, working in groups or alone, are assigned different pages on the same topic from different organizations and asked to answer a list of questions (e.g., the page on immigration put together by the Brookings Institute, cis.org, the Pew Research Center, and heritage.org).

In the list of questions, students are first asked for their initial impression of a website:

- Take a look around the website. What are your first impressions? Does it look credible? Why or why not?
- What kind of information does it contain? News? Original research? Government information? Something else?
- Who is publishing this website? What individuals are involved?

Next, the activity takes students beyond both their initial impressions and the website itself; students are asked to find out how their assigned website is described, cited, lauded, or criticized by other sources of information. Questions include the following:

- Google the organization or individuals. What do other websites tell you about them?
- What is this website's perspective on the issue?
- Who is this website written for?

This activity not only addresses familiar questions about credibility but also introduces the idea that authority is not innate in an information source. A website can appear to be current, relevant, or accurate, but there may be less visible issues like bias, funding sources, or author credentials. These issues are difficult to uncover using the website alone, and initial impressions should be corroborated with further sources. Of course, each source used to evaluate the initial website could itself be evaluated, highlighting the iterative nature of research. This activity is also a way to talk about the kind of checking that goes into the peer-review process.

Street Harassment and Research Questions

Threshold Concepts: Research Process
Activity time: 25 minutes
Prep time: 20–30 minutes

Start by watching the viral video titled "10 Hours of Walking in NYC as a Woman" commissioned by Hollaback, an anti-street harassment organization. This two-minute video shows a woman being followed, propositioned, and harassed.

After the video ends, we ask students two questions via anonymous poll:

- What do you think the makers of this video used as their research question?
- What racial patterns did you see in the video?

Next, show excerpts from a blog entry written by Zeynep Tufekci titled "Hollaback and Why Everyone Needs Better Research Methods and Why All Data Needs Theory" published on Medium.com. Despite purporting to represent a walk all over New York City, 59 percent of the interactions that made it into the short video took place in Harlem. And, as many viewers pointed out, only men of color are shown harassing the woman. In fact, the filmmaker admitted to editing out the Caucasian men captured on film for various reasons, like unclear audio.

Class discussions can cover whether the filmmaker was justified in his decisions, whether the criticisms of the video were fair, and students' own experiences with street harassment. Bring it back to the assignment by revisiting their perception of what the video's research question is. Having a good research question is key, and their suggestions were good research questions. But, when evidence is flawed, skewed, or biased, the argument will be weak.

The Daily Show Is a Primary/Secondary Source

Threshold Concepts: Format, Research Process
Activity time: 35 minutes
Prep time: 20–30 minutes

This activity addresses the difference between primary and secondary sources. Rather than treating the two categories as silos, engage students in a conversation about why these distinctions are slippery or confusing. Why does the value of information shift depending on the question you're asking and the means by which it was created or will be used?

To do this, students are given links to two or three different sources and allowed time to explore. Then, they're asked to vote: Is this a primary source, a secondary source, both, or neither? Discuss each source, asking students to defend their positions. This activity generates the most discussion with recognizable, but difficult to classify, media types like Victorian conduct guides for gentlemen, an interactive *New York Times* article about an avalanche, or a clip from *The Daily Show* from the night of the 2008 election.

The responses to these sources are likely to be mixed, leading to discussions about context and function. The conduct guide quotes from many sources so it's secondary, but since it was published in the 1800s, it does tell us something authentic about Victorian standards for proper behavior, so it's also a primary source. When Jon Stewart shows clips from Fox News or CNN, he's quoting like we would in a research paper, which is what secondary sources do; if we were using this clip in 2008, it might be a secondary source. But, if you use it today, and take into account the immediacy of Jon Stewart's reaction to the 2008 election, you can use it as a primary source.

This activity stresses that the important questions you have to ask are "How are you going to use this?" and "What are you trying to prove?"

Net Neutrality Is No Time for Neutrality

Threshold Concepts: Information Commodities, Organizing Systems
Activity time: 40 minutes
Prep time: 30–40 minutes

Following a lecture on net neutrality, the class is divided into four groups and assigned one of the following roles:

1. The founder of Venmo, a start-up
2. The CEO of Netflix
3. The CEO of Time Warner Cable
4. A college student

Students are asked, "Do you support net neutrality?" Together, they answer the question as their designated identity and report to the class.

After explaining the Federal Communications Commission's (FCC) ruling in December 2017, students are asked to answer a second question: What does the FCC decision mean for you? Students are asked to defend their stance and make a recommendation for the future that is in line with the priorities of their assigned identity. This activity asks students to consider the competing interests that dictate information access and delivery and the extent to which their interests as students can and should be represented or made more visible.

This Is Not a Book Report: Writing a Literature Review

Threshold Concepts: Research Process

Activity time: 50–60 minutes

Prep time: 50–60 minutes

After talking about the function of a literature review in scholarly writing, students work together in small groups to look at seven article citations and abstracts, all pulled from the literature review of a single published article. Make sure that students understand that the literature review should never be a book report. It is not a review, a summary, a critique, or a dump of whatever you can find. Instead, scholars use the literature review to look for relationships between publications and to identify major themes, concepts, gaps, and disagreements.

To practice this skill, students are asked to map out the relationships between the seven article abstracts they have been given, creating a concept map or outline. A sample topic for this activity is the impact of parental employment on childhood development. Each article in the set fits the topic, but students can further group the articles by type of methodology, whether the focus was on two-parent or single-parent households, whether the impact studied was academic versus emotional, and so on. As these relationships are mapped out, students can also start to see which authors agree or disagree, or which demographics have not been the subject of a study.

Citation without Bibliographies

Threshold Concepts: Research Process, Information Commodities

Activity time: 60 minutes

Prep time: 50–60 minutes

In advance of the library instruction session, students read an article that quotes from outside sources (newspaper articles, videos, research studies, books). Sample articles are "Small Change" by Malcolm Gladwell in the *New Yorker* and "The Millennials Are Generation Nice" by Sam Tanenhaus in the *New York Times*. During the library instruction session, students are introduced to the basics of Google advanced search and finding sources using library databases. In groups of two or three, students are given one of the quoted or referenced sources from the article. Working together, they track down the full text of the quoted or referenced source, creating hyperlinks throughout the text of the original article. Students running into paywalls on the open web are shown how to locate the sources within library databases.

The prep level for this activity is high because you will likely need to do a trial run to find out how each the quoted or referenced sources can be (or not be) found. For instance, if the article quotes from an Alabama newspaper that is only available on microfiche at your institution, you may or may not want to assign it to a group. Similarly, we've had some student groups tell us that they've "found" an essay online, but checking in advance prepares us to point out that only the first page is available while the rest is paywalled.

Assignments

Time Traveling: Primary and Secondary Sources

Threshold Concepts: Format, Research Process
Prep time: 10–20 minutes

Students pick one historical event and use online archives, library resources, and the open web to find one primary and one secondary source related to the event. For each source:

1. Describe the source:
   a. Format: Is it a photograph, a diary entry, a book, a magazine or newspaper article, etc.?
   b. Background information: Who created this and why? What is the context of the source or what is it about?
2. Explain why they think each resource is primary or secondary.
3. Identify which source tools they used; describe in detail how they located each one (including any search terms or the path they followed to get there).

Sample question prompts:

- How does the author/creator of this source know these details (names, dates, times)?

- On the basis of the information available (book record, article abstract, reviews, etc.), can you tell if the author's conclusions are based on a single piece of evidence, or perhaps many sources have been taken into account (e.g., diary entries, along with third-party eyewitness accounts, impressions of contemporaries, newspaper accounts)?
- How distant is the researcher from the event or action? Days? Years? Decades?

Not All Search Is Created Equal

Threshold Concepts: Format, Organizing Systems
Prep time: 10–20 minutes
Students are asked to select a topic of their choice and go through a process similar to the "Why Buy the (Library) Cow" activity. For their topic, students must find

- one book in the library catalog;
- one article in a library database; and
- one item in Google.

Then, they answer the following questions:

- What is your research question?
- What are the keywords on the basis of your research question?
- What is your search query? (Hint: keywords and Boolean operators—AND, OR, NOT)
- What is the *MLA* citation for each result?
- What kinds of results show up in each search?
- How useful are the results for your research question?

Movie Views and Reviews

Threshold Concepts: Authority
Prep time: 10–20 minutes
Students choose a classic or acclaimed movie and find a popular review and a scholarly review. They fill out a chart that compares the characteristics of the two reviews: Who is the audience? What are the author's credentials? When would you need this information? Is the review easy to understand? Students then write a paragraph using specific examples from the reviews to compare the scholarly and popular categories.

Who Can See My Stuff?

Threshold Concepts: Information Commodities
Prep time: 10–20 minutes

In preparation for class, students read "The Laborers Who Keep Dick Pics and Beheadings Out of Your Facebook Feed" by Adrian Chen in *WIRED*. This assignment asks students to position themselves socially and ethically as information consumers. Students are asked to check the privacy settings on their social media accounts and to answer the following questions:

1. Were you surprised by how much you are revealing on Facebook and to Google? If you do not have Facebook or Google accounts, what do you use instead? Why?
2. Adrian Chen's article, "The Laborers Who Keep Dick Pics and Beheadings Out of Your Facebook Feed," talks about the way that social media companies try to protect you from disturbing content using low-cost labor. What are some of the problems with this system? What was your reaction to this article?
3. Consider your experience as a user of web services. How has using Facebook, Instagram, Twitter, Google, and other services shaped your thoughts about online privacy? Do you think you are *more* or *less* concerned about privacy because you use these services?
4. Look into one of the following privacy tools: DuckDuckGo, Privacy Badger, TOS Didn't Read, and CCleaner. Which of these tools did you find the most valuable? Why?

Citation Sleuthing

Threshold Concepts: Authority, Research Process
Prep time: 30–40 minutes

This assignment was adapted from an activity developed by Jenna Kammer in *Let the Games Begin*, edited by Thomas R. McDevitt. As in the "Citations without Bibliographies" activity, students read an article in a popular or trade publication that refers to outside sources of information but doesn't have a citation list. They track down the sources of information and arrange them into an annotated bibliography. Students assess how effectively the author of the article used the information sources. For instance, were the original author's points accurately represented in the new work? This assignment also asks, "What are the sources considered to be authoritative evidence by the person writing the article? How does the author incorporate that evidence in order to make his or her case?"

Purpose, Process, Product

Threshold Concept: Format, Information Commodities, Research Process
Prep time: 30–40 minutes
Looking in print publications, online, or on social media, students are charged with finding examples of information as follows:

- Education: This example should exist to inform people about an event, increase awareness about a cause, or to teach them something new.
- Entertainment: This example is primarily used to entertain people.
- Commercial: This example is primarily used to sell something.

In a 300–500 word reflection, students describe their examples and answer the following questions:

- How did you decide if the purpose of your example was Education, Entertainment, or Commercial?
- How was your example created? What was the process?
- Did any of your examples feel like they could be in more than one category? Why?
- On the basis of the examples you selected and modern trends in information delivery, how do you think we will get information in the future?

This assignment can be expanded into a research paper. In this paper students will choose one of their examples to explore in depth via a research question of their own creation. For instance, if the example is a campaign advertisement, the paper could ask, "How do political advertisements complicate ethics in elections?" Students could investigate the election that produced the advertisement; the accuracy of the claims in the advertisement; the changing regulations related to campaign advertising; and the extent to which race, class, and gender are targets or liabilities in campaign messaging. This paper should contextualize the example in its historical, social, and cultural place, examining the purpose and process that created the product, in order to analyze its impact on individual or collective decision making.

Course Outline

In Chapter 1, we noted that the threshold concept approach is most useful in the context of a credit course. Complex topics can be introduced, integrated, and developed over the course of the term rather than treating the course like 10 one-shots. In Table 9.1, we share an outline for a

Table 9.1 Course Outline for 13-Week, 1-Credit Information Literacy Course. Reprinted with permission from LaGuardia Community College Library and Media Resources Center.

Week	Theme	Topics	Threshold Concepts	Activities & Assignments
1	History of Information	The Print Revolution History of the Internet Public and Academic Libraries	Authority Organizing Systems	
2	Information Cycle & Evaluation (1)	Format as a Process Scholarly and Popular Sources Information and Research Cycles	Format Research Process	Movie Views and Reviews Purpose, Process, Product
3	Information Cycle & Evaluation (2)	Primary and Secondary Sources Controlled Vocabularies Social Tagging	Authority Format Organizing Systems	The Daily Show Is a Primary/ Secondary Source Time Traveling: Primary and Secondary Sources
4	Finding Information	Search Engines Narrowing and Relevancy Research Questions	Organizing Systems Research Process	Citation Sleuthing I Am an Expert—Ask Me Anything Not All Search Is Created Equal Street Harassment and Research Questions Why Buy the (Library) Cow
5	Choosing Information	The Open Web and the Invisible Web Filter Bubbles Evaluating Sources	Authority Organizing Systems	Are You in a Filter Bubble? Beyond the CRAAP Test Web Evaluation: Don't Take Their Word For It

(continued)

Table 9.1 *(continued)*

Week	Theme	Topics	Threshold Concepts	Activities & Assignments
6	Information Integrity: Preventing Plagiarism & Citation Management	Intellectual Property Paraphrase, Summary, and Direct Quotation Zotero	Information Commodities Research Process	Citation without Bibliographies This Is Not a Book Report: Writing a Literature Review
7	Midterm Project			
8	Using Statistics	Census Data Market Research Reports	Authority Information Commodities	
9	Copyright & Open Access	Copyright Law Fair Use Open Access Creative Commons	Format Information Commodities	
10	Net Neutrality	The FCC, Internet Service Providers, and Content Providers	Authority Information Commodities	Net Neutrality Is No Time For Neutrality
11	Social Media Information & Privacy	Social Media Activism Hidden Labor Privacy Strategies	Information Commodities Organizing Systems	Who Can See My Stuff?
12	Review for Exam			
13	Final Exam			

semester-long information literacy course, including the theme of the week, information literacy topics, and the associated threshold concepts. Where applicable, we include suggestions about which activities and assignments from this chapter are relevant (though you would not use all of them on one day). You'll notice that a number of activities and assignments fall into the "finding information" and "choosing information" topics. Since those are the skills we address most often in one-shot sessions, we've developed a broader variety of activities in those areas. For the weeks where no activity or assignment is listed, you can assume we lectured, led a database demonstration, or gave a quiz.

A More Complete Picture

The threshold concept approach expands the boundaries of the classroom and anchors our information literacy content within the disciplinary curriculum. At a basic level, these activities and assignments still lend themselves to the same kind of informal assessment we've always done: we watch student reactions, we build in time to work with students one on one, and we listen carefully to the questions being asked or not being asked. Used alongside formal assessment, these activities and assignments can help you form a more complete picture of student understanding and their progression through the liminal space of a threshold concept.

After one library instruction session, Silvia was approached by the disciplinary faculty member. "I used to think that the library visit was about library topics that took away from my teaching time," she said, "but this was the first time that I realized that it could be complementary. The discussion that was happening was useful for what I was doing in my class, but it wasn't anything I would cover in my class." How we wish all faculty already knew this! We credit the threshold concept approach with helping us take the information science content that has always interested us the most into our information literacy sessions.

Takeaways

- Conceptual teaching can have a place in one-shot or bibliographic instruction sessions.
- Threshold concepts address content, not pedagogy—you don't need to teach them in any particular way.
- Threshold concepts describe overlapping and integrative content in our field. For this reason, activities may touch on more than one concept.

For Further Consideration

- Consider implementing one of the activities described in this chapter. What would you need to change in order to use it effectively in your context?
- Pick a place where your students often get stuck. What can students practice in an assignment or activity in order to move past this stuck place?
- Pick a threshold concept (either as described in this book or that applies to your teaching practice). How would you design an activity to introduce this concept?

References

Cousin, G. (2009). *Researching learning in higher education*. New York, NY: Routledge.

explore. (2018). Brooks Falls brown bears. Retrieved from https://explore.org/livecams/brown-bears

Meriam Library, California State University, Chico. (2017, September 17). Evaluating information—Applying the CRAAP test [Assessment Instrument]. Retrieved from https://www.csuchico.edu/lins/handouts/eval_websites.pdf

Rothstein, D., & Santana, L. (2014). The right questions. *Educational Leadership, 72*(2). Retrieved from http://www.ascd.org/publications/educational-leadership/oct14/vol72/num02/The-Right-Questions.aspx

Shesgreen, S. (1973). *Engravings by Hogarth*. New York, NY: Dover Publications.

CHAPTER TEN

Case Study: Fake News (and Other Information Crises)

The threshold concepts for information literacy described in this book are a series of interconnected understandings. While aspects of some concepts may overlap, taken together, they introduce a distinct disciplinary perspective that librarians bring to instruction. This chapter offers a case study to demonstrate how librarians can use a threshold concept approach to guide teaching content on one familiar topic: misinformation.

"Fake news" is a punchy, evocative phrase that feels more of the moment than the broader term "misinformation." When we are aiming for complete accuracy, we say that this chapter is about misinformation. This is because fake news is used as a category that includes satire from the *Onion*, clickbait titles, outright lies, erroneous interpretations of a fact, native advertising, and news delivered with a strong partisan bias. Stefanie Bluemle has a helpful way of explaining how *misinformation* and *fake news* can at times seem interchangeable:

> "Fake news" became ubiquitous during and after the United States presidential election campaign of 2016. Originally referring to fabricated stories on the Web that were shared as genuine news, the phrase quickly became more encompassing, coming to mean potentially any source that intentionally misleads, presents news in a hyper-partisan fashion, or even publishes satirical stories that could accidentally be taken as true. (2018, p. 266)

At the time of this writing, the misinformation crisis is not only top of mind but also illustrates how the threshold concepts proposed in Part II of this book can be used to explore the same topic from multiple angles. Librarians have been quick to claim fake news as an information literacy issue, but what can we uniquely bring to a discussion of this topic?

Librarians' concerns over the quality of online information coincide with the advent of the web. The early years saw a flurry of publications by librarians attempting to establish the scope of the problem and generate models for evaluating information found online (e.g., Fitzgerald, 1997; Floridi, 1996; Fritch & Cromwell, 2001). However, misinformation has long gone hand in hand with information; fake news is as old as news itself (Soll, 2016). Online misinformation seems to be the problem at the moment because so many people consume most of their information via online sources, and social networks have unique characteristics that make users more likely to spread lies than truth (Vosoughi, Roy, & Aral, 2018), but the mode of discovery itself is not the central problem.

So should we talk about standards for information evaluation? It can certainly seem that the problem of misinformation is primarily one of quality control. Checklists for evaluating information found online take this approach; they assume that if students were offered better guidance on the markers of credible information, they would not fall prey to misinformation. As it relates to authority, evaluation is one of the ways that librarians might teach to this issue, but there are other productive lessons to be introduced around other information literacy threshold concepts discussed in this book. In this chapter, we'll consider how misinformation can be approached with students in the context of three threshold concepts: authority, format, and information commodities. For each learning threshold, we include sample discussion questions to share with students.

Authority

> Authority is a form of intellectual trust granted by an individual or community to an information source. It is both constructed, built through expertise and persistent reliability, and contextual, limited to certain knowledge domains or situations and shaped by community norms.

The term "fake news" implies that there is such a thing as real news. In fact, there is: with some variation, credible news sources tend to agree on a common set of ethics communicated through professional standards. The Society of Professional Journalists (2014), the *Washington Post* (2016), National Public Radio (n.d.), the *New York Times* (n.d.), and the *Los Angeles Times* (2014), for example, all state a commitment to accuracy, truth, fairness, objectivity, independence, transparency, and accountability. Likewise, these news sources all include language in their standards stating that reporters will not misrepresent their identity to get a story and will attribute material from other media. In the field of journalism, ethics and standards signal an intention to report facts, to be transparent when reporting opinions, and to serve as a trustworthy source. A clear and unequivocal statement of ethical and professional standards by a publication can thus serve as a marker of authority, one indication among others that encourages the consumer to trust the information conveyed. When users trust journalists to uphold these ethics and standards to produce objective reporting, they are likely to confer cognitive authority to these news organizations.

A common source of misinformation related to authority, and the one most closely aligned with fake news, comes from users who confer cognitive authority to sources on the basis of their "intrinsic plausibility"—in other words, on whether those sources pass the sniff test on a very subjective level (Wilson, 1983, p. 25). Intrinsic plausibility sounds reasonable, except that relying on our own judgment about the content of a source when we are not content experts can lead us to trust a source simply because it confirms previously held beliefs and feels right. This is what happens when users share memes featuring unsubstantiated or distorted claims, as was the case when a doctored image of student activist and Stoneman Douglas High School shooting survivor Emma Gonzalez was shared on Twitter and then retweeted 1,500 times within a few hours. The original image of Gonzalez, from a *Teen Vogue* story, showed Gonzalez ripping up a poster of a shooting target; the edited image shows Gonzalez tearing up a copy of the U.S. Constitution (Mezzofiore, 2018). The image was first posted by Gab, a "free speech social network," known to be a platform for white supremacists with a frog logo that is a clear nod to Pepe the Frog, a cartoon adopted as a mascot by the alt-right. This context was lost, however, after the image was reposted on message boards and retweeted by actor and conservative commentator Adam Baldwin, accounts run by bots, and many private citizens (Danner, 2018). Users shared the altered image, trusting it to be true because it made sense to them, despite the absence of any markers of authority or indications of format that would help them figure out whether that was the case.

Valuing the intrinsic plausibility of a source over conventional markers of authority does not, however, always lead to the proliferation of fake news or hate speech. At times, it is the only way that users can access information on certain topics. Much of the initial reporting on the Black Lives Matter and Dakota Access Pipeline protests took place on social media, with Twitter threads and hashtags appearing weeks, if not months, before articles in major newspapers. Jenna Wortham (2016) notes that the use of Twitter made it possible for the Black Lives Matter movement to avoid the top-down, male-leader structure of previous movements. Instead, Black Lives Matter used social media to amplify the message that "lesbian, gay, queer, disabled, transgender, undocumented and incarcerated black people's lives matter too." By departing from the conventions of civil rights activism of the 1950s and 1960s, the movement has been able to bring forward the voices of people who for a variety of reasons have been marginalized from conventional markers of authority. In the absence of attention from mainstream media, users looked to these alternative spaces where credible second-hand knowledge could be found, even though it came without the masthead or vetted credentials that serve as journalistic markers of authority. Authority in this context can be more directly communicated through relationships with information creators and is signaled through the community's trust in that source. Does the community find this source to be a reliable narrator?

Another type of imbalance occurs when users dismiss a source as fake news even though it is marked by indicators of credibility, as when it adheres to journalistic ethics and standards. Users in this case prioritize intrinsic plausibility over all other factors. While mainstream media outlets are far from infallible, this particular scenario has been taken to extremes and popularized by Donald Trump, who rejects any unfavorable or critical reporting as fake news. Discrediting and devaluing the free press has far-reaching implications, as the *New York Times* editorial board points out: "When the president calls every piece of information he does not like 'fake news,' he also encourages politicians in other countries who are not constrained by constitutional free speech protections or independent judiciaries to more aggressively squelch the press" (2018). Another outcome of this unbalanced view of cognitive authority is the mislabeling of neutral mainstream news organizations, like NPR and PBS, as partisan. Years before the 2016 presidential election, Democrats were already 21 percent more likely than Republicans to believe most or all of what they heard on NPR (Shepard, 2011). This credibility gap can be attributed to issues of trust, as it is not supported by facts; a report by the Pew Research Center (2009) found that "NPR and PBS offered the highest percentage of neutral stories of any outlets studied." When working with students on the concept of authority, this is an area of particular concern: What makes neutral sources seem partisan? How should you react when you encounter credible reporting that contradicts what you believe to be true?

In this context, librarians can help students consider why it's important to seek out reporting with which we disagree or that we find implausible. Intellectual freedom is undermined if it is not exercised; even though the United States protects dissent, information users can find themselves inside an echo chamber of their own making. In a 1951 speech at the Conference of the Association of College Reference Libraries, Louis Shores, director of the School of Library Training and Service at Florida State University offered some answers (while confirming that misinformation is a long-standing dilemma). Shores warned,

> We in the United States provide all kinds of newspapers, with all shades of opinion. We provide all kinds of radio programs, with a variety of points of view. Diversified problems and diversified solutions are presented in our movies. However, we, as Americans, tend to read what we want to read, tend to hear what we like to hear, tend to go to the movies we like to see. The result is an unintentional line for many Americans. (1951, p. 702)

Librarians, however, can help users rebalance their model so that they both look for and accept markers of authority, in addition to going with their gut, when conferring cognitive authority.

What happens, then, if users prioritize markers of authority more than intrinsic plausibility when seeking cognitive authorities? One outcome is that when a user encounters an ambiguous source that has markers of authority, they may opt to confer cognitive authority in spite of their suspicion. Another outcome is that the user might seek out additional sources as a second opinion from a different cognitive authority on the matter. This scenario may come into play if the user is uncertain about how financial support might affect journalistic standards, as when the *Washington Post* reports on Amazon, the company founded by the paper's owner, or when objectivity might be at risk, as when Fox News reports on sexual harassment allegations against their own anchors.

Finally, on a related note, students can consider how information creators build cognitive authority by following journalistic ethics. When a source is trustworthy, but the markers of quality are missing, the information creator might decide not to use the information even though their gut tells them that it's probably true. For example, a journalist may opt out of writing a story if their sources are unwilling to go on the record. While these decisions reinforce the value of journalistic ethics and standards, they also explain why it took decades before allegations of sexual harassment and rape against Harvey Weinstein were made public. In explanation, Ronan Farrow (2017) writes,

> [Weinstein's] behavior has been an open secret to many in Hollywood and beyond, but previous attempts by many publications, including *The New Yorker*, to investigate and publish the story over the years fell short of the demands of journalistic evidence. Too few people were willing to speak, much less allow a reporter to use their names, and Weinstein and his associates used nondisclosure agreements, payoffs, and legal threats to suppress their accounts.

We realize, of course, that there is no checklist that can show students exactly how to appropriately evaluate information, which is ultimately more art than science. Markers of quality, such as journalistic standards, are relatively straightforward to define and identify in the wild. But because those markers are only one part of the puzzle and cognitive authority is subjective, it opens up an affective side of evaluation that is less clear-cut and can't be addressed with a tool like the CRAAP test (Currency, Relevance, Authority, Accuracy, and Purpose) for evaluating sources (Meriam Library, 2017).

Mike Caulfield's work on involving students in fact-checking on the web suggests an entry point to evaluating authority. Just as students learn about the natural environment through service learning cleanup days, they can take a civic interest in cleaning up the information environment by creating content that checks dubious claims and corrects the record (American Democracy Project, 2016). Caulfield's openly licensed textbook, *Web Literacy for Student Fact-Checkers*, takes an approach that encourages students to use the type of concrete techniques that fact-checkers employ:

- **Check for previous work:** Look around to see if someone else has already fact-checked the claim or provided a synthesis of research.
- **Go upstream to the source:** Go "upstream" to the source of the claim. Most web content is not original. Get to the original source to understand the trustworthiness of the information.
- **Read laterally:** Read laterally. Once you get to the source of a claim, read what other people say about the source (publication, author, etc.). The truth is in the network.
- **Circle back:** If you get lost, hit dead ends, or find yourself going down an increasingly confusing rabbit hole, back up and start over knowing what you know now. You're likely to take a more informed path with different search terms and better decisions. (Caulfield, 2017, p. I.2)

Using these techniques allows students to move past looking for markers of authority or relying on their own evaluative efforts to judge the content of the source. It encourages students to seek out additional second-hand sources to confirm the information offered by a source or to evaluate the general consensus on the authority of the source itself.

In order to help students better understand the role that emotions play in source evaluation, Lori uses the "PAWS" approach, as shown in Figure 10.1. This is not an acronym—PAWS is a pun on *pause*. It's a reminder to take a moment and reflect: How does this headline or information source make you feel? Students can become acclimated to

Figure 10.1 PAWS.

constant distraction via content feeds. When you ask them to stop and think, they have to disengage, and that can be boring. Librarians can interrupt the habit of passive information flow and encourage students to stay with the discomfort or boredom to reach a deeper understanding. Rather than engaging in a battle over what is true or not true, students can make personally relevant decisions about whom to trust or not trust.

Discussion Questions

- How do you decide whether to trust a source of information? Do you look for markers of authority or do you go with your gut? How much weight do you give to each aspect of evaluating information?
- In a media landscape where many organizations, sources, or individuals do not adhere to journalistic ethics and standards, what other markers of quality can you look for?
- What do you think about the decision made by previous reporters to not publish stories about Harvey Weinstein because they didn't have enough evidence?

Format

> Each instance of a format shares a common intellectual and physical structure with others like it, and is intentionally produced to support or effect action. Intellectual structure refers to the textual and visual content of a format. Physical structure refers to the organization, design, and medium of a format. These categories are not strict and may overlap.

In Chapter 4 we offered three elements by which to understand format: product, purpose, and process. While genre theory emphasizes process to create effective communication in the mode of a discipline, librarians typically investigate format by first looking at the finished product and then evaluating it with a tacit understanding of its purpose and the process by which it was created.

Newspapers are a long-used information format with a long-used method of distribution. Fake news mimics this established format and takes on superficial format indicators to mislead people into thinking it is credible content. Fake news is especially misleading when it is stripped of format indicators, as it is on social media and message boards. In this section, we take an extended look at how format intersects with fake news as a product, purpose, and process.

First, let's consider format as a product—that is, as a news story. Every episode of *Wait Wait . . . Don't Tell Me*, NPR's weekly news-based quiz show, features a segment called "Bluff the Listener" where a contestant hears three news stories—two fictitious and one genuine. To win, the contestant must choose the real news story. Typically, the segment is structured so that all three news stories sound equally unlikely; the best strategy by far for a contestant is to be an omnivorous news consumer who has, hopefully, heard the real story reported elsewhere. Barring that, contestants have to rely on a combination of deductive reasoning and lucky guessing. If you've ever listened to *Wait Wait* and thought, "I would be so good at this segment; as a librarian, my information evaluation skills are off the charts. This would be a piece of cake"—well, here's your chance. Without doing any fact-checking or looking at the citations, using only the text of the news stories in Table 10.1 (Dolan, 2014; Rizzo, 2015; Stevan, 2016), can you tell which news stories are true?

"More people have died from selfies than shark attacks this year," published by *Mashable*, is, unfortunately, completely true. "Creationist Carl Kerby insists dinosaurs were on Noah's Ark: They took the younger ones," published on the Raw Story, is also true, though it needs context: the site self-identifies as a progressive news organization. That being said, the Raw Story posted the original video quoted in the title alongside the article, confirming that Carl Kerby did, in fact, suggest that baby dinosaurs could fit on Noah's ark. Finally, we have "Arizona Republican suggests 'sterilizing women as a condition for receiving food stamps,'" a truly insidious piece of semi-fake news. Published on Newslo, which bills itself as a hybrid news/satire site, the article combines a factual first paragraph featuring an accurate quote from former senator Russell Pearce with a series of fabricated quotes. Though the site includes "show facts" and "hide facts" buttons to help distinguish between fact and fiction, the layout, tone, language, and general presentation of the story is clearly intended to mislead and misinform readers.

So. How did you do?

Table 10.1 Three News Stories

Creationist Carl Kerby Insists Dinosaurs Were on Noah's Ark: They Took the Younger Ones	**More People Have Died from Selfies Than Shark Attacks This Year**	**Arizona Republican Suggests "sterilizing women as a condition for receiving food stamps"**
One of the founding board members of the Creationist organization Answers in Genesis believes that dinosaurs accompanied Noah on his Ark as the entire world was flooded by God. Speaking to Bryan Fischer, formerly of the American Family Association recently, Carl Kerby insisted it wasn't infeasible for the giant reptilian creatures to have been on Noah's Ark. The self-described "creation scientist" said he had debunked the notion that two of every animal could not have possibly fit on Noah's Ark. The Bible states that the boat was about 450 feet long, 75 feet wide and 50 feet high, Kerby explained.	A 66-year-old Japanese tourist has died, and his travel companion has been injured, after falling down stairs while attempting to take a selfie at the Taj Mahal. The man's death raises the selfie-related death toll this year—to 12. To put that in perspective, in 2015 there have so far been eight deaths caused by shark attacks. The deaths are a tragic reminder to travelers that focusing on a phone screen instead of unfamiliar surroundings is not safe. Four of the selfie deaths this year, like the tourist, identified as Hideto Ueda, were caused by falling. It's not clear if the number of daredevil selfies is increasing, but more and more tourists are making headlines because of their dangerous attempts at a memorable photo. Parks have closed because	The far-right former lawmaker who helped push Arizona's "papers please" immigration law has resigned as a top official with the state GOP after making comments about sterilizing poor women. The state Democratic Party recently highlighted comments made by Russell Pearce, a former state senator, on his radio show. Discussing the state's public assistance programs, Pearce declared: "You put me in charge of Medicaid, the first thing I'd do is get Norplant, birth-control implants, or tubal ligations . . . Then we'll test recipients for drugs and alcohol, and if you want to [reproduce] or use drugs or alcohol, then get a job." . . . Pearce then went on to explain how "we need to limit food stamp access to women

(continued)

Table 10.1 *(continued)*

Creationist Carl Kerby Insists Dinosaurs Were on Noah's Ark: They Took the Younger Ones	**More People Have Died from Selfies Than Shark Attacks This Year**	**Arizona Republican Suggests "sterilizing women as a condition for receiving food stamps"**
"I see some people that like to mock and ridicule, especially about the dinosaurs, how did they put the big old dinosaurs on there?" he said. "Well, I would suggest to you they didn't take the big old dinosaur—they would have taken the younger ones. You think of a guy like me, if you're going to go repopulate a planet, you're not taking me with you. I'm old. My repopulating days are done. You take my son or my grandson. My grandson is a whole lot smaller than I am."	visitors keep trying to take selfies with bears, bull runs—an already dangerous activity—have had to expressly outlaw selfie-taking, and even Tour de France cyclists are concerned about selfie danger.	who have been sterilized," and how "that's the only way of separating the ones who are willing to work for food from those who aren't."

If you found it difficult to analyze the above stories, you're not alone. Lori gave Silvia the text of the news stories to use in this section without any commentary about which of the three was true or false. Even though she shamelessly broke the "no fact-checking" rule, it took Silvia an outrageously long time to decipher the accuracy of these three stories. Unless you are Wolverine, Daredevil, or Emma Swan, it is extremely unlikely that you can automatically tell a truth from a lie; more often than not, you need specialized knowledge about the news story at hand. If these stories stumped (at least one) midcareer librarian, what chance do our students have?

What made the aforementioned news stories so tricky? When we receive news stories in this way, we are missing out on necessary context. In Table 10.1, the news stories appear the way they do when they appear in our social media feeds. They appear as nothing more than shocking headlines, lacking any external clues that hint at quality. The news stories have been stripped of format indicators, leaving only words on a page. Format indicators used to be a critical part of how we related to the news. Opening a physical newspaper, there was an expected geography of information from section to section; the front page was distinct in nature and function from local news, op-eds, the business section, the real estate section, marriage announcements, and obituaries. Bylines made authorship clear, we could get a sense of context by looking at the other articles on the page, and we could judge the relative significance of a story on the basis of the type size of the headline and whether it appeared above the fold. Today, however, many of us encounter news stories within organizational systems—like Facebook and Twitter—that flatten our information experience. Without other stories on the page, a byline, or even the name of a website, it is difficult to *know*, unequivocally, that something is fake or incorrect just from reading it. As a product, fake news and real news are disturbingly similar.

Next, let's look at format as a reflection of purpose. The purpose of Facebook is not to deliver news; it is an advertising platform that delivers ads using a social media network designed to funnel users into like-minded groups to amplify a sense of community. Throughout 2017 and into 2018, Facebook has been the venue by which anti-Rohingya propaganda has spread in Myanmar, making the social media giant complicit in an ethnic cleansing. Phil Robertson, a deputy director of Human Rights Watch in Asia, observed that "Facebook has become a bit like an absentee landlord in Southeast Asia." Even as NGOs flagged and reported posts containing propaganda, hate speech, and misinformation, Facebook lacked the third-party reviewers and Burmese language reviewers to keep up with complaints. "Instead," Robertson continues, "it's sort of, complain into the void and hope some relief arrives before it's too late" (Larson, 2017). Similarly, Max Fisher described nine lynchings in rural Indonesia that were linked to anti-Chinese rumors on Facebook about child kidnapping gangs. "It could not happen," Fisher holds, "without Facebook and social media and without hate speech and misinformation coursing through it the way that it does" (Fisher, Taub, & Barbaro, 2018). While propaganda, hate speech, and misinformation are problematic in any format, they are particularly troubling when Facebook functions as a stand-in for news media in developing countries. The most credible post on Facebook will still fall short of the quality standards necessary for responsible news stories. The explicit purpose of Facebook communication is at direct odds with the purpose of news journalism, leading to the proliferation of fake news.

Finally, we argue that a closer look at process can help separate real news from fake news. To illustrate this point, Table 10.2 compares the process for planning a week's worth of content for the *Onion*, a satirical newspaper, with the process by which the *Washington Post* broke the story on allegations of sexual misconduct against candidate for Senate, Roy Moore (Couch, n.d.; McCrummen & Reinhard, 2017).

Table 10.2 illustrates the vast gulf between fake news (in this case, satire) and real news by pinpointing the disparate processes by which the two formats were created. While we respect and appreciate the hard work and value of well-crafted satire, there is a clear escalation in rigor and complexity once journalistic standards are applied.

Traditional markers of quality that rely on how a format looks and how we experience it can be mimicked, borrowed, or disregarded in a fake news context. A completely fabricated story can be made to emulate the tone of an authentic news story and be posted on a website that echoes the layout of legitimate news sites. Or, all of those trappings can be removed from both true and false stories when they are reposted in a social media space. As new formats emerge in a digital information explosion, visual shortcuts for quality cease to be reliable. Instead, we should focus on content creation. Analyzing fake news using the purpose and process elements of the format threshold concept helps us, and our students, identify misinformation.

Discussion Questions

- Does real news look different from fake news? Does real news *feel* different from fake news?
- To what extent is the violence in Myanmar and Indonesia Facebook's fault? Can you think of other examples where a platform or an information source was used for an unintended or problematic purpose?
- When you are looking at an information product, what do you look for in order to figure out the process by which it was created?

Table 10.2 The *Onion* versus The *Washington Post*

The *Onion*	The *Washington Post*
1. Research real news stories and how they are presented 2. Pitch headlines (up to 500/week) 3. Pick ~15 headlines to title stories for the week 4. Cross-check Twitter and Facebook to make sure the jokes are original and do not overlap, even unintentionally, with what others have said 5. Write drafts of stories 6. Revise and complete stories 7. Prepare for public reaction to story 8. Repeat	1. Stephanie McCrummen goes to Alabama to write a story about Roy Moore's supporters 2. While conducting interviews, some sources mention Moore's affinity for younger women; McCrummen is skeptical until names of specific women start to emerge 3. Upon finding out that Moore liked to hang out at the mall, McCrummen and her team verify this by locating mall employees from the relevant time frame, 1977–1982 4. As they conduct interviews, McCrummen and her team follow up on names mentioned until they have a long list of people to talk to in-person 5. Beth Reinhard, McCummen's colleague, arrives in Alabama to assist with verification of emerging allegations 6. Reporters have off-the-record interviews with Moore's accusers where no notes were taken 7. McCrummen listens to sources and offers them the chance to go on the record if they want to; she does not attempt to convince them to go on the record, nor does she pay sources for their stories 8. Reinhard and McCrummen prepare sources for the scrutiny they will face upon publication of the story 9. All statements from sources are verified and fact-checked; when a long drive is mentioned, the reporters replicate the drive 10. "The agenda is to figure out what the reality is, what the truth is, of a story. That's it," McCrummen explains

Information Commodities

> Information is a commodity because it can be described by Marx's model: it is a good or service, has value, and is produced by human labor. Like other commodities that can be bought and sold, information is property that can be either privately owned or publicly available in the commons.

In Chapter 5, we used Marx's model of commodities as a way to understand how economic factors affect the way we relate to and interact with information. Information, viewed as a commodity, is a good, with value, created through labor. However, we also considered how information is more difficult to evaluate when any of the three characteristics in Marx's model is not clear to the user. In this section, we will look at how the rise of influencer culture via personal brands on social media platforms like Instagram has led to the sharing of intentionally misleading information. Exploring information commodities using this example can help students understand the concept without the distraction of controversial or inflammatory political topics that evoke emotional responses.

Influencer culture relies on social media stars with follower counts in the tens or hundreds of thousands, if not millions, to share content that strikes the perfect balance between authentic and aspirational. One thinks of a lithe young woman walking down the cobblestones of Paris in a Burberry trench coat and worn-out Converse sneakers, or a trio of laughing children decorating sugar cookies in a forest clearing. Despite the frequent display of luxury goods, many influencers take care to cultivate personal brands that emphasize relatability and normalcy, which belie the incredible financial stakes associated with convincing users to interact with their content. When people flip through a catalog, or visit a store, they know the kind of transactions they are agreeing to. When people consume information and content from these influencers, they contribute to ad revenue, generate referral payments from affiliate links, increase follower numbers, and help land the next big contract—without exactly knowing when they are doing which of these things. This section will uncover the ways that influencers hide the extent to which their content functions as information commodities.

First, let's look at how influencers obscure the good or service they are selling. Courted by both niche start-up brands and major corporations, influencers are subject to Federal Trade Commission (FTC) regulations against deceptive marketing; they are required to disclose any financial arrangements made with brands. This process may be straightforward if an influencer has been paid to post a picture to advertise a resort in Hawaii. But what about the sandals, swimsuit, mascara, and beach towel the influencer wears (and tags) in the same picture? According to the FTC, these peripheral endorsements should also be regulated, even if the influencer is sharing a genuine preference for a specific beach towel, because information users should know when the influencer benefits from a relationship with a brand. Without disclosures, users may not be able to tell which goods or services are actually for sale and may mistake these endorsements, however sincere, for unpaid opinions. Enforcement in this area is lax, however, and repercussions have so far been limited to warning letters (Dalton, 2017).

Indeed, for every influencer that dutifully documents their financial stake in the products they are endorsing, there are twice as many who appear to be in violation of, or ambiguously complying with, FTC regulations. Amber Fillerup Clark, for instance, posting under *Barefoot Blonde*, runs a lifestyle blog and Instagram account; Fillerup Clark is considered among the most successful influencers in the mommy blogging category. She also co-owns, with her husband, a company using the *Barefoot Blonde* name to sell hair extensions, gummy biotin hair supplements, and various accessories. Most of Fillerup Clark's posts highlight her long, lush hair, a de facto advertisement for her products, though disclosures are rarely made, if at all. This means that in a typical post, Fillerup Clark is selling a number of goods: a sponsored advertisement for a product or service, everything else she is wearing (and tagging) in the picture, her hair extensions, and her personal brand as an effortlessly winsome young mother. In a profile of Fillerup Clark in the *Atlantic*, Bianca Bosker (2017) spoke with one of Fillerup Clark's fans, revealing the effectiveness with which she is able to translate her explicit and implicit endorsements into purchases for her sponsors:

> Twenty-nine-year-old Gena Baillis, who lives with her husband and their infant son in Charleston, South Carolina, has followed Fillerup Clark for three years and looks to her "to help me become a better version of myself." On Fillerup Clark's recommendation, Baillis has bought nail polish, camera gear, sports drinks, healthy snacks, and workout equipment. (For her birthday, Baillis said, her husband "bought me a spinning bike because Amber takes spinning and I swore that's what would work.") "My husband's like, 'You aspire to be like her, so this is what you need to do,' " said Baillis. "They kinda seem to live a fantasy life, but they seem pretty down-to-earth. It doesn't seem fake at all."

For women like Baillis, Fillerup Clark serves as a moving target of ideal femininity and maternity, making it very complicated to parse what the actual good or service in this situation is.

Next, we'll consider what happens when the value of a commodity is hidden by influencers. While some people are influencers because they are celebrities (like Selena Gomez, the Kardashian and Jenner sisters, and The Rock), many influencers are formerly private citizens who have built lucrative empires out of good taste, photogenic surroundings, and friendly recommendations. According to Karen Robinovitz, a cofounder of the agency that represents *Barefoot Blonde*, "Bloggers at [Fillerup Clark's] level can earn between $1 million and $6 million a year" (Bosker, 2017). Influencers do not, however, foreground the value of their product (their personal brands) because they want participation to feel like a visit with a friend—and this illusion does not stand up to the awareness that followers are tracked and monitored for economic gain.

Naomi Davis of *Love Taza* is particularly successful at cultivating the right blend of relatability and charming authenticity. Davis and her husband started their family blog to document the early days of their relationship as undergraduates in New York City, then as young newlyweds in Washington, DC, and now as a family of seven back in New York City with their five young children. While much about their life together has changed, the tone of the blog has not. Despite regular sponsorships, including from HomeAway, for a weekend in the Catskills (Davis, 2015); Amazon Prime Pantry (Davis, 2016); Anthropologie, for remodeling their living room (Davis, 2017); and DSW (Designer Shoe Warehouse; Davis, 2018), Davis still maintains that the blog is simply a space "where i share bits and pieces of my family's adventures in new york city. i love celebrating motherhood, family, travel, good food, and life's simple joys. life is beautiful!" (n.d.). This kind of positioning is not only misleading but it is also the standard for most lifestyle blogs and influencers. For another example, we can look to Jean Wang of *Extra Petite*. Wang started her style blog when she was a twentysomething working in financial services and documenting attempts to tailor her own suits and build a professional wardrobe. Today, she partners with a number of major brands, including participation in a sponsored trip with skincare company L'Occitane to pose in the company's lavender fields in Provence, France (Wang, 2017). Yet, Wang's "About" page describes her site not as a successful new media company but rather "my outlet for sharing the things I'm most passionate about—classic, timeless style, good food (all the noodles, please!), and traveling to new places" (n.d.). When influencers obscure the value of their personal brands with language suggesting that they are altruistically documenting their lives for their follower-friends, users will struggle to understand the economic implications of interacting with their information commodities.

Finally, let's consider the way hidden labor works in influencer culture. Taken at face value, the influencer lifestyle is an envy-inducing showcase of Sunday brunches, weekend getaways, and lattes enjoyed in Nordic-chic cafés. This is especially true of travel bloggers, who use their Instagram accounts to post pictures of themselves hammock-lounging before a sweeping vista without ever mentioning the hours they must spend waiting in airport security. Liz Carlson of *Young Adventuress* spoke to *Condé Nast Traveler* about the hidden labor of traveling professionally, revealing that

> [s]he often has a contract, and a list of deliverables for a brand when it's a sponsored trip. She meets with hotel management, photographs rooms, goes on tours, meets with locals, interviews staff, and hopes to get an hour or two of free time to actually, well, travel. She says she often ends up going days without sleep. (Carey, 2018)

Kiersten Rich, of *The Blonde Abroad*, adds that in addition to working constantly, most influencers have to master a range of complex skills, including photography, customer service, video editing, public relations, and contract negotiation, and for travel bloggers, all of this must be done on spotty Wi-Fi (Halpern, 2017). Why conceal the labor that produces a successful product? This approach is a unique form of misinformation in that most information commodities seem more valuable when you know how much work it took to produce them; the opposite is true for influencers. Just as some influencers hide the value of their accounts and personal brands by presenting them as noncommercial spaces, so, too, do influencers hide the labor associated with maintaining these media empires in order to preserve a sense of effortlessness.

For every great success, however, there are many more influencers who go into debt building a personal brand that never takes off. Brooke Erin Duffy, a communications scholar, argues that the influencer market is a false meritocracy that has become just as exploitative as unpaid internships. The social media economy asks influencers to make "investments of time and energy as a form of work, but they're often seen as leisure, they're seen as fun, and they're seen as something that shouldn't be materially compensated" (Kessler, 2017). Influencers are predominantly women, and, not surprisingly, their labor in this sphere is treated like other types of women's work, including child care and domestic work.

While most influencer content drifts more toward the line of entertainment, much of it takes the form of (or mimics) recommendations, tutorials, and other types of instructive information. For many students, social media content represents a significant percentage of the total information commodities they consume; knowing how to identify misinformation tactics used by influencers will prepare students to move through digital landscapes with sophistication.

Discussion Questions

- Do you think FTC regulations that require influencers to disclose financial regulations should be stricter? Why or why not? How do you interact with influencer culture? Have you ever bought something recommended by an influencer?
- Why do you think influencers try to downplay the way their content functions as a commodity?
- Marx's model of commodities contains three parts: goods and services, value, and labor. When one or more of the three parts are obscured, our ability to evaluate information as a commodity is compromised. Which part do you find to be the most important for evaluating information?

Conclusion

Misinformation can be funny and outlandish, cruel and scandalous, or a matter of life and death. To borrow a metaphor from author Neil Gaiman (2013), the current challenge is "not finding that scarce plant growing in the desert, but finding a specific plant growing in a jungle." Due to the way that many formats are now presented on the web, the challenge feels more like we are trying to find one life-saving plant in a jungle full of identical plants—many innocuous, some poisonous. This is a topic that students need to learn about and that librarians have a unique way to teach. Thinking about misinformation through the lens of the threshold concepts discussed in this book shows how the disciplinary content behind information literacy instruction prepares librarians to offer meaningful instruction and prepares students to bring deeper understandings about information into their academic context and beyond.

Teaching conceptually can feel overwhelming because it raises the stakes. Librarians know that it's difficult enough covering the essentials of library services and resources in an hour, without tossing in the contextual underpinnings of the information landscape. Engaging with threshold concepts, however, is less about trying to teach five separate and complex concepts in one class, and more about shifting priorities. Introducing a learning threshold, maybe helping it to come into view, circling back many times, all help plant a seed that may finally result in an "aha" moment.

Perhaps most important, reflective teaching is something that we do together. Thinking about threshold concepts has helped us see anew our students' experience and question why we do what we do. We question assumptions and potentially make changes on the basis of those reflections. Engaging with threshold concepts turned us into a community of practice around a better understanding of student learning; it keeps us critical, it lets us be skeptical, and it brings up difficult questions. And, in our experience, shifting the focus from skill-based training to conceptual teaching has been energizing and stimulating, a nonquantifiable benefit but one that contributes to sustainable teaching. We hope it does the same for others.

References

American Democracy Project. (2016, December 22). WSU Vancouver's Mike Caulfield to lead new ADP Digital Polarization Initiative. *AASCU's American Democracy Project*. Retrieved from https://adpaascu.wordpress.com/2016/12/22/wsu-vancouvers-mike-caulfield-to-lead-new-adp-digital-polarization-initiative/

Bluemle, S. R. (2018). Post-facts: Information literacy and authority after the 2016 election. *portal: Libraries and the Academy, 18*(2), 265–282. Retrieved from https://digitalcommons.augustana.edu/cgi/viewcontent.cgi?article=1009&context=libscifaculty

Bosker, B. (2017, March). Instamom. *The Atlantic*. Retrieved from https://www.theatlantic.com/magazine/archive/2017/03/instamom/513827/

Carey, M. (2018, April 2). What it's really like to turn travel into a full-time job. *Condé Nast Traveler*. Retrieved from https://www.cntraveler.com/story/what-its-really-like-to-turn-travel-into-a-full-time-job

Caulfield, M. A. (2017). *Web literacy for student fact-checkers*. Retrieved from https://webliteracy.pressbooks.com/

Couch, C. (n.d.). Anatomy of a joke: Dissecting "The Onion." Retrieved from Get in Media website: http://getinmedia.com/articles/film-tv-careers/anatomy-joke-dissecting-onion

Dalton, M. (2017, December 15). Social-media stars are turning heads—of regulators. *The Wall Street Journal*. Retrieved from https://www.washingtonpost.com/lifestyle/home/after-a-year-out-of-the-spotlight-a-new-kind-of-young-house-love/2015/09/14/fd75c12e-4502-11e5-846d-02792f854297_story.html

Danner, C. (2018, March 25). People are sharing fake photos of Emma González tearing up the Constitution. *New York* magazine. Retrieved from http://nymag.com/daily/intelligencer/2018/03/some-conservatives-are-sharing-a-fake-photo-of-emma-gonzalez.html

Davis, N. (n.d.). About. *Love Taza*. Retrieved from http://lovetaza.com/about

Davis, N. (2015, February 23). A weekend in the Catskills! *Love Taza*. Retrieved from http://lovetaza.com/2015/02/a-weekend-in-the-catskills/

Davis, N. (2016, October 26). 3 ways I'm simplifying life! *Love Taza*. Retrieved from http://lovetaza.com/2016/10/3-ways-im-simplifying-life/

Davis, N. (2017, October 12). Our new apartment living room reveal! *Love Taza*. Retrieved from http://lovetaza.com/2017/10/our-new-apartment-living-room-reveal/

Davis, N. (2018, May 1). Breakfast in bed! *Love Taza*. Retrieved from http://lovetaza.com/2018/05/breakfast-in-bed/

Dolan, E. W. (2014, April 18). Creationist Carl Kerby insists dinosaurs were on Noah's Ark: They took the younger ones. *Raw Story*. Retrieved from https://www.rawstory.com/2014/04/creationist-carl-kerby-insists-dinosaurs-were-on-noahs-ark-they-took-the-younger-ones/

Farrow, R. (2017, October 23). From aggressive overtures to sexual assault: Harvey Weinstein's accusers tell their stories. *The New Yorker*. Retrieved from https://www.newyorker.com/news/news-desk/from-aggressive-overtures-to-sexual-assault-harvey-weinsteins-accusers-tell-their-stories

Fisher, M., Taub, A., & Barbaro, M. (Host). (2018, May 16). *When Facebook rumors incite real violence* [Audio podcast]. *The Daily*. Retrieved from https://www.nytimes.com/2018/05/16/podcasts/the-daily/facebook-sri-lanka-violence.html

Fitzgerald, M. A. (1997). Misinformation on the internet: Applying evaluation skills to online information. *Emergency Librarian, 24*(3), 9–15.

Floridi, L. (1996). Brave.net.world: The internet as a disinformation superhighway? *Electronic Library, 14*, 509–514. doi:10.1108/eb045517

Fritch, J. W., & Cromwell, R. L. (2001). Evaluating internet resources: Identity, affiliation, and cognitive authority in a networked world. *Journal of the American Society for Information Science and Technology, 52*(6), 499–507. Retrieved from https://pdfs.semanticscholar.org/a5da/c52e47c5965cbb7a4771c44ad111edb0af85.pdf

Gaiman, N. (2013, October 15). Why our future depends on libraries, reading and daydreaming. *The Guardian*. Retrieved from https://www.theguardian.com/books/2013/oct/15/neil-gaiman-future-libraries-reading-daydreaming

Halpern, A. (2017, October 6). Coolest travel jobs: What it's like to be a social media celebrity. *Afar*. Retrieved from https://www.afar.com/magazine/coolest-travel-jobs-what-its-like-to-be-a-social-media-celebrity

Kessler, S. (2017, August 10). Becoming a social media "influencer" is the new unpaid internship, and just as exploitative. *Quartz*. Retrieved from https://qz.com/1049408/becoming-a-social-media-influencer-is-the-new-unpaid-internship-and-just-as-exploitative/

Larson, C. (2017, November 7). Facebook can't cope with the world it's created. *Foreign Policy*. Retrieved from http://foreignpolicy.com/2017/11/07/facebook-cant-cope-with-the-world-its-created/

Los Angeles Times. (2014). Los Angeles Times ethics guidelines. Retrieved from http://www.latimes.com/la-times-ethics-guidelines-story.html

McCrummen, S., & Reinhard, B. (2017, December 8). How to be a journalist: How Stephanie McCrummen and Beth Reinhard broke the Roy Moore story. *The Washington Post*. Retrieved from http://wapo.st/2AFhQjJ

Meriam Library, California State University, Chico. (2017, September 17). Evaluating information—Applying the CRAAP test [Assessment Instrument]. Retrieved from https://www.csuchico.edu/lins/handouts/eval_websites.pdf

Mezzofiore, G. (2018, March 26). No, Emma Gonzalez did not tear up a photo of the Constitution. CNN. Retrieved from https://www.cnn.com/2018/03/26/us/emma-gonzalez-photo-doctored-trnd/index.html

National Public Radio. (n.d.). *NPR ethics handbook*. Retrieved from http://ethics.npr.org/

New York Times. (n.d.). *Ethical journalism: A handbook of values and practices for the news and editorial departments*. Retrieved from https://www.nytimes.com/editorial-standards/ethical-journalism.html#

New York Times Editorial Board. (2018, April 4). The true damage of Trump's "fake news." *The New York Times*. Retrieved from https://www.nytimes.com/2018/04/04/opinion/trump-washington-post-amazon.html

Pew Research Center. (2009, April 28). Obama's first 100 days. Retrieved from http://www.journalism.org/2009/04/28/obamas-first-100-days/

Rizzo, C. (2015, September 22). More people have died from selfies than shark attacks this year. Retrieved from Mashable website: https://mashable.com/2015/09/21/selfie-deaths/#Z6PwdLt_2aqc

Shepard, A. (2011, April 28). Views of NPR's credibility tend to be partisan-based. NPR Ombudsman. Retrieved from https://www.npr.org/sections/ombudsman/2011/04/28/135775694/views-of-nprs-credibility-tend-to-be-partisan-based

Shores, L. (1951). Library logistics in teacher education. *Vital Speeches of the Day, 17*(22), 701–703.

Society of Professional Journalists. (2014, September 14). SJP code of ethics. Retrieved from https://www.spj.org/ethicscode.asp

Soll, J. (2016, December 18). The long and brutal history of fake news. *POLITICO Magazine*. Retrieved from https://www.politico.com/magazine/story/2016/12/fake-news-history-long-violent-214535

Stevan, A. (2016, May 29). Arizona Republican suggests "sterilizing women as a condition for receiving food stamps." Retrieved from Newslo website: http://politicops.com/arizona-republican-suggests-sterilizing-women-condition-receiving-food-stamps

Vosoughi, S., Roy, D., & Aral, S. (2018). The spread of true and false news online. *Science, 359*(6380), 1146–1151. doi:10.1126/science.aap9559

Wang, J. (n.d.). About. *Extra Petite*. Retrieved from http://www.extrapetite.com/about

Wang, J. (2017, August 7). Postcards from Provence, France with L'Occitane. *Extra Petite*. http://www.extrapetite.com/2017/08/provence-france-loccitane.html

Washington Post Staff. (2016, January 1). Policies and standards. *The Washington Post*. Retrieved from https://www.washingtonpost.com/news/ask-the-post/wp/2017/01/01/policies-and-standards

Wilson, P. (1983). *Second-hand knowledge: An inquiry into cognitive authority*. Westport, CT: Greenwood Press.

Wortham, J. (2016, September). Black tweets matter. *Smithsonian*. Retrieved from https://www.smithsonianmag.com/arts-culture/black-tweets-matter

Index

About the Authors

AMY R. HOFER, MLIS, is Coordinator, Statewide Open Education Library Services at Open Oregon Educational Resources. Along with Lori Townsend and Korey Brunetti, she is the coauthor of the article "Threshold Concepts for Information Literacy," which won the 2013 Association of College & Research Libraries Instruction Section Ilene F. Rockman Publication of the Year Award. She received her master's degree in library and information science from San Jose State University.

SILVIA LIN HANICK, MLIS, MA, is the First Year Experience librarian and an associate professor at LaGuardia Community College, a City University of New York (CUNY) institution. She received her master's degree in library and information science from the University of Illinois at Urbana–Champaign and her master's degree in English literature from the University of New Mexico (UNM). She previously worked at UNM as an access services librarian.

LORI TOWNSEND, MLIS, is Learning Services Coordinator and an associate professor for the University Libraries at UNM. In this position, she oversees and coordinates the instruction program for the University Libraries. She holds a bachelor's degree in history from the UNM and a master's degree in library and information science from San Jose State University. Before joining UNM, Townsend worked as the electronic collections librarian at California State University, East Bay, from 2005 to 2010.